Free Market Madness

Free Market Madness

WHY HUMAN NATURE

IS AT ODDS WITH ECONOMICS—

AND WHY IT MATTERS

Peter A. Ubel

Harvard Business Press

Boston, Massachusetts

To Paula

Library of Congress Cataloging-in-Publication Data

Ubel, Peter A.
   Free market madness : why human nature is at odds with economics and why it matters /
Peter A. Ubel.
     p. cm.
   ISBN 1-4221-2609-9
   1. Free enterprise.   2. Economics.   3. Human behavior.   I. Title.
   HB95.U24 2009
   330.12'2—dc22

                                                              2008029735

The paper used in this publication meets the requirements of the American National Standard for Permanence of Paper for Publications and Documents in Libraries and Archives Z39.48-1992.

CONTENTS

Is there any place where freedom is more apparent than a super-market? Walking the aisles of your local grocery store, you can freely choose from among dozens of shampoos, scores of cereals, and hundreds of frozen delicacies.

But are you as free as you think? In some supermarket today, an anthropologist is wandering the aisles watching how you shop, observing whether your eyes roam the shelves from top to bottom or bottom to top, and measuring how long you linger in front of display cases if you have toddlers in tow. Meanwhile, over at the kitchen store, the proprietors have just placed an expensive new rice cooker onto the shelves, a deluxe model with a control panel that would put a 1990s VCR to shame. At nearly double the price of their next-best model, almost no consumers are willing to buy this new product. But that doesn't matter to the kitchen store, because the next-best model (which used to be its high-end, slow-selling brand) now races off the shelf, appearing to be a veritable bargain in comparison with this newer product.

The simple fact is, you know less about your own shopping behavior than the people running the stores that you shop at. Is it any wonder, then, that people have purchased themselves into debt, with the American citizenry demonstrating a negative savings rate in recent years? And is it really surprising that our hospitals are teeming with people whose diseases are a result of smoking, drinking, and overeating?

Western-style democracies pride themselves on freedom: freedom to assemble, freedom to elect legislators, and freedom to interact in the marketplace. Indeed, capitalism and democracy seem to go hand in hand. How else do you explain that Thomas Jefferson proclaimed the importance of life, liberty, and the pursuit of happiness in the same year, 1776, that Adam Smith wrote his great economic masterpiece, *The Wealth of Nations*, a book that established much of the intellectual basis for defending capitalism against its critics?

I am lucky to live in a free democratic and capitalist country. Liberty is a precious commodity, good in its own right—a gift so special that many of us would die for it. Freedom is also valuable as a means to other ends. Freedom allows people to pursue their goals, goals that vary from one person to another. It allows us to choose what career to pursue, what person to marry, how many kids to have, and (to return to the grocery store) what bottle of shampoo to buy.

But freedom to choose is accompanied by the freedom to make bad choices. And in the current marketplace, filled with companies that make a practice of studying human behavior, freedom too often leads to harm and misery. Procter & Gamble owns multimillion-dollar functional MRI (fMRI) machines, which enable the company to visualize which part of your brain "lights up" when you view its products. Psychology and sociology PhDs leave academia to work for industry or Madison Avenue, where they can employ their knowledge of human behavior in the service of selling consumer goods. We might think that we are impervious to television ads or supermarket sales schemes. But marketers and sales experts know more about our behavior than we do, and they know how to influence us without our awareness.

I wrote this book to highlight some of the dangers of liberty, but even more importantly to show how restricting some kinds of liberty can improve people's health and well-being. I intend to highlight the harms that can befall people when capitalism meets human nature—when their freedom to behave in the marketplace confronts their propensity to make flawed decisions.

Who am I, to write this book? For starters, I'm a physician caring for patients whose illnesses are frequently caused by decisions they've made and behaviors they've, um, behaved. The majority of my patients are eating too much and exercising too little; they are suffering the harmful consequences of trans fat and tobacco; in short, they are consuming themselves to death.

But I am more than just a physician. I've been trained in psychology and behavioral economics, and I've spent the better part of fifteen years researching the forces that influence the way people make decisions. I've studied the errors people make when facing difficult choices. And having helped uncover the forces that lead to such errors, I've become acutely aware of the dangers of unfettered markets. I think the time is ripe for some fettering. I can hear Larry King introducing me: "Coming up next, an egomaniacal physician who has wasted the better part of his adult years studying decision making spouts off on why free markets give people too many opportunities to make irrational decisions." A risky message for me to convey, in these days of Rush Limbaugh and Fox News.

Besides, there's nothing new about criticizing capitalism. Ever since Adam Smith defended capitalism, with his appeal to the wonders of the invisible hand, people have been trying to restrain the free market, handcuffing the economic system, so to speak, to rein in its excesses. Moreover, many of the criticisms people have heaped on capitalism have been misinformed and prejudicial. For example, many people have opposed free trade without grasping what economists, beginning with Smith, have learned about the ability of free trade to benefit people on *both* sides of the trading border. Similarly, critics like Marx were convinced that capitalism would never benefit the broad masses, because so much power was concentrated in the hands of people with capital, people with large bank accounts or vast property holdings. Marx didn't anticipate, among other things, that the power of capitalists would be reduced by labor unions. Many people still oppose free trade, and the world still has its share of Marxists. But these are no longer the most numerous or credible of capitalism's critics.

Instead, the most credible critics of capitalism today have settled into a two-front war against free markets. On one front, they try to beat back capitalism by pointing out its moral failings. In an entirely free market system, it is pointed out, people who can't afford health care won't receive it, meaning they will be essentially a ruptured appendix away from the grave. In such a system, people who can't find jobs will be left homeless, begging for spare change. Morally outraged at the heartlessness of unfettered markets, these critics contend that capitalism should be smoothed over on its rough edges, to take care of people who would suffer under its relentless competition.

On the second front, people fight back capitalism because free markets fail to protect people from spillover effects of market activity. Economists call these *externalities*. When a factory is allowed to dump toxins into a river, people living downstream are harmed. When a teenager revs up his mufflerless sports car at 2:00 a.m., he disturbs the sleep of the neighbors. An economic system that doesn't regulate water quality or noise pollution will seriously diminish the quality of life of its citizens. Once again, this critique of capitalism is put forward to address important problems that markets alone would never solve.

Let me state up front: I don't plan to debate either morality or externalities in this book. Instead, I plan to mount a third front against unfettered markets. Think of this attack as one designed neither to defeat free markets nor to force capitalism to surrender, but rather to prevent markets from gaining more territory than they deserve. To beat markets back when they've crossed the wrong boundaries.

Think of this third front as an example of "third-way" politics. I'm neither promarket nor antimarket. Free market capitalism has helped many people thrive and has created social conditions that have alleviated much suffering. But markets always need to be restrained, sometimes for reasons of justice, other times for reasons of the greater good. And they also need to be restrained for a third reason—that when people operate, their unconscious behaviors too often cause them to act against their own best interests.

In this third front against capitalism, I want to show what happens when the invisible hand meets the unconscious brain. You see, defenders of free markets and other libertarian positions have long been able to pull out some very strong ammunition when battling those forces that restrict people's freedoms. For when critics of free markets complain about wealth inequality, libertarians can always point out the injustice of limiting people's freedoms. And to strengthen their position even further, these libertarians will also point out that different people value different ends in life: some people care a lot about money, while others want to spend more time with their families. Why should a policy address wealth inequality, when wealth inequality arises at least in part from these different preferences? If some people want to spend their cash on luxury cars, and others on college educations for their children, why should we stop them from doing this? Given the different values that people hold, libertarians can always argue that society should simply step out of the way and let people make their own choices.

Backing up this defense of libertarianism have been a series of brilliant nineteenth- and twentieth-century economists, who took the initial insights of Adam Smith and developed them into the most influential of the social sciences. Indeed, while there have always been left-wing and right-wing economists—with Karl Marx and Milton Friedman both belonging to the discipline—most academic economists by the middle of the twentieth century had embraced the libertarian view of individuals as the best promoters of their interests. The economic theories that came to dominate the discipline embraced a mythical being, *Homo economicus*, who made rational decisions that reflected his own preferences.

Because of the power of this myth, free markets have encroached on an increasingly large part of people's lives. Kids who struggle with basic math skills can rattle off a thousand consumer brands. New stadiums no longer don the names of famous politicians or athletes, and instead drape themselves in corporate logos. Pharmaceutical companies now convince us to "talk to our doctor" about diseases that they hope to convince us we have. It is this encroachment that I plan to fight.

I will show how economists came to hold a belief in human rationality, and how that faith has come under question by developments in neuroscience and behavioral economics. More importantly, I will raise questions about what the limits of human rationality imply for the proper limits of free markets. In doing so, I plan to show, in broad outline, what markets can look like when they are designed to take account of human nature.

ACKNOWLEDGMENTS

First and foremost, I owe this book to Charles Darwin. OK, not to Darwin exactly, but instead to evolution—to the amazing forces that caused human brains to evolve in such a way not only to give me (and most other members of my species) the ability to read and write, but also to give me the irrational desire to wake up at five every morning and delude myself into believing that I could write a book that thousands (nay, tens of thousands) of people would read. With the average American reading less than one book per year, it takes a certain kind of irrationality to spend hundreds of hours writing books. But people like you, holding this book (or e-book) in your hand right now, are clearly not average, and it is for people like you that I've written this book.

In writing this book, I'm lucky to have worked with many brilliant people who have given me helpful feedback on earlier versions. At the Center for Behavioral and Decision Sciences in Medicine, where I work, I had the privilege of bouncing ideas off of many wonderful people. I am grateful to Dylan Smith, Angie Fagerlin, Brian Zikmund-Fisher, and Scott Kim for commenting on specific chapters. Michele Heisler, another Michigan colleague, once again has proved to be an incredibly enthusiastic but critical reader. I also received invaluable advice from colleagues around the country, and am especially grateful to George Loewenstein, Dan Ariely, and several anonymous reviewers for their feedback. This book is better because of their efforts.

When I discuss my own research in this book, I am always referring to collaborative studies. Almost none of the research I do is done just on my own. That's one of the joys of science. I'm sure that George Loewenstein, Heather Pond Lacey, Angie Fagerlin, Brian Zikmund-Fisher, Dylan Smith, Ellen Hummel, and Scott Halpern will all recognize our collaborative efforts peeking out through the pages of this book.

Thanks to Sarah Conner, Sandra Serna Smith, Melissa Shauver, Sarah Scheitler, and Lauren Bailey for helping me with multiple drafts of this book. Special kudos to Sarah Scheitler for taking every one of my requests three steps further than I anticipated, and enriching my understanding of this topic in the process.

My agent, Rob McQuilkin, has once again been an amazing help, full of encouragement, enthusiasm, and great advice. Jacque Murphy has shown me the benefits of getting a top-notch editor involved early in the drafting of the manuscript. I am really lucky to have been able to work with her. Special thanks to John Lofy for making it through an early version of this book. And my final thanks, and the dedication of this book, go to "my first wife"— Paula. Thanks for setting aside your love of fiction long enough to read and reread so many chapters of this book.

PART I

Maximizing Our Best Interests by Expanding Our Waistlines?

CHAPTER ONE

The Invisible Hand Meets the Unconscious Brain

JOHN HOWARD has always been a man of rituals. Back in high school, he owed much of his success as a star wrestler and sprinter to his mastery of each sport's rituals. During the winter wrestling season, he would starve himself to slim his 6-feet 2-inch frame down to 170 pounds, a feat he accomplished the night before weigh-ins by spitting intermittently into a cup to take off the last few ounces of water weight. In springtime, when training for the 100-yard hurdling competition, he would tirelessly practice his leaping form each day after school. He mastered these rituals well enough to earn a college wrestling scholarship and to win the city hurdling championship his senior year.

Fifty years later, John finds himself immersed in a whole new set of rituals that begin every day at the crack of dawn. Waking up, he rubs the sleep out of his eyes, pulls open his bedside drawer, then takes out a vial of insulin, a syringe, and a glucometer. Pricking his finger, he squeezes a drop of blood onto a test strip so his glucometer can calculate his blood sugar, and, glancing at the reading, he quickly determines how much insulin to draw up into the syringe—10 units if his sugar is in the normal range, 15 units if last night's banana cream pie is still circulating through his system. Then he puts down the vial and, matter-of-factly, plunges the needle into his belly.

Thanks to his diabetes medicines, John is already ten years older than his father was when he died, succumbing to complications of diabetes at age fifty-eight. In fact, members of John's generation on average are living almost twenty years longer than their grandparents, proof, it might seem, of the miracles of modern medicine.[1]

The longevity of John's generation, however, is hardly attributable to medical science alone. If anything explains their health and well-being, it is the modern evolution of free markets.

That's right. The marketplace has saved John's life.

Take a moment to imagine the needle poised above his abdomen. Now back up from this view, as if you were looking at John through the Google Earth Web site. Zoom out, above John's bedroom, and you'll see the top of his condominium. Back out farther, and you will see the city of Scottsdale, where he lives; soon you'll see the whole state of Arizona. Now travel across the Atlantic Ocean to the Terumo needle factory, in Leuven, Belgium (about 10 miles outside of Brussels), where, if you zoom back in during working hours, you can watch workers making the kind of needles that people like John use every day to give themselves their insulin.[2]

It will look like an ordinary modern factory. The factory floor will be an elegant synchrony of humans and machines. One group of workers, standing next to large vats of molten steel, will be pouring the liquid out and drawing it into the casts, which will be fitting the steel into the proper shape to become a needle. As the steel moves along the production line, it will be further formed into a continuous hollow wire by another series of machines. Yet another set of machines will be cutting the wires to form the needles. Along all these production lines, some workers will be monitoring the machines, while others will be bringing materials back and forth to different parts of the manufacturing site. In one day, the workers and machines at this factory will make 4.5 million needles.

But needles alone will not suffice to allow John to administer his daily injection. Those needles need to be attached to syringes. To see a typical syringe being made, you could zoom back out and zip across the globe to a factory in India or China. There's also John's insulin, the most important part of this marketplace miracle. The insulin John uses is manufactured by people who look more like laboratory researchers than factory workers. Rather than monitoring heavy machinery, they supervise colonies of bacteria that have been genetically altered to produce insulin.

John Howard's morning insulin shot, then, is the product of a great many people's labors. In the kind of factories that manufacture his needles, syringes, and medicines, the people who made these products for John number well into the dozens. But dozens, even hundreds, of other people played a role in this morning's insulin shot, too. Scores of additional workers, for instance, were needed to transport the needle, the syringe, and the insulin to John's pharmacy. Countless others mined the metals melted into the steel that became John's needle; drilled for the fossil fuels that became the plastics that became John's syringe; and labored in the manufacturing plants that produced the trucks and boats and trains that transported these materials around the globe.

And the market forces providing John with his medication extend well beyond such mines and factory floors. Consider the venture capitalists who funded the biotech firm that made his insulin; the banks that loaned money to the trucking companies that transported the medicine; and the business schools that trained the financiers and managers who developed the operating procedures that made this all possible.

And so we see that the medicine John takes each day is, in fact, produced by *thousands* of people. Amazing to think of, when that same medicine, something with the potential to save his very life, costs him all of $1.75—roughly half the price of a ham sandwich.

How could the product of so many thousands of people's labors cost so little money? The answer to this question was given to us in 1776 by Adam Smith in his revolutionary book, *The Wealth of Nations*. Early in this masterpiece, Smith describes a pin factory in his native Scotland:

> *One man draws out the wire, another straights it, a third cuts it, a fourth points it, a fifth grinds it at the top for receiving the head; to make the head requires three distinct operations; to put it on is a peculiar business, to whiten the pins is another; it is even a trade by itself to put them into the paper; and the important business of making a pin is, in this manner, divided into about eighteen distinct operations, which, in some manufactories, are all performed by distinct hands, though in others the same man sometimes performs two or three of them.[3]*

This may seem like a mundane way for Smith to begin a book that he had labored over for more than a decade.[4] But Smith was illustrating a profound point, a point that echoes in the halls of academia and government buildings to this day. For he was showing why national wealth, and therefore the well-being of humankind, was strongly dependent on the division of labor. Smith showed that the making of a pin, which a single man on his own would be hard pressed to accomplish in any given day, was accomplished so efficiently through the division of labor, that ten men could now make 12 pounds of pins in a day—some 48,000 pins.

Of course, Smith himself did not invent the idea of a division of labor. The pin factory he described was already in business when he wrote his book. What Smith *did* accomplish was to explain to people how free markets could benefit humankind, by promoting the division of labor and, therefore, increasing societal wealth and well-being.

Smith's book was immediately influential because it addressed and effectively allayed people's fear of free markets. As Robert

Heilbroner eloquently explains in *The Worldly Philosophers*, Adam Smith lived at a time when economic activity was controlled by tradition or determined by fiat.[5] Free markets didn't decide how many people would be hired to manufacture pins or bake bread. There was as yet no invisible hand guiding people's career decisions or determining what products manufacturers made. Instead, people's jobs were determined by king or caste systems. The workplace was dominated by rigid rules and traditions, and when people deviated from these rules or traditions, they were punished or ostracized or harassed by local authorities. The world was an orderly place, but it was also a place where progress was slow and the rewards of innovation small.

Smith had close knowledge of these noncapitalist traditions, which in his life had not yet released their grip on Scottish society. For he had befriended a bright young man, James Watt, who was looking for work as an instrument maker.[6] Though Watt had an uncommon knack for mechanics, he was banned from the workplace, not being the son of an instrument maker. Through Smith's intervention, Watt was offered a job as instrument maker at the university, an offer possible only because universities were allowed to make their own hiring decisions. And Smith's faith in the younger man's talents would prove well founded: Watt would later become famous for inventing the steam engine.[7]

As entrepreneurial energy transformed eighteenth-century Europe, the old social order was beginning to crumble, and Edinburgh, where Smith lived, was a major center of capitalist enterprise. Thousands of workers were finding jobs that had no relation to the jobs of their fathers. No longer were all of the pin makers in the local pin factories the sons of pinsmiths. Indeed, new industries were blossoming in Edinburgh, creating a demand for altogether new types of jobs—jobs that *no* one's fathers had previously held. And so to fill these jobs, employers were forced to break from tradition. This rapid break from tradition was exciting, but also frightening. The thriving new economy felt chaotic to many people: how could anything good come out of the chaos created by free markets? If people aren't told what careers to enter into, how can they be expected to pick the right careers? How will society end up with the right number of physicians and farmers and instrument makers if no central authority, or no sense of tradition, determines who ends up in each of these occupations?

Economists like to tell a joke about the chaos of free markets, involving an argument among a surgeon, an engineer, and an economist, about whose profession is the oldest. The surgeon points out that his profession is the oldest, because when God took a rib out of Adam to make Eve, God obviously needed a surgeon on hand. The engineer claims that her field was first, pointing out that God made the world before making people and must have needed an engineer to separate the land from the sea. Undaunted, the economist points out that "before God made the world, what was there? Chaos. And who do you think was responsible for *that*?"

The Wealth of Nations created a stir in large part because Smith explained, in elaborate detail, with rich anecdotes, why free markets would not lead to chaos. To the contrary, Smith showed that only by shedding tradition, and letting free markets operate by the laws of supply and demand, would the correct number of people become farmers and instrument makers. He explained how such markets, through the workings of an invisible hand, would determine not only how many people would work in pin factories, but also how many pins they would make. He showed how, through the division of labor, factories could have fewer pin makers and still make more pins, freeing up laborers to manufacture other goods and thereby increase the wealth of the nation, with each worker "led by an invisible hand to promote an end which was no part of his intention," an end, Smith concludes, that promotes the general well-being of humanity.[8]

Since at least the 1870s, in what is called the neoclassical revolution in economics, the theories of Adam Smith have dominated economic thinking.[9] Many economists believe, as Smith did, in the wonders of free markets.[10] Many economic theories are grounded on the view, often attributed to Smith, that human beings are motivated by rational self-interest to make decisions that, when guided by an invisible hand, lead to happiness and well-being.

Charles Wheelan, a reporter for the *Economist*, illustrates the wonders of the invisible hand by describing a Coca-Cola executive living in West Berlin at the time the wall to East Berlin was coming down. The executive had the idea to hand out free bottles of Coke through holes in the wall: "In a sense, it was Adam Smith's invisible hand passing Coca-Cola through the Berlin Wall. Coke representatives were not undertaking any great humanitarian gesture as they passed beverages to the newly liberated East Germans . . . They were looking after business—expanding their global market, boosting profits, and making shareholders happy."[11] No doubt, the Coke executive made a brilliant decision, and I'm sure people were delighted, at that moment in time, to gulp down a bottle filled with such a powerful symbol of Western culture. But was Coca-Cola the very best thing that the invisible hand could bring to people just escaping from decades of communism? And should we, then, celebrate the increase in tooth decay and diabetes diagnoses now spreading through Eastern Europe?

Consider how John Howard has functioned as a marketplace consumer over his adult life, purchasing thousands of meals at fast-food restaurants, and reaching for junk food out of his kitchen cabinets a dozen or more times each day. When we visited the factories that manufactured John's needles, syringes, and insulin, we got a good view of the wonders of free markets. But we could have just as easily looked at another series of businesses that have influenced John's diabetes. We could have visited his butcher, where John bought the ground beef and steaks that contributed to his adult weight gain; or the bakery, where he picked up cinnamon rolls and donuts every weekend; or the Idaho potato farms that grow the potatoes for the french fries John has munched on over the years.

As Eric Schlosser described in *Fast Food Nation*, the fast-food industry itself is an example of amazing market efficiency.[12] The production of french fries, hamburgers, and Coca-Cola have all resulted from the same divisions of labor that led to the production of John Howard's insulin treatments. Indeed, because of these efficiencies, food calories have never been as cheap to produce and consume as they are today.[13] Without a doubt this is a miracle of modern markets. But it is a miracle whose implications clearly do not lead, in all cases, to the best of all possible worlds.

John Howard is not only a member of the longest-living generation to date. He may be a member of the longest-living generation ever. Because by some estimates, the obesity epidemic rampant in industrialized countries, and emerging in many developing countries, has become so severe that, notwithstanding modern medicine, today's children may not, in fact, live as long as their parents.[14]

Research has shown that genetics contributes to diabetes and obesity: you're more likely to be fat if your father is fat, and are more likely to develop diabetes if your identical twin is diabetic.[15] But genetics is not the only cause of diabetes or obesity—indeed, not even the main cause. We know this because obesity rates have risen dramatically over the past few decades. In 1991, only four states in the United States had obesity rates of 15 percent or higher; by 2001 some thirty-seven states did.[16] In fact, the proportion of overweight teenagers roughly doubled in Great Britain between 1984 and 1993. Trust me, the genetic code of people in the United States and Great Britain has not changed substantially over the past few decades. The primary cause of obesity, then, is not genetics; it is free markets.

Free markets have created tremendous wealth—of opportunity and of consumer goods. Free markets have encouraged the expansion of human liberties, giving people more choice in the workplace (no longer forced to follow in dad's career path) and in the shopping market (no longer limited to a choice of only two or three shampoos). In theory, these liberties and these choices should work out for the best. People will make choices based on their preferences and values. They can decide whether to work overtime at 150 percent of their normal wages or, instead, spend the weekend wrestling with their kids. According to their own idea of the "good life," they can decide whether they would be better off spending money on TiVo or on a college savings account for those same kids. They can choose whether to spend an hour cooking every night or to simply pick up some KFC on the way home from work. And the market will respond to each of these choices, erecting more KFC franchises as demand rises, and increasing overtime pay as the number of workers willing to put in weekend time falls.

I could easily write a book trying to convince people of the wisdom of markets. Not so long ago, after all, two of the largest countries in the world, the USSR and China, more closely followed the anticapitalist teachings of Karl Marx than the procapitalist views of Adam Smith. Indeed, even in predominantly capitalist countries, free trade is constantly under threat across the industrialized world.

But with all the wonders of free markets, with all the freedom brought by markets, comes the freedom for people to make bad decisions. Adam Smith famously wrote, "It is not from the benevolence for the butcher, the brewer, or the baker that we expect our dinner, but from their regard to their own interest."[17] Consider Smith's butcher, brewer, and baker in the context of today's obesity epidemic. On the supply side, the free market does a good job of determining how many butchers, brewers, and bakers there need to be in order to meet people's demand for butchered, brewed, and baked goods.

But what about the people buying such goods? When a sixty-year-old diabetic man purchases a pound of beef from a butcher, a six-pack of beer from the liquor store, and a dozen donuts from the bakery, how convinced would any of us be that he has just maximized his best interests?

What about the twenty-year-old who purchases a carton of cigarettes at the drugstore—has she maximized her best interests? Or the exhausted mother who relents to her child's demand for a PlayStation—has she maximized her own best interests or those of her child?

The structure of most industrialized countries is a reflection of people's response to market forces and to the pressures people exert on markets by demanding specific market goods. To the extent people make wise purchasing decisions, this is all for the better. But it isn't hard to look around and see evidence that many of the purchasing decisions we make are having less than ideal effects on our well-being, to say nothing of society more generally.

If we hope to understand not just the strengths but also the weaknesses of free markets, we need to understand the strengths and weaknesses of human nature.

CHAPTER TWO

Is the Obesity Epidemic
a Consequence of
Rational Choices?

MUCH OF THE POWER of economics as a social science resides in its ability to reveal the logic underlying a wide range of human behaviors. Economists have developed mathematical tools that elucidate the kinds of cost-benefit calculations that influence everything from criminal behavior to marital decision making. Indeed, economists have even done a good job of highlighting the rational choices that have contributed to the obesity epidemic.

It is strange, of course, to describe obesity as a rational choice. All else equal, few people choose to be fat. To call obesity a consequence of rational choice, however, is not to say that the John Howards of the world want to be fat. Instead, it amounts to saying that John has faced a series of choices in his life and has largely made them rationally; that some of those choices concerned the food he ate—he knew that Big Macs weren't helping him squeeze into his old trousers; and that John decided that the pain of forgoing delicious meals was greater than the benefit of reducing his caloric intake.

By this same reasoning, John has contemplated, on many nights, heading to the gym or walking around his neighborhood to burn off calories. But on most of these nights, tired from a hard day of work, he decided against such exercise and partook, instead, in the pleasures of a cold beer and a *Gunsmoke* rerun. As a consequence of these rational cost-benefit calculations, John became obese.

The case for rational obesity is strengthened by the fact that most obese people know the causes of their body size. When markets don't provide consumers with the information they need to make good decisions, the markets have failed, and policy makers need to decide whether to take steps to make sure consumers get such information. I will return to this information idea later in this book. But it is only minimally relevant to the obesity epidemic. After all, people have known for a long time that obesity is caused by consuming more calories than you burn. And while most of us don't know how many calories are in our Big Macs, we know that our waistlines are expanding in large measure as a result of our eating habits.

Rationality, as I've mentioned, is a common assumption underlying many economic studies of human behavior. Consider what Paul Samuelson and William Nordhaus write in their best-selling economics textbook, a view that captures the dominant strain of twentieth-century economic thinking: "We do not expect consumers to be wizards. They may make most decisions in a routine and unthinking way. What is assumed is that consumers are fairly consistent in their tastes and actions—that they do not flail around in unpredictable ways, making themselves miserable by persistent errors of judgment or arithmetic. If enough people act consistently, avoiding erratic changes in buying behavior and generally choosing their most preferred commodities, our scientific theory will provide a reasonably good approximation to the facts."[1] In other words, people aren't perfect, but they come close enough to perfection in their consumer behavior that it makes scientific sense to assume that consumers are making rational decisions. Indeed,

Trenton Smith justifies the presumption of rationality underlying much economic theory on the basis that a productive social science "must focus on the systematic (rather than the idiosyncratic) aspects of behavior if it is to have any hope of generating a theory with substantive predictive power."[2]

Many economists, steeped in neoclassical theory, have used this assumption of rationality to predict wide-ranging behaviors. Robert Lucas, for instance, a University of Chicago economist and Nobel Prize winner, writes that unemployment is a rational decision people make: "To explain why people allocate to unemployment, we need to [know] why they prefer it to all other activities."[3]

Another Chicago laureate, Gary Becker, and his MacArthur-winning colleague, Kevin Murphy, have written that addiction is a rational response to circumstance: "People often become addicted precisely because they are unhappy," they write, but go on to add, "However, they would be even more unhappy if they were prevented from consuming the addictive goods."[4] According to rational choice theory, people only take drugs because drugs maximize their well-being. Then why do so many addicts try so hard to kick their habits? Becker and Murphy have an answer: "The claims of some heavy drinkers and smokers that they want to but cannot end their addictions seem to us no different from the claims of single persons that they want to but are unable to marry or from the claims of disorganized persons that they want to become better organized."

At first glance, these statements may strike many people as foolish. But Lucas, Becker, and Murphy are not fools, by any measure, and they are hardly fringe economists. They are espousing views that were *central* to twentieth-century economic thinking and that continue to influence scientific thinking today.

Indeed, the ideas of people like Lucas, Becker, and Murphy in many ways are the culmination of two hundred years of economic thinking. In the eighteenth century, a philosopher and political activist named Jeremy Bentham developed an influential moral and political philosophy called utilitarianism. Bentham equated utility with happiness and spent much of his life persuading people that the goal of human activity and of government legislation should be to maximize the overall happiness of the general public.[5] In the nineteenth century, economists transformed Bentham's ideas from these vague hedonistic terms into more precise scientific measures, equating utility not with happiness per se but with rational choice. These nineteenth-century theories were quite profound and deserve a brief introduction here, in order to set the stage for a fuller look at what it would mean for a person to make rational choices that lead to obesity.

Water and Diamonds

It was during the nineteenth century—a time of relative peace and prosperity—that economics came into its own as a profession. In the hundred years between Napoleon's defeat at Waterloo and the beginning of World War I, leading research universities began to establish economics departments separate in identity from moral and political philosophy. No longer was economics led by moral philosophers. In their place arrived men who were more interested in mathematics than moral philosophy, more likely to be versed in engineering than psychology. And this new breed of mathematically inclined economists revitalized the economic understanding of utility.

They would start by revisiting a conundrum identified by the founding father of their discipline: they would help explain, in a way Adam Smith had not foreseen, why diamonds are more valuable than water.

Adam Smith was not the first person to ponder the relative value of water and diamonds,[6] but he is responsible for making the conundrum famous: "Nothing is more useful than water," he wrote, "but it will purchase scarce anything; scarce anything can be had in exchange for it. A diamond, on the contrary, has scarce any value in use; but a very great quantity of other goods may frequently be had in exchange for it."[7]

Smith understood value in two ways: the value in *use* of an object or its value in *exchange*. A hundred-dollar bill, by this distinction, has very little value in use. You can use it to help start a fire, or if you roll it up, I am told, you can use it to snort drugs. But the real value of a hundred-dollar bill is its value in exchange. You can trade it for hordes of useful things.

Water, for all its uses, is not so valuable in exchange, unless you happen to have an extra jug of it and come across a wealthy man lost in the desert. In normal situations, you cannot exchange a bucket of water for anything, because the person you are trading with can fill up his own bucket for free. Water's value is all about value in use. You can drink it; water a plant with it; wash your clothes, your dishes, or your hair with it; and even fill a swimming pool with it.

So why doesn't something with such great value in use have more value in exchange? Smith answered this question by tying the price of goods, their value in exchange, to the amount of labor it took to produce the good. If you want to know how much something costs, Smith suggests that you find out how much labor it took to produce it: "If among a nation of hunters, for example, it usually costs twice the labor to kill a beaver than it does to kill a deer, one beaver should naturally exchange for or be worth two deer." Most early economists followed Smith's lead, in attributing the exchange value of goods to the labor that produced them.[8]

I expect many of you have noticed that something doesn't seem right about Smith's solution to the water/diamond conundrum. For by Smith's logic, if it took the average hunter twenty hours to chase down and kill a squirrel, and only an hour to shoot a deer, then people should be willing to trade twenty deer for one squirrel. That simply doesn't jibe with common sense. For all his insight, Smith didn't successfully isolate why diamonds had more value in exchange than water. The understanding came instead from someone who spent many hours intensely pondering the mysteries of water, a hydraulic engineer named Jules Dupuit.

Water Under the Bridge

Jules Dupuit was born in Fossano, Italy, in 1804, at a time when Napoleon still ruled much of Europe.[9] When he was ten years old, his family moved to France, where the studious child, who won numerous academic awards, grew up to become a studious young adult, graduating from the Ecole Polytechnic with a degree in civil engineering. After graduation, Dupuit remained in France, designing roads and bridges and water systems. In conducting this work, he thought deeply about the financial costs and benefits of these systems and how best to pay for them. What, for example, is the right toll to charge when people cross a public bridge? To answer this type of question, Dupuit taught himself economics.

Perhaps if he had been on the receiving end of formal economics lectures, he would have been indoctrinated into the classical line of thinking. Maybe he would have become convinced that the value of a bridge depends on the labor that went into building it. But that logic didn't make sense to Dupuit. If a bridge cost 100,000 francs to build, that still doesn't tell us how much to charge any single person to cross the bridge. Even if your sole goal were to recoup the 100,000 franc investment, the correct toll would depend on how many people crossed the bridge, and the number of people who would cross the bridge would depend on the price of crossing.

What about the price of water from a public water system? Surely, you won't try to recoup the cost of the system with the first cup of water. But how much should you charge for each cup of water? Here, Dupuit settled on the idea of *marginal utility*. Dupuit recognized that the value of water—its value in use—is not constant, but declines as more water becomes available.

Suppose, for example, that a hectoliter of water costs 50 francs. Dupuit concluded that every hectoliter of water consumed in these circumstances has a utility of *at least* 50 francs, because otherwise people wouldn't purchase the water. But that doesn't mean that every hectoliter is worth only 50 francs to people. In fact, the first hectoliter of water I buy at 50 francs will be very valuable to me, staving off dehydration. If water were scarce enough, I would gladly part with the better portion of my fortune to procure a hectoliter of water. The next hectoliter will still be valuable, but not quite as valuable. My immediate life will not depend on it. At some point, I will consider whether to buy another hectoliter of water, and decide that it is not worth 50 francs. That means the value of use of that first hectoliter (its utility) is not equal on average to the utility (or value in exchange) of 50 francs. Instead, it is the *last* bit of water I buy that is actually worth at least 50 francs to me.

Adam Smith was correct in writing that water often has tremendous value in use; fending off dehydration is a valuable thing. But lower the price of water enough, and people will use it for much less valuable things: lawn watering, car washing, and water balloon fights. To know the utility, then, of any consumer good, Dupuit directed people to look at the margins. If you look at how people use water when it's priced at 40 francs per hectoliter rather than 50, you'll know which uses bring somewhere between 40 and 49 francs of utility per hectoliter.

Comparing Apples to Oranges

Dupuit's insight would launch economists on a revolution in thinking, known as the *marginalist revolution*.[10] Fittingly enough, one of the next great thinkers to develop this marginal theory of utility, Stanley Jevons, attended school at the University College of London, the school founded by Jeremy Bentham. In Benthamite fashion, he wrote, "A true theory of economy can only be attained by going back to the great springs of human action—the feelings of pleasure and pain."[11] But Jevons's theory didn't remain in the vague form Bentham had left it in. Instead, in his theory Jevons attempted to quantify utility—pleasure and pain. To do this, he took advantage of the fact that people's market behaviors are grounded in monetary decisions. Do I water my lawn? Not if water costs $1 per gallon. Because gallons of water (and milk and Silly Putty) cost money, people need to decide whether the benefit of any given purchase, the utility of that purchase, is worth that cost.

Jevons began developing his theory while working as an assayer at the Royal Mint in Sydney, Australia, where he was responsible for testing whether coins had the right amount of gold in them.[12] The job was not very demanding for a man of his intellect, so in his free time he investigated topics like weather and geography, studied plants and rocks, and began reading up on economics. Quickly absorbing the rather scant literature available on this last topic, he became convinced that the discipline needed a shot of mathematics if it was to unlock market mysteries.

He made his way to London in 1859, at age twenty-four, to attend university, focusing his energy on logic, mathematics, and economics. Jevons sparked the marginalist revolution in economics by taking Dupuit's concept of marginal utility and showing how it explained consumer choices. His starting point, like Bentham's, was the psychological importance of pleasure and pain. But to these strong emotions he wedded a belief in the rationality of people's decisions: "Our estimation about the comparative amounts of feeling is performed in the act of choice or volition. Our choice of one course out of two or more proves that, in estimation, this course promises the greatest balance of pleasure."[13] People making rational choices should spend money in a way that brings the same utility per dollar with each purchase they make.

To illustrate his point, Jevons compared apples to oranges. Suppose apples sell for 10¢ each and oranges sell for 20¢. If I like apples just as much as oranges, and I plan to spend 20¢, I will buy two apples, because I get more utility—pleasure—out of two apples than I do out of one orange.

But suppose I am spending $3 on fruit. I won't necessarily buy thirty apples. By the time I own twenty-eight apples, I might feel that the utility of a 20¢ orange is greater than that of a twenty-ninth and thirtieth apple. With each 20¢ increment, I will consider how much pleasure I will get from two apples versus one orange. The only rational way to spend money in this situation is for me to purchase apples and oranges so that the marginal utility—the extra utility—that I get from the last two apples I buy is the same as the marginal utility I get from the last orange.

Now how does this explain water and diamonds? Jevons extended his reasoning beyond consumer purchasing decisions, the demand side of the economy, to include as well things like selling decisions—the supply side. Suppose I am in possession of a hundred apples and you own a hundred oranges. As neither of us is making applesauce or orange juice for a living, we have pretty much maxed out the utility we can get out of our respective fruits, and I will receive very little additional utility by holding on to that 100th apple. So I propose an exchange—I will give you one apple if you give me one orange. I gain utility from this exchange, since the utility of the first orange will far exceed that of the 100th apple. You gain for similar reasons. As Jevons interpreted this type of situation, we will continue to trade apples and oranges as long as at least one of us is gaining from the trade.

Jevons showed that the value in exchange of any good, from an individual's perspective, depends on the marginal utility that the seller will forgo and that the buyer will receive. If you and I are lost in the desert, I won't trade you my canteen for your diamond ring. But if, as in most cases, water is plentiful, then I give up very little utility by parting with a liter of water and would gladly trade that for your ring.

With the work of Jevons and contemporaries such as Leon Walras, the marginalist revolution was now in full force. And as a result, the concept of utility was being explored with a level of mathematical rigor that would have pleased Bentham.

We will soon shift from healthy foods like Jevons's apples and oranges back to the processed foods that have contributed to the modern obesity epidemic. At that time, I'll show how those nineteenth-century ideas have influenced contemporary theories of rational obesity.

But first we must complete our brief historical with a quick discussion of jam. You see, with the increasing quantification of utility, you might imagine that the concept of utility was becoming more abstract. But to the economists of the time, the more they could characterize utility in the language of mathematics, the *realer* utility felt to them. To those men, concepts like "the balance of pleasure and pain" had been unsatisfying abstractions, so vague as to border on meaningless. But by expressing utility mathematically, it became real. In fact, Nobel laureate Paul Samuelson once remarked that for Francis Edgeworth, another contemporary of Jevons, the concept of utility was "as real as his morning jam."[14]

Edgeworth's Jam

Edgeworth's father was a Cambridge-educated and thoroughly impractical man, too interested in literary pursuits to establish much of a career. He died at age thirty-seven, during the height of the potato famine, but not before he'd sired a gaggle of children, having married a sixteen-year old when he was twenty-two, a girl he enthusiastically described as being "fat, voluptuous and made for love."

Young Francis didn't share his father's infatuation with the fairer gender, remaining unmarried throughout his life. A kind and courteous eccentric, he was too absorbed in deep thoughts to concern himself with which women might or might not be made for love. Trained as a lawyer, Edgeworth was not cut out for real-world pursuits, and so lived his life as an academic, where he was renowned for the way he avoided normal conversational English. Legend has it that he once asked T. E. Lawrence whether it was "very caliginous in the Metropolis," to which Lawrence replied (well aware of Edgeworth's Latinate proclivities), "Somewhat caliginous but not altogether inspissated."

To give you a feel for how Edgeworth developed the mathematical side of utility, we need to map out my feelings toward apples and oranges. Fair minded as I am, let us say I am equally pleased at possessing one hundred apples as I am at possessing one hundred oranges. Let's further suppose that I would be equally happy (because of the declining marginal utility of each fruit) to have twenty-five apples and twenty-five oranges as I would be to have one hundred of either fruit.

Edgeworth would map out my feelings in a manner like figure 2-1, in which every point on this curve brings me an identical amount of utility.

In this example, I'm pretending that apples and oranges bring me similar utility. This wouldn't need to be true. If I were a huge

FIGURE 2-1

Utility curve

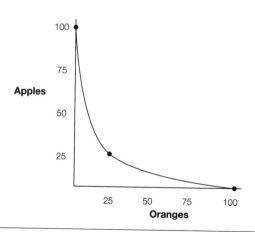

fan of oranges, then this curve might intersect the Y axis at one hundred apples and the X axis at, say, fifty oranges. Economists call this an *indifference curve*, because it shows the distribution of apples and oranges that bring similar utility and that, therefore, I should be indifferent between. In other words, I should feel just as happy receiving one hundred apples as I do receiving twenty-five apples and twenty-five oranges.

Now consider what might happen if you have one hundred oranges in your possession and I have one hundred apples, and we begin to trade fruit to maximize our respective utilities. Suppose I trade fifty apples to you in exchange for fifty oranges. That means I now possess fifty apples and fifty oranges. Where is this mixture on our figure? It is to the right of my initial indifference curve. It sits in the middle of *another* indifference curve (see figure 2-2), and the utility of that curve—of every point on that curve—is greater than the utility of my initial indifference curve.

I'm not doing justice to the brilliance of marginalists like Edgeworth. But I hope you can begin to glimpse the power of their ideas. Here, with a simple pair of indifference curves, Edgeworth has illustrated how free trade in the marketplace increases the

FIGURE 2-2

Indifference curve

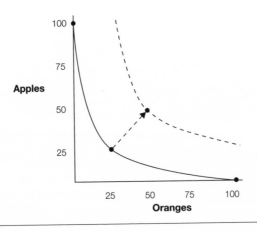

utility—the well-being—of both trading partners, moving them off one curve to a better one.

The eloquence of Smith's *Wealth of Nations* had eased many people's fears about the impact of free markets on people's lives. Now, with the marginalists' equations and graphs, people had scientific *proof* that markets benefit people. People like Dupuit, Jevons, and Edgeworth had made the benefits of market exchanges so obvious—you give me two apples, I'll give you two oranges, and we'll both be better off—that it seemed only rational for people to behave the way Edgeworth's indifference curves would suggest they ought to behave.

Back to Rational Obesity

Thanks to this brief historical tour, you now understand the famous joke: "Why did the chicken cross the road? To maximize his utility, of course."

I said famous, not funny.

But in any case, more important than understanding or appreciating this joke is the job of understanding how these ideas of rational choice and utility maximization translate into theories of rational obesity. Economic science often focuses on the decisions people face when their wants can't all be met at once. John Howard wants to be thin, and, yet, he also wants a slice of cake for dessert. In opting for the dessert, he is telling us something about his preferences. Economists have shown that the choices people make are influenced by the costs and benefits of their alternatives. If that dessert is a bit less appetizing, John might choose to adhere to his diet for the evening. If the cost of baked goods rises enough, people like John won't eat as many cakes and brownies.

One rational explanation for the rise in obesity, then, focuses on the change in food prices that market economies have experienced over the past few decades.

In 1998, Adam Drewnowski, a professor at the University of Washington, walked around his local grocery store calculating how many calories per dollar he could get from the food located in various aisles. At that time, he discovered that $1 of carrots contained around 250 kilocalories of energy, just enough energy for a person to bike 5 miles. That same $1, if spent on cookies, would garner 1,200 calories and propel a biker more than 20 miles.[15] For people with spare cash, the caloric inefficiency of carrots is generally not an issue. But for people who don't have so much money, the cost of carrot calories can be prohibitive. For instance, when researchers have surveyed low-income families, they have found that the price of healthy foods—like fruits, vegetables, and whole grain breads—creates a significant incentive for the families to purchase less-healthy foods.

If your income was above the U.S. median in 1997, you had a 15 percent chance of being obese. If you were living near the poverty line, these odds climbed to almost 30 percent.[16] Drewnowski's research presents a market-based explanation for this strong association between obesity and poverty—only people with high incomes, it seems, can afford healthy foods. Low-income families, in an effort to spend less money on groceries, are stuck with junk food.

At the same time that low-income families have faced increasing pressure to eat junk food rather than healthy produce, these same families have encountered an increasingly steep price to exercise. I am not referring to the cost of joining the local fitness center. Instead, as Thomas Philipson and Richard Posner from the University of Chicago put it, technology changes at the workplace have reduced the number of calories expended by laborers. "In an agricultural or industrial society," they write, "work is strenuous; in effect, the worker is *paid* to exercise."[17] But now, workers must exercise on their own time, and thus the cost of exercise has risen for them. Rationally speaking, if the cost of exercise goes up, people will exercise less.

The increasing cost of exercise hasn't occurred only in the workplace. For when people come home from work, they face an increasing number of attractive choices about how to spend their time. When John Howard considers a brisk walk through his neighborhood to burn off some calories, he has to balance the costs and benefits of that activity with the costs and benefits of watching television for thirty minutes. As Philipson and Posner put it, the existence of entertaining television shows increases the cost of exercise. Forgoing *Gunsmoke* can take its toll on people.

When economists think about costs, they don't limit themselves to sticker prices. Their theories are powerful in part because they hold an expansive view of costs, considering not just monetary costs, but time costs, opportunity costs, sunk costs, and the like.

Indeed, one of the most profound economic analyses I have seen on obesity attributes the rising girth of Americans not to the monetary cost of junk food versus healthier alternatives, but instead to the relative time costs of these food categories.[18] Harvard economist David Cutler and his colleagues present compelling evidence that obesity has risen more from an increase in calories than from a reduction in exercise. People eat more fast food and snack food than they used to.[19] The reason they do so, Cutler and colleagues argue, is that technology has allowed people to spend less time cooking and cleaning in their kitchens than they used to. In the old days, if a person wanted french fries, he would have to thinly slice some potatoes, season them, fry them, and then clean up the splattery mess. Quite a series of disincentives. Now, a french fry craver can pop frozen fries into the microwave, or, better yet, pick up a bag from one of the fast-food joints that lie on their commuting route. The same goes for potato chips. Is it any surprise that potato consumption has risen more than 30 percent since the late '70s?

Because cooking takes less time and labor now than it used to, the cost of eating has dropped. People can pull fresh cake out of their cupboards, hermetically sealed and taste tested. Home-baked cake can't linger in the cupboard for long, and so cake used to be less attractive to consume.

This is what I mean when I say that free markets have created the obesity epidemic. Advances in food technology have reduced the monetary and time costs of eating, and these technological advances are a result of free market enterprises responding to consumer demand. Some market defenders might dispute me on this matter, pointing out that the obesity epidemic has only taken off in the last several decades, whereas capitalist enterprise has been around for at least two hundred years. But by this reasoning, we'd also be forced to conclude that free markets aren't responsible for HDTVs, or iPods, or aluminum siding, none of which existed at the dawn of time.

Market forces are the main cause of obesity, which only became an epidemic when the food industry developed more efficient ways to manufacture cheap, energy-dense foods and perfected ways of storing and packaging these foods that reduce the time cost of eating them.

Rational Predictions

Cutler and colleagues don't simply assert their "time cost" theory of obesity. Instead, like good social scientists, they test their theory to see whether it predicts who is more likely to have become obese in recent years. For example, high-income families have historically eaten out more often than lower-income families. Therefore, lower-income families have experienced a bigger change in the time cost of food preparation in recent years than have higher-income families. As a result of these cultural differences, Cutler's theory correctly predicts that the rise in obesity over the past couple decades has been greater in poor families than rich ones. Similarly, men have historically eaten out more than women, often eating out while at work or while traveling. Once again, Cutler's theory has correctly predicted that women have gained more weight in the past several decades than men, thanks to the advent of processed food. Cutler's theory also correctly predicts that the increase in caloric consumption that has occurred in the past several decades hasn't been equal across all food groups, but has been tilted toward processed food.

By looking for the logic underlying obesity, economists have broadened our understanding of the epidemic.

Policy Responses to Rational Behavior

Given evidence for the rationality underlying the obesity epidemic, Philipson and Posner conclude that words like *overweight* are misnomers: "In a rational choice model," they write, "there is no such thing as being 'overweight.' Weight is the result of personal choices along such dimensions as occupation, leisure time, activity or inactivity, residence, and, of course, food intake."[20] They go on to posit that this "rational choice perspective calls into question the case for public interventions designed to reduce obesity."

According to Philipson and Posner, consumers have shown us through their choices that they prefer being obese to the alternative—to exercising more, to forgoing their favorite snack foods, and to taking the time to prepare healthier food. By this reasoning, if the government intervened to combat obesity, it would be going against its citizens' own preferences.

It is very important to recognize that views like this are not shared by all economists; nor are economists the only people to hold such views. (Posner, in fact, is a law scholar, not an economist.) In this book, I am not critiquing economists, who after all are a diverse group of people who hold a wide range of world views. I am not critiquing economic theories either, which are also quite diverse. Indeed, I'm a huge fan of economics and have collaborated with economists in numerous research studies. Economics has greatly enriched our understanding of human behavior and stands to further enrich this understanding now that more of its practitioners are collaborating with noneconomists.

I am not critiquing economics. Instead, I am exploring alternatives to a "hands-off" approach to problems like obesity. Proponents of laissez-faire government still justify their political philosophies in part by appealing to rational choice theory, to the idea that people are better at choosing their course in life than their government would be. As a group of market enthusiasts wrote in a Department of Agriculture publication, "If consumers willingly trade off increased adiposity for working indoors and spending less time in the kitchen as well as for manageable weight-related health problems, then markets are not failing." Using this reasoning, they conclude that "federal policy to curtail overweight and obesity could cause more harm than good."[21]

Belief in rational choice does not wed one to a libertarian view of how to deal with problems like the obesity epidemic. But it surely stands as the foundation of many libertarian arguments. To better understand the pros and cons of this hands-off approach to the obesity epidemic, then, we need a better understanding of the irrational forces that stand alongside the more rational causes of obesity.

Behavioral economics, which draws much of its worldview from disciplines like cognitive and social psychology, offers a less rational take on the world. As a consequence, behavioral economists have been espousing new reasons for regulating markets, to better serve people's interests. Before returning to the obesity epidemic, and to other potentially troubling consequences of the modern marketplace, we should explore the origins of behavioral economics, and what it means when people in this field say that humans are not as rational as nineteenth-century economists once believed them to be.

PART II

The Rise of Behavioral
Economics and Soft
Paternalism

CHAPTER THREE

Bank Tellers, Fighter Pilots, and the Limits of Rationality

THE U.S. MILITARY is second to none in its size and scope, in its sheer power and reach. But many contend that the Israeli military, pound for pound, is unparalleled. Indeed, the U.S. military has frequently consulted with the Israeli military to learn from its advanced training techniques. When Israeli officers tell you that such and such technique is the best way to improve troop performance, they speak from experience. But what are the lessons of experience?

Daniel Kahneman, a young psychology professor in Israel, asked himself that same question. It was the 1960s, the decade of the Six-Day War, and the Israeli military was at the height of its powers. Kahneman was teaching flight instructors about the value of praise in promoting performance. His teaching was met with incredulity, with one instructor taking it upon himself to lecture the young professor: "On many occasions I have praised flight cadets for clean execution for some aerobatic maneuver, and in general when they try it again, they do worse. On the other hand, I have often screamed at cadets for bad execution, and in general they do better the next time. So please don't tell us that reinforcement works and punishment does not, because the opposite is the case."[1] In fact, because of these experiences, the instructors had instituted a training policy in which they would criticize pilots *no matter how* they performed.

Neither intimidated nor persuaded by this speech, Kahneman found himself pondering the psychological implications of the profound error in judgment that these flight instructors had made. You see, they had ignored a statistical phenomenon known as *regression toward the mean*. Think of regression like this: suppose you play golf tomorrow and perform the best that you ever have. Now, whether I praise you or criticize you for your performance, you are likely to perform less well the next time you go out, because you will regress (move) toward your mean (average)—your next eighteen holes will be more like your typical performance. Therefore, if I praise you for doing well, only to then watch you perform less well next time, I would be mistaken to conclude that my praise caused you to hit all those fairway bunkers.

At the time he was teaching these flight instructors, Kahneman was not an expert in decision making. But he would soon encounter a new professor on the faculty, Amos Tversky, who had studied decision making at the University of Michigan under the tutelage of Ward Edwards, a pioneer in the field. The two young professors began swapping stories of strange judgments they had seen people make, judgments that flew in the face of statistical teaching.

Kahneman shared a few more stories with Tversky from his days in the Israeli military, including work he did helping the military evaluate the leadership potential of new enlistees. In one part of the evaluation, the young soldiers were placed in small groups and directed to carry a telephone pole through an obstacle course. Observing the performance, the evaluators would quickly converge on what seemed the obvious leaders of each group, with little controversy. Unfortunately, these evaluations had almost no predictive power. The "leaders" identified through these exercises were no more likely to distinguish themselves as leaders in their military careers than the followers. Nevertheless, the military continued these evaluations, unable to shake the belief that the evaluations had diagnostic value.

Kahneman and Tversky realized they were on to something and began a series of studies that would raise fundamental questions about human rationality. Their scientific output over the next decade was full of more insights than I can describe in this book. But just to give you a flavor of their collaboration, let me introduce you to Linda.

What's My Line?

Linda is thirty-one years old, single, outspoken, and very bright. She majored in philosophy. As a student, she was deeply concerned with issues of discrimination and social justice, and also participated in antinuclear demonstrations. Given this information, what do you think are the odds that the following statements are true about Linda?

Linda is a teacher in elementary school.

Linda works in a bookstore and takes yoga classes.

Linda is active in the feminist movement.

Linda is a psychiatric social worker.

Linda is a member of the League of Women Voters.

Linda is a bank teller.

Linda is an insurance salesperson.

Linda is a bank teller and is active in the feminist movement.

When I first read the article in which Kahneman and Tversky posed this question, I thought about how well Linda fit the stereotype of each statement.[2] Linda sounded to me like just the kind of person who would be active in the feminist movement. By contrast, she did not sound at all like a bank teller. So, I rated the likelihood of Linda being a feminist as being significantly higher than her chance of being a bank teller. Was I right? Well, actually, we don't know, because Linda is a mythical woman, invented to illustrate the power of what is called the *representativeness heuristic*.

Heuristics are rules of thumb that we use to make judgments about the world. When you walk down a dark alley and veer away from the five kids walking toward you brandishing knives, you are relying on a potentially lifesaving heuristic. You don't know for sure that this is a dangerous group of kids. They might simply be walking home from a cooking class. But the odds of something less benign are simply too high for you to take any chances.

The representativeness heuristic guides many of our judgments. When I decided how likely Linda was to be a feminist or a bank teller, I thought about how representative she was of the typical person in each group. But this type of thinking can lead us astray. Consider, for example, the possibility of Linda's being a bank teller who is active in the feminist movement. Now I have to admit, Linda does not sound like a bank teller to me. But when she is described as a bank teller who is active in the feminist movement, the description starts sounding plausible. Maybe she is making a feminist point, rising up through the male-dominated banking system to prove that women can handle large sums of money. So when I first met Linda, I rated her chances of being a bank teller who is active in the feminist movement as being greater than her chances of being a plain old bank teller.

But let's look at this situation more logically. What is more likely: that Linda is a bank teller or that Linda is a bank teller who is active in the feminist movement? The latter *feels* more likely, because it better fits our representation of Linda. But logically speaking, the former *has to be* more likely, because the category of bank tellers who are active in the feminist movement is subsumed by the broader category of all bank tellers.

To better understand how the representativeness heuristic works, imagine that I flip a coin six times, and write down the result of each toss. I then show you two sequences of results and ask you to guess which one was the actual outcome of my coin flips: H-T-H-T-T-H or H-H-H-T-T-T. If you are like most people (and you're not, of course, because you're reading this book), you will pick the first sequence, because it is more representative of what coin-flip sequences are like—it is more random looking. But if you think about this carefully, you will realize that each sequence is equally likely. The odds of getting H-T-H-T-T-H are just the same as getting H-H-H-T-T-T, which happen to be exactly the same odds of getting six heads in a row, for that matter.

Does this example sound too artificial to ever influence real judgments? Unfortunately for my social life, the answer is no. One night, we had a family of four to our house for dinner, hoping to get to know them better. Our boys attended school with their boys, so we hoped the two families would hit it off. The night was going well—our kids were playing with their kids, and at low enough volumes that the four of us adults had a chance to converse. At one point in the evening, Dave, I will call him, commented on the collection of songs he had been hearing over our loudspeakers, and I geekily pointed out how they were being randomly generated by my new iPod. He shook his head in disagreement, pointing out that on a couple of occasions, two Elvis Costello songs appeared in a row, so my iPod must not really be selecting songs randomly. I pointed out the flaws in his logic, going off on an erudite explanation of how he had been fooled by the representativeness heuristic.

I successfully made my point, and we never saw the couple again.

What Comes to Mind

When George W. Bush decided to invade Iraq, he no doubt reflected on some probabilities. He contemplated the odds of finding weapons of mass destruction and of the U.S. troops' being greeted as liberators. He is not alone in thinking of probabilities when making decisions. Even mundane decisions often hinge on our probability judgments. A commuter might decide on a back road one morning rather than the highway when he guesses the odds of highway congestion are high. But how do people make judgments about the chance of various things happening in the world? Kahneman and Tversky's work on the representativeness heuristic raised the troubling possibility that people's likelihood judgments are biased by rough rules of thumb that don't always work.

Consider another rule of thumb, which they called the *availability heuristic*.[3] Assuming you do not have a photographic memory, try to guess how many words, in the past two thousand words of this book, have the following sequence of letters:

- _ _ _ _N_

- _ _ _ _ST

- _ _ _ING

It is easy to imagine lots of words ending in *ing*, like the word *ending*, which I have now used twice in this sentence. Such words are highly available—easily retrievable—from our brains. It is much harder, however, to retrieve words ending in _ _ _ _N_. We don't have a place in our brain where we store words according to the second-to-last letter they contain. But of course, every word ending in the letters _ _ _ING is subsumed by the words ending in _ _ _ _N_.

Biased by the availability heuristic, people guess, on average, that there were five words (out of the last two thousand) ending in _ _ _ _N_, and 13.5 words ending in the letters _ _ _ING.[4] (As it turns out, the correct answers for this book are 212 and 79.) The availability, the easy retrievability, of *ing* words leads people to make inaccurate judgments.[5]

As soon as they began to work together, Kahneman and Tversky found themselves discovering a whole series of strange judgments that people make, judgments that defy the laws of probability and the rules of logic.[6] They showed that they could influence people's estimates of how many countries there are in Africa by having them write down the last two digits of their Social Security number before making their guess. This essentially random number *anchored* people's estimates, so that someone whose last two Social Security digits were 93 would estimate a larger number of African countries than someone whose last two numbers were 16.[7]

Kahneman and Tversky's work made an immediate splash, challenging people's faith in the pervasiveness of human rationality. Belief in human rationality, after all, had been thought of as our species-distinguishing characteristic since at least the time of Aristotle. So, Kahneman and Tversky's findings shook up many people—philosophers, who prided themselves on being rational, would read their scenarios and find themselves making the same mistakes that ordinary mortals made; even statisticians found themselves responding to Kahneman and Tversky's surveys in ways that violated basic principles of their own discipline.[8] Many people were concerned that Kahneman and Tversky must be wrong, with Stephen J. Gould, the famous evolutionary theorist, claiming that if Linda was a bank teller, she simply *had* to be active in the feminist movement.[9]

But at least one group of thinkers was largely unmoved by this research—and that group was economists. Nothing about bank tellers and random iPods could threaten their theory of human rationality. That's when Kahneman and Tversky got serious and turned their sights on money.

Gambling Time

Imagine that I have just offered to give you $3,000. Yours for the taking, no questions asked. If you are feeling lucky, however, you can forgo that $3,000 and take a chance at making even more money, but at the risk of losing it all. Your hypothetical choice is laid out below:

(a) a sure $3,000

or

(b) 80 percent chance of $4,000

and

20 percent chance of (gulp) nothing

If you are like most people, you will take the sure $3,000. This choice is not a foregone conclusion, of course. Nothing in the traditional economic view of rationality favors one of these options over the other. Instead, the best choice for any person depends on the relative utility they place on $4,000 versus $3,000. So far, so good.

But now imagine a different choice, illustrated below:

(c) 25 percent chance of $3,000

and

75 percent chance of nothing

or

(d) 20 percent chance of $4,000

and

80 percent chance of nothing

In this situation, the majority of people choose (d), reasoning that if they are likely to end up with no money, they might as well take a chance at the larger sum. But let's look at these two choices more closely. People who prefer (a) over (b) have revealed the utility—the preferences—they have for these two sums of money. Their choice reveals the relative utility of the two sums of money: $u(\$3,000) > .8u(\$4,000)$.

By contrast, if you prefer choice (d) over (c), then you have revealed that, for you, $.2u(\$4,000) > .25u(\$3,000)$, which, if we remember our high school algebra, means that $.8u(\$4,000) >$

u($3,000). In other words, those people who prefer (a) in the first choice and (d) in the second choice have given us completely different information about the relative utilities of these two sums of money.[10] If you chose this way, my friend, you have contradicted yourself.[11]

But at least you are in good company. Leonard "Jimmy" Savage, a University of Michigan–trained mathematician who had gained fame developing axioms of rational choice, made this same pair of inconsistent choices when faced with these gambles. When someone pointed out that he had violated the very same standards of rationality that he had helped to make famous, Savage stubbornly replied, "Since my axioms are totally evident, my answers, which are indeed incompatible with my axioms, are explained by the fact that I did not give the matter enough thought."[12]

A Matter of Certainty

Savage was convinced that, with proper reflection, he would have obeyed his axioms. But Kahneman and Tversky were convinced he was wrong—they were certain of it, in fact. They theorized that when people make risky decisions, they overweigh outcomes that they perceive as being *certain*.

To grasp the power of certainty, imagine for a moment that you have just been diagnosed with a uniformly fatal cancer: 0 percent chance surviving for one year. Suppose a new chemotherapy has been developed, not yet covered by your insurance company, that will raise your odds of survival to 3 percent. How much would you pay out of pocket for that treatment? Now imagine, instead, that you have a life-threatening, but much more treatable cancer, and your insurance company will pay for standard chemotherapy, which has a 50 percent chance of saving your life. How much would you pay out of pocket for a new chemotherapy not yet covered by insurance that will raise your odds of survival to 53 percent? Whatever that number is, I expect it would be a lot less than the amount you would have paid for the drug that bumped your survival from 0 percent to 3 percent.

In both cases, you are paying money to increase your chance of survival by 3 percent. In the first situation, that felt like a huge difference. But in the second situation, it felt almost trivial. In the first situation, the psychological power of certain death magnified the value of the 3 percent improvement in survival.[13]

The two psychologists worked long hours, developing a theory that would highlight the strategies that influence people when they are making risky choices. Their partnership settled into a biorhythm, with Tversky drafting ideas late into the evening and Kahneman rising early in the morning to do his own thinking. Their conversations would begin each day at lunch and often last through the afternoon.[14]

As a result, their insights just kept on coming. One day, in fact, as they were pondering the decision-making literature, it struck the two men that almost all the gambles that people studied were based on positive sums of money. Researchers might ask people to choose between a sure $3,000 or an uncertain, say, $4,000, but they never asked people to choose between sure and uncertain losses. They quickly rectified that oversight and in the process made a discovery that would become a crucial part of their Nobel-winning work.

Loss Leaders

Kahneman and Tversky discovered that people view situations quite differently when the situations are described in ways that focus on losses. People are much more likely to undergo a surgical procedure advertised as having a 90 percent survival rate, for instance, than one described as having a 10 percent mortality rate. When considering the latter procedure (which of course is the same surgery as the former), they focus on the mortality rate and become averse to the potential loss of life.[15]

People's aversion to losses can be downright irrational. Imagine, for instance, that I have just given you $1,000 and am now offering you a chance of receiving either an additional $500 or of taking a fifty-fifty chance at earning another $1,000. In other words, you face a choice between a sure $1,500 ($1,000 plus $500) or a gamble that will leave you with an equal chance of ending up with either $1,000 or $2,000. If you are like most people, you will take the sure $1,500. Nothing about this choice contradicts the standard economic view of rationality. You simply thought about the relative utilities of $1,000, $1,500, and $2,000 and made your choice.

Now consider a different situation: I have just given you $2,000 (after an appearance on *The Daily Show* boosted my book sales) and am now offering you a choice between giving $500 back to me or taking a fifty-fifty chance of either giving me $1,000 back or keeping all the money. Once again, you face a choice between a sure $1,500 or a gamble that will leave you with an equal chance of ending up with either $1,000 or $2,000. Exactly the same choice as before. Yet in this situation, because the gamble takes place in the domain of losses, the majority of people take the gamble and forgo the sure $1,500. Their decision in this case is completely at odds with their previous decision. They don't simply ponder the relative utilities of $1,000, $1,500, and $2,000 and decide what to do. Instead, they place dramatically different weights on the three values of money depending on whether they are focused on wins or losses.

In 1979, Kahneman and Tversky pulled their ideas together into an article that they innocuously named "Prospect Theory."[16] They published their new theory in a journal called *Econometrica*, not because they wanted to challenge economists but, rather, because this journal was the best place to publish mathematically oriented manuscripts on decision making.

They had no idea that their paper would shake up the economics establishment to the degree it did, spurring on the development of subdisciplines like behavioral economics and its stepchild, neuroeconomics. They had no aspirations of winning a Nobel Prize, either. They were psychologists, after all, and there *is* no Nobel Prize for psychology. Indeed, nothing happening in economics at that time pointed toward a future where members of the discipline would challenge the view of humans as rational decision makers. Just that same year, Theodore Schultz, from the University of Chicago, won the Nobel Prize. Other notable Chicagoans would win the prize in subsequent years, people like George Stigler, Ronald Coase, and Gary Becker, all steeped in the traditions of rationality. Economists of the time were slow to accept Kahneman and Tversky's insights, vehemently opposing what they described as "parlor game experiments," and ridiculing their outlandish view of human fallibility.[17] Kahneman and Tversky were accused of playing "stupid human tricks," and of creating clever little experiments that merely tricked unsuspecting participants.

Without a doubt, Kahneman and Tversky's experiments *were* clever. Too clever, perhaps, to persuade reluctant economists to accept their findings. You see, because of their psychology training, Kahneman and Tversky were accustomed to designing experiments that elucidate the working mechanisms of the brain. Take the Ames room reproduced in figure 3-1.

No doubt you have seen a picture like this before. The geometry of the room creates a visual illusion that makes it nearly impossible to dispel the notion that the person at the front is a giant. Most readers will be familiar with a host of such visual illusions, tricking us into thinking a short line is longer than a longer one, and so on.

The existence of such illusions does not prove that our visual systems are horribly flawed. People don't walk into walls by accident or misjudge the size of people they encounter on the street. Instead, the existence of such illusions reveals how our brains work, identifying how our brains make sense out of what we see.[18]

Psychologists have been relying on errors to understand the brain since the nineteenth century. Hermann von Helmholtz, a

FIGURE 3-1

Ames room

pioneer of visual illusions, described this approach as far back as 1881, writing, "It is just those cases that are not in accordance with reality which are particularly instructive for discovering the laws of the processes by which normal perception originates."[19]

By conducting so many clever, memorable studies, in manuscripts filled with sparkling prose and wonderful illustrative examples, Kahneman and Tversky drew attention to the many forces that nudge people away from rationality. The only question now was whether economists would ever act on their insights.

CHAPTER FOUR

Cashews, Coffee Mugs, and the Birth of Behavioral Economics

DICK THALER had a dirty little secret. A notebook full of dirty secrets, in fact—observations he had made of economists behaving irrationally. Thaler was not an anthropologist, hiding in the back of economics seminars taking notes on an alien culture. Rather, he was, himself, a card-carrying economist, having received his PhD from the University of Rochester, in a program that indoctrinated its students into the neoclassical, rational-choice way of thinking.[1]

But this indoctrination failed to take hold. Thaler simply could not accept that people were as rational as he had been taught. One night, for example, Thaler was entertaining a group of economists at his house for dinner. During the cocktail hour, he put out a bowl of cashews for people to snack on. The cashews began disappearing at an alarming rate, a rate that threatened to ruin people's appetites for dinner. Thaler grabbed the bowl of cashews and put it back in the kitchen. When he returned to the living room, Thaler's guests thanked him enthusiastically for removing the otherwise irresistible snack. In other words, the economists—all deeply committed, at that time, to the idea that people left to their own devices will make decisions that maximize their best interests—were actually thanking him for stripping them of the freedom to munch on cashews.

The irony was not lost on Thaler, who jotted the story down in his notebook and filed it away for future reference.

In that same notebook, Thaler reflected on how his colleagues behaved when playing poker. The games were typically low stakes but nevertheless involved real money, so if an economist could ever be expected to follow his own theories, this would be the time; economists, after all, take money very seriously. Nevertheless, Thaler kept noticing strange behavior. When one of the players made some early cash, he would begin betting recklessly. Gamblers call this "playing with house money." This behavior, though hardly unique to these economists, did not make rational sense to Thaler. If at the beginning of the evening, you would fold with a pair of eights and a $2 bet on the table, why wouldn't you do the same thing when you were up $20?

The people who fell behind early in the evening also behaved in strange ways. They would get very cautious, folding more often than they had earlier in the evening, until a good hand came around, whereupon they would make the kind of bets that gave them the chance of recouping all of their losses at once, like a football team that falls behind in the first quarter and abandons its running game, even though it has plenty of time to catch up. These poker players, after all, had their entire *lives* to catch up—if they were to lose $10 now, they could always make it up the following week. Surely, their betting strategies should have been based on their odds of long-term success, not on some desire to break even that same evening.

Thaler couldn't shake the idea that if economists, when trying to make money at poker, didn't behave rationally, then the nineteenth-century economic view of human nature—of people as rational utility maximizers—must be horribly flawed. He knew that this idea was heretical. So when he spoke to colleagues, he did so carefully and somewhat tangentially, whispering anecdotes of these strange behaviors but not raising some kind of fundamental theoretical crisis. He wrote up his notes, in hopes of publishing a manuscript describing some of the anomalous behaviors he had witnessed. But he could not find a coherent way to frame his ideas or a new theory that could replace the standard theory of rational choice.

Then, in the summer of 1976, Thaler attended a conference that explored, among other things, how to value life-threatening risks. How much extra money, for example, should a worker be paid if his job carried a risk of serious injury? The conference was attended not only by economists, but also by a young group of psychologists, people like Paul Slovic and Baruch Fischoff, who were probing many of the same topics that Kahneman and Tversky had been working on. Thaler was intrigued by what he saw that day. He gave Fischoff a ride in his car after the conference ended, and shared some of his observations on people's anomalous behaviors. Fischoff nodded knowingly, as if unsurprised at what Thaler had observed, and promised to send Thaler a few papers in the mail (this was before e-mail, after all) that would provide context for these anomalies. Among the papers that Thaler received in the mail that next week was an early paper on heuristics and biases by Kahneman and Tversky. Thaler felt as if he had discovered a gold mine, barely able to contain himself as he rushed to the library to find more of their papers.[2] Finally in possession of a theory that explained the anomalies he had observed, he published his notebook of dirty secrets in an economics journal, and the discipline of behavioral economics was born.

People are more resistant to new ideas when those ideas come from outsiders. Nixon was able to go to China, and Clinton was able to "end welfare as we know it," because the political parties most resistant to such ideas were their *own* parties. As insiders, they were able to take advantage of relationships that they had forged and the "street cred" they had built up within their respective parties. Having trained in psychology, Kahneman and Tversky had few close relationships with economists. But Thaler was able to use his insider status to begin reforming the discipline.

But he didn't do it alone. In the summer of 1977, Thaler heard through the grapevine that Kahneman and Tversky would be visiting scholars at Stanford, where he would also be spending the year. Placed on the same campus, the three men began to talk. Thaler quickly realized that Kahneman and Tversky's ideas provided the underlying framework to explain many of the anomalies he had been collecting in his notebook.

From Kahneman and Tversky, he learned about loss aversion, to start with, and immediately recognized that this psychological phenomenon explained the first anomaly he had identified, back when he was a graduate student. At that time, he had been pouring through large databases to find out how much extra money people needed to be paid in order to take on hazardous jobs. While conducting this painstaking work, he had tried to take a shortcut, by surveying people and asking them how much they would have to be paid to accept, say, a one-in-one-thousand risk of immediate death. Playing around with the wording of his questionnaire (since he hadn't been trained in how to do survey research), he asked the question a different way to some people, inquiring about how much they would pay to rid themselves of the same risk. He figured this was basically two ways of asking the same question.

But to his amazement, people's answers varied dramatically across these two types of questions. Asked to imagine that they had already assumed a hazardous job, they told him they would be willing to pay about $200 to reduce the risk, barely the price of a good hard hat. Getting rid of such a risk at work, when framed this way, would be viewed as a gain, in Kahneman and Tversky's scheme. By contrast, if they did not yet face such a risk at work, meaning that the risk itself would be viewed as a loss, they told Thaler that they would require a *huge* raise in their salary to accept the risk, on the order of $50,000. Hard to imagine, but the same basic question led to an answer of either $200 or $50,000. Even then, as a graduate student, Thaler recognized that something strange was going on. But only now, spending time with these two brilliant psychologists at Stanford, did he realize *why* people were acting this way: they were irrationally averse to losses.

Before long, he would be collaborating with Kahneman (and Jack Knetsch) on a series of clever experiments that would show how such loss aversion influenced even the simplest of market interactions. And together, these three men would establish the power of what they called the *endowment effect*.[3]

A Mug in the Hand

In a typical demonstration of the endowment effect, Kahneman, Knetsch, and Thaler would arrange students into pairs and give a Cornell coffee mug to one member of each pair, saying it was now theirs. They would encourage both students to examine the mug— to see it, to feel it. They would then ask each of the students to place a value on the mug. Those who already owned the mug— who had been endowed with the mug—would decide the lowest price at which they would sell it to their partner, while those who did not already own the mug would decide on the highest purchase price at which they would buy the mug from their partner. The average selling price was greater than $5, while the average purchase was barely more than $2. Clearly, the mugs were being viewed as more valuable by the students who already owned them.

In another experiment, Thaler and his colleagues gave each student a mug for participating in a study, but told them that they could exchange the mug for a large bar of chocolate, if they so desired. Only 11 percent of students made the exchange, exhibiting a preference for the mug that would force a traditional economist to conclude that it was worth more than the chocolate bar. But no longer a traditional economist, Thaler then turned around and gave chocolate bars to a separate group of students and told them that they could exchange it for a mug, if they so desired. If the mug was really so much more valuable to the typical student than the chocolate bar, then 90 percent of the students should make the exchange. But only 10 percent chose to do so. Whichever object Thaler endowed the students with became the more valued one.

Thaler had first recognized the endowment effect as a graduate student. When he came across Kahneman and Tversky's papers, he realized that the endowment effect is a consequence of loss aversion. Losing a chocolate bar is a bigger deal than gaining a coffee mug; by the same token, losing a coffee mug is a bigger deal than gaining a chocolate bar. Thus, the value of any good is not simply a function of the utility of that good, but also a function of whether a person already *owns* the good. And by ownership, I don't mean some prolonged relationship that has generated its own utility. I'm not talking about the emotional attachment people develop for their favorite sweater or for the baseball glove that they broke in just right. I'm talking about a coffee mug that they held in their hands for less than ten seconds.

Not long ago, the *New York Times* published a very moving example of the endowment effect. In the essay, Elizabeth Fitzsimons relayed the story of what had happened when she and her husband, Matt, flew to China to adopt a baby girl. Knowing that some of the children being put up for adoption were less than perfectly healthy, they fully expected their girl would be malnourished, perhaps even a bit neglected. But they had filled out forms before arriving, indicating the kind of health conditions that would be too much for them to handle. They didn't want to come off as heartless, but they weren't prepared to adopt a girl with, say, a major heart ailment or spina bifida.

So you can imagine their surprise when they met the girl they came to adopt and noticed a two-inch scar at the base of her spine. When people at the orphanage acted surprised at this hint of trouble, the parents-to-be asked them to bring in a doctor to evaluate the girl. The doctor was concerned, noticing that her rectal tone wasn't quite up to snuff. He wondered if she had some kind of spinal abnormality. A CT scan confirmed that there had been a tumor that "someone, somewhere had removed." All medical people evaluating her assumed she was on her way toward a life of multiple disabilities.

But Elizabeth and her husband had already held her. They had already fallen in love with this little girl. And that checklist, those health conditions they had previously said they couldn't handle, didn't seem so important anymore. They wanted this girl, and this girl alone, no matter what medical problems they would face. In fact, they couldn't imagine flying home with any other child.[4]

Living, breathing human beings, of course, lead to very different endowment effects than coffee mugs. It even seems crass to categorize these parents' behaviors in behavioral economic terms. But the psychology of coffee mugs and adoptable children really is parallel. Imagine two couples are hugging their new, healthy adopted baby girls, when they are suddenly told that the Chinese adoption agency messed up the paperwork, and each couple is hugging the wrong kid. I expect both couples, if given a choice, would rather trade paperwork than swap children.

Mental Accounting

Thaler identified another phenomenon early in his anomaly-collecting days, which also meshed well with Kahneman and Tversky's theories. Thaler's insight, which he dubbed "mental accounting," was that even though money is fungible—a $10 gain added to a $10 loss leaves a person right where he began—people's experience of money, the way they keep mental tabs of their gains and losses, often belies this fungibility.[5] Consider a woman who wins $100 in the office fantasy football league but who, that same day, breaks a piece of office equipment and must fork over $50 to replace it. Do you think she feels the same as someone who just found a $50 bill? Fifty-dollar bills aside, the woman experienced two events: a $100 gain and a $50 loss. The displeasure of the $50 loss will take away more than half of the pleasure she experienced from the $100 gain. Now if this woman were rational and treated money as being fungible, she would simply convert her day's events into a single monetary value, and celebrate making 50 unexpected dollars.

But people aren't that rational. When they experience events, they don't enter these events into some kind of utility function. Instead they . . . experience the events!

Consider the way people experience good events. A child who opens up all his birthday presents in one ten-minute frenzy has pretty much maxed out his joy meter (to say nothing of his parents' auditory cortex) by minute number five. By contrast, a kid who opens up one present before going to school in the morning, a few more that evening, and another present when grandma visits the next weekend will experience several joyous moments, perhaps none quite matching the intensity of the ten-minute frenzy, but more than likely yielding greater overall gift-opening pleasure.

In other words, it feels better to experience lots of small gains than to experience one big gain. That's why TV marketers like to throw in that small slicing knife at the end of the advertisement. And that's why when one of my boys plays a piano piece really well, I don't just say, "Great job"; I tell him all the reasons the piece sounded so good: "You really brought out the dynamics, Taylor, and the phrasing, and you know what else you did? . . ."

In addition, Thaler's idea of mental accounting led him to predict that, while people like to experience good things independently, they prefer to lump losses together in their mind. Thaler figured that when people experience losses, they will instinctively lump them together. They'd rather lose $100 on a single day than lose $50 two days in a row. To test his theories, Thaler would pose hypothetical scenarios to people and show that their responses fit his theory better than they fit standard economic theory. He also bolstered the credibility of his theories by pointing out real-world situations that reflected the power of his theories.

For instance, he pointed out that sales experts like to lump losses together. That's why once you've spent $20,000 on a new car, they convince you to throw in another $200 for the gizmo add-on or another $500 for the factory-finished whatchamacallit. They realize that you won't be able to tell the difference between forking over $20,000 versus $20,700.

The car salespeople also recognize another aspect of mental accounting—the value of silver linings, of receiving small benefits in the face of large losses. What feels better: spending $20,000 on a car or spending $21,000 on the same car while receiving a $1,000 rebate? You can't tell much difference between spending $20,000 or $21,000. But you can definitely feel the difference between receiving no rebate or a $1,000 rebate. Suppose that car salesperson throws in an upgrade to the car's sound system for free. Wouldn't that feel better than having her simply put a lower price tag on the car and leave you with enough money to pay for the sound system yourself?

Winning Over Hearts and Minds

Darwin needed Huxley to win people over to his ideas on evolution. Jesus, it could be argued, needed Paul to spread his teaching to non-Jews. By the same token, Kahneman and Tversky needed Dick Thaler to spread their theories among economists. Thaler, being a card-carrying economist, wrote articles in economics journals, presented his ideas at economics meetings, and began to chip away at his colleagues' resistance.

But even so, things were slow going at first. Economists were understandably skeptical about the rampant irrationality that these upstarts seemed to be uncovering. If people are so irrational, why do market economies do such a good job of producing goods and distributing them to the people who want them? These biases, or heuristics, struck most economists as being artifacts of the methods that people like Thaler were using. Take, as an example, one of the first economists to follow in Thaler's footsteps, George Loewenstein. In his PhD dissertation, Loewenstein surveyed undergraduates and asked them how much they would pay to avoid receiving an electric shock immediately or to avoid receiving one after a three-day delay. According to standard economic theory, people should prefer the delayed shock because of something called a "discount rate" and therefore should be willing to pay less to avoid it than the immediate shock. Nevertheless, the students offered to pay Loewenstein almost twice as much to avoid the delayed shock as the immediate one. The students wanted to get the shock over with so they wouldn't fret about it for three days.[6]

Loewenstein quickly rose to become a leading behavioral economist, and his insights have challenged many assumptions of the Chicago school. But early in the development of behavioral economics, much of the research that Thaler and Loewenstein and their colleagues conducted involved hypothetical surveys, using far-fetched but wonderfully clever scenarios. These behavioral economists were working in the psychology paradigm, using surveys to draw attention to plausible truths about how people make decisions. The strength of these studies was that they lined up with most people's intuitions about how they would behave in such situations, even if such situations were not part of ordinary life. Indeed, the researchers invented outrageous situations not despite their implausibility but *because* of their implausibility, recognizing that the way people think about such strange experiences would tap into their underlying decision processes, much as an optical illusion taps into the workings of our visual cortex.

But given the methods that people like Kahneman, Tversky, Thaler, and Loewenstein were using (surveys), the kind of questions they asked (the number of countries in Africa, electric shocks), and the populations they studied (nineteen-year-olds), the economics establishment was not exactly quaking in its hyperrational boots. Economists trained in neoclassical traditions knew that their models did a wonderful job of predicting a wide range of market behaviors. If behavioral economists and their friends in psychology wanted to challenge economic dogma, they would need to collect much more convincing evidence that things like anchoring effects, endowment effects, and other such phenomena influence actual market behavior.

Behavioral economists needed to get real!

Getting Real on eBay

When we named our first child Jordan, we recognized some of the benefits of that first name. For one thing, we knew that we could settle on the name before Jordan was born, regardless of whether Jordan turned out to be a boy or a girl. (He ended up as a he.) Having lived in Chicago when the Bulls dominated the NBA, we also knew that the name would carry many positive connotations. But we did not realize that the enduring popularity of Michael Jordan would reap yet other benefits for our basketball-obsessed boy, who spent much of his ninth year wearing a sleeveless T-shirt that bears the name Jordan on the front, with a silhouette of Michael Jordan, mid-dunk. He loves the idea that his own first name sits on the front of this "very cool" shirt.

We also failed to realize that if we wanted to get a bargain on such a shirt, we should check out eBay and find those unfortunate sellers who'd mistakenly spelled the word *Michael* as "Micheal." Most people looking for such shirts on eBay, you see, type in Michael Jordan's name correctly and see what apparel is available, utterly unaware of all the T-shirts that are listed under the *wrong* spelling. With less traffic coming to the misspelled merchandise, the selling prices of these shirts are significantly lower.[7]

Sounds like classic supply and demand. Misspell Michael Jordan's name, and there will be less demand for your product, forcing you to settle for a lower sales price. But the story is not so straightforward. As it turns out, eBay auctions provide a wealth of data about how people make real purchasing decisions, and this data has allowed behavioral economists to move beyond their undergraduate surveys, to show how irrational forces can influence market transactions.

Take Kahneman and Tversky's anchoring effect, for example. On eBay, some items are listed with a "must sell for at least" price, signaling to potential buyers that they must bid at least, say, $20 on that Michael Jordan shirt, or the seller won't part with it. The "must sell for" price serves as an anchor, influencing people's purchasing behavior. That means that if two sellers list the same Michael Jordan shirt on eBay (and spell his name correctly), and one of them places a "must sell" price that is $5 higher than the other seller, then that first seller stands to make more money, as his higher listing price will influence people's bids, anchoring them on the higher number.[8]

But what about the starting price of goods on eBay? Does it make sense to anchor people on higher numbers there, too? Turns out, that would be a mistake. If you want to make money on eBay, you should make it easy for people to bid on your goods, because a low starting bid makes your item look more popular. Suppose you and I are selling identical digital cameras, and you let people start bidding at the ridiculously low price of $1. Someone will bid $1 on your camera, prompting someone else to bid $5, until things quickly heat up and you get bidders willing to fork over serious money. Meanwhile, if I require a minimum starting bid of $75, I will find customers willing to pay that much for my camera. But by the end of the sales period, your camera should sell for more than mine. Why? Because lots of people bid on your camera, making it look more attractive. You see, eBay prominently displays information on the number of people bidding on any given object, so people searching for cameras would see that your camera is generating more interest than mine, and a great many of them would wrongly conclude that your camera must be better.[9]

In addition, your low starting bid has accumulated traffic to your camera, thereby creating endowment effects: once someone places the highest bid on your camera, she will feel as if she owns it. So, when someone places a higher bid on it an hour later, the early bidder will feel as if they have taken it away from her, which will make her even *more* desirous of the camera. Pretty soon, she will have sunk a fair amount into time on this object—bidding on it, watching other people's bids—and won't want all of this time to have been wasted, causing her to jack the price up even higher.

Sunk costs, endowment effects, anchoring heuristics . . . behavioral economists have shown that all these seemingly irrational phenomena influence cold, hard market behavior. Moving out of their laboratories—abandoning their surveys and their undergraduate volunteers—behavioral economists evaluated eBay bidders and found that they behaved irrationally.

Savvy Consumers

Standard economic theory cannot account for the way people behave on eBay. Still, a defender of rationality could point out that many of the people surfing eBay are not necessarily the savviest consumers on the planet. Maybe a more informed consumer would not fall prey to something as silly as an anchoring heuristic.

A traditional economist would, no doubt, be equally unimpressed by a study conducted by Gregory Northcraft and Margaret Neale, which found that undergrads are susceptible to anchoring effects when estimating the price of a new house.[10] Northcraft and Neale let undergraduates walk through a house that was on the market, after providing them with a fact sheet describing how many square feet of living space the house had, how many bedrooms, and other facts, including the suggested listing price. They then asked students what the lowest offer was that they would accept if they were selling the house. Across the sample of students, Northcraft and Neale randomly varied the listing price, however, and just as predicted, discovered that students anchored on this price when saying what price they would sell the house for. Those told that the listing price was $125,000 were willing to sell the same house for less money than those who believed it was listed at $150,000.

This is an easy study to criticize, of course. What do these students know about buying and selling houses, after all? Besides, the market has a simple way to take care of this problem, since most house buyers and sellers work with highly educated consumers of houses. We call them Realtors. So even if these college students are too inexperienced to know what a house is worth, their Realtors ought to put them straight.

There's only one problem with this line of criticism: when Northcraft and Neale ran this same experiment with real estate agents, they found the same results! Realtors were just as susceptible to anchoring effects as the undergrads.

It is beginning to look as if this behavioral economics stuff is not simply an artifact of clever survey experiments. Sometimes even the savviest consumers cannot live up to the standards of rational choice.

When Unsavvy Consumers Subsidize Savvy Ones

There are very few contexts in which I can be characterized as a savvy consumer. Men's suits? Not even a touch of savviness: my dad helped me buy sports coats when I worked at the Mayo Clinic in the late '80s, and I've stuck with those outdated fashions ever since.

Hotel services, on the other hand? I'm a certifiable expert, mainly because most of my hotel stays are for business trips, where

I am responsible only for incidental expenses. Tempted by the $3 Snickers in the hotel minibar? Not when it would be *my* $3. How about $15 an hour for Internet usage? Actually, I rather enjoy being offline for a couple of days. Want to call home to say goodnight to the kids? Sure, but I will use my cell phone (long-distance calls for free), not the hotel phone, where they would charge me 10 bucks just to call a 1-800 number.

When theories of rationality evolved in the nineteenth and twentieth centuries, people were viewed not only as being extremely rational, but also as being thoroughly knowledgeable about information relevant to their market behavior. People were savvy consumers, knowing just which features of a new product to pay attention to and which to ignore. Economists recognized, of course, that no one was perfectly knowledgeable. They knew that experienced consumers would have advantages over less experienced ones. But they figured that with common purchases, most people would become quite savvy, and therefore the marketplace would quickly adapt to make these savvy consumers happy.

Of course, when these theories evolved, times were much simpler. Local markets didn't stock 150 kinds of beer. When choosing a bank, people had to research only one or two attributes, like the interest rate and the institution's chance of surviving a market downturn; people chose hotels on the basis of location and the cleanliness of their rooms. There wasn't much to learn back then, and so it was reasonable to assume that consumers did a good job of making purchasing decisions.

Have you tried to choose a bank lately? There are likely to be a half-dozen different savings plans. You need to consider not only the interest rate at which your savings will grow, but the fees you will have to pay when you use the bank's ATM, when you use someone else's ATM, when your balance goes below some pre-specified limit, and when you, God forbid, bounce a check. In the midst of such a confusing array of charges and fees, not every consumer will be equally good at figuring out which bank is truly a low-cost bank. This creates an opportunity for banks to hide their true costs from unwitting consumers.

Would the market ever tolerate such underhandedness? By the standard economic account, such trickery should be weeded out by competition. A hotel that charges exorbitant fees for using telephones, for instance, will be punished by enough savvy consumers that it will lower its fees. And yet such fees remain, as if purposely shrouded from consumers.

A pair of behavioral economists, Xavier Gabaix and David Laibson, have an explanation for the persistence of such fees. They have shown that if a hotel starts advertising its telephone and parking costs up front (on its Web site, for example, when people are searching for rooms), it will lose out in competition to a hotel that fails to advertise such costs. Why? Because the sneakier hotel will attract some savvy guests, who like the hotel's low room prices and who are smart enough to avoid the extra charges. It will also attract some less savvy customers, whose unwitting use of the telephone and the minibar will increase the hotel's profits, the very same profits that allow it to offer low-cost rooms to the savvy consumers. The unsavvy customers, in other words, will subsidize the savvy customers' room charges by purchasing candy bars from the minibar. The transparent hotel, on the other hand, will not be able to match the overnight rate of the sneakier hotel, since the transparency of its add-on fees will reduce the telephone and minibar usage. That means savvy customers will avoid this hotel and go somewhere where they can get a subsidy. As will less savvy customers, who won't realize that they are going to end up paying more for the other hotel, because they will unwittingly use its expensive and shrouded services.

Gabaix and Laibson's theory is quite profound, demonstrating that behavioral economists, far from abandoning the idea that people behave rationally, have shown that the market is determined by a much more subtle and fascinating mix of rational and irrational decision making.[11] In a world where people were rational supercomputers, hotel minibars would not contain $3 candy bars. On the other hand, in a world where all people were complete idiots all the time, no one would even know how to manufacture a minibar. Behavioral economists do not assume, then, that people are idiots. Rather, they simply recognize that people are imperfect decision makers, and that the market evolves in response to both their smart and their not-so-smart decisions, their rational choices and their irrational impulses.

In this book, I am not setting out to attack the discipline of economics. Traditional economic theories of rationality still offer insight into a wide range of human behaviors, as I'll show throughout upcoming chapters. And newer economic theories, that emphasize the irrational side of human nature, are also relevant to many human behaviors.

My target in this book is not economists. It is free market evangelists—people who think that things like obesity are a result of rational behavior and, therefore, that we should leave the free market unimpeded so that people can continue to eat their way into bliss.

Behavioral economics has not only highlighted flaws in the way people make important decisions but also, as we will see, has pointed us toward ways of tweaking markets so that the markets mesh more successfully with both the rational and irrational sides of human nature.

CHAPTER FIVE

Kinder, Gentler Paternalism

BY MANY OBJECTIVE MEASURES, John Howard (the former track star we met in chapter 1) is better off than ever. The tiny black-and-white TV of his childhood has been replaced by a large color set with more than two hundred channels of available programming. The rickety old sedan of his early adulthood has been exchanged for a minivan loaded with a CD player, dual side air bags, and a GPS device that put an end to his wife's complaints about his refusal to ask for directions. His grocery store is stocked year-round with fresh fruits that, in his youth, were available only a few weeks a year. He can whip out his cell phone and call any of his four children at the drop of a hat. And at age sixty-nine, he can still hope, with the help of modern medicine, to live for another decade or two.

But of course, John's life is not perfect. His chronically stiff lower back is a constant reminder of all those hours he spent on the road, commuting during his work life. With so many TV shows available, he spends too much time vegging out in front of the screen and too little time walking outdoors or socializing with friends. His joints would hurt less if he could drop 20 pounds. He gets short of breath walking up a flight of stairs. And he worries that he didn't save enough money during his working years and might not be able to afford to live the extra decades that modern medicine has offered him.

He is convinced that his life would be improved if he could eat better, exercise more regularly, turn off the TV more often, stop wasting time visiting mindless Web sites, and remember to watch movies with actual characters in them. (Seriously, he *knew* that *The Silver Surfer* would be a waste of two hours, but he somehow couldn't resist.)

If John is correct in believing that these changes would improve his life, then we need to ask what society should do, if anything, to improve his life. Certainly, we aren't going to limit his freedom to subscribe to cable TV or to turn on the E! channel. We aren't going to forbid him from purchasing potato chips or compel him to work out with a personal trainer. John has the power, within himself, to improve his own life. But should society do anything to make it easier for him to do so?

One of the advantages of the nineteenth-century economic view of human nature is that it leads to straightforward answers to those kinds of questions. To almost any policy problem, the believer in rationality replies: leave it up to the market. Like the *Far Side* cartoon about treating horse injuries: broken leg → shoot; pneumonia → shoot. Obesity epidemic? Leave it up to the market. If people truly care about flat tummies, the market will find a way to meet those desires. Or so the theory goes. But unfortunately, freedom is not the cure-all that its strongest proponents claim it to be. Even when people know what they want out of life, they often lack the decision-making competence to obtain these goals.

In the early days of behavioral economics, people like Dick Thaler and George Loewenstein conducted imaginative surveys that highlighted the limits of human rationality, thereby exposing flaws in the standard economic view of human nature. As the discipline matured, its practitioners increasingly located their studies in the real world, further demolishing the myth of human rationality. And they were joined in this pursuit by scientists from many different disciplines—social psychologists, political scientists, marketing experts, and food scientists. These and other groups, as we'll see in upcoming chapters, have expanded our understanding of the strange mixture of rationality and irrationality that guides human behavior. This mixture can lead people astray—causing people to live where they probably shouldn't live, eat what they probably shouldn't eat, and smoke what they definitely shouldn't smoke.

What should we do about these problems? Is it ever appropriate to restrict people's liberties to protect them from their own bad decisions? Should society step in and stand strong when people are prone to weak wills?

In recent years, behavioral economists have begun pondering these very questions, seeking alternatives to the libertarianism they were steeped in during their economic training. Not surprisingly, their initial forays into the policy arena have been cautious. Having been trained in economics departments, most behavioral economists have made friends with more than their fair share of libertarians, and they care about the opinions of such colleagues. Indeed, they strive to publish their most important studies in traditional economics journals rather than in new behavioral economics publications. Some would no doubt love to join Daniel Kahneman in winning a Nobel Prize.

So when behavioral economists began to critique libertarianism, they directed their arguments at the audience they most cared about influencing—they targeted traditional economists. And thus, they worked hard to find a kind of paternalism that even a libertarian might appreciate. Soft paternalism. Paternalism lite, you might say. They worked hard to show people that society doesn't face an all-or-nothing choice between liberty and coercion. To illustrate their approach, consider the unconscious behaviors that influence the way people save for retirement.

Planning for Retirement

Savings rates vary dramatically across the developed world. In China, for example, the rate for fiscal year 2005–2006 was 25 percent, while in the European Union it was 11 percent.[1] Compare that with the United States, where savings rates have, in recent times, plunged below zero, meaning that Americans as a whole are borrowing more than they save.[2] Many financial experts are concerned that people in the United States are not saving enough money. Trying to encourage more savings, the U.S. government has allowed people to put money into retirement savings accounts on a pretax basis. That portion of their earnings, in other words, that they put into retirement accounts won't be taxed as income. To encourage even more savings, many companies offer to match a portion of their employees' contributions to these retirement accounts. For instance, if I put 5 percent of my earnings into a 403(b) plan, the University of Michigan will toss in another 10 percent. If I don't max out my retirement contribution, I will essentially be turning down free money.

Now almost no one wants to turn down free money, so we should expect most people to take advantage of this opportunity. Yet when companies create new programs to match employee contributions, many people don't take advantage of them for quite a while. Eventually they catch on. Within five years, most companies offering such matching plans can expect 80 percent or more of their employees to enroll. Many of the employees who don't contribute to such plans are too strapped for cash to put anything away for retirement. So it looks as if people are pretty rational when it comes to making retirement decisions. If you encourage people to save by paying them to do so, most people eventually catch on.

But what is going on with this "eventually" thing? If by year five more than 80 percent of people have figured out that 401(k) and 403(b) contributions are a good idea, why haven't 80 percent figured that out by year one or year two?

As it turns out, these slow adopters are being influenced by what behavioral economists call a *status quo bias*.[3] Rationally speaking, people should reevaluate their employee benefits each year, considering what health insurance plan, for instance, makes the most sense this year given any changes in their family's health or in the insurance plan offerings. But people often don't do this. Stuck in their ways, they're slow to take on new opportunities, hesitant to learn new tricks.

Aware that these status quo biases are often at odds with people's best interests, behavioral economists have proposed that we overcome these biases by taking advantage of another bias: a bias toward sticking with default options. Think of a default as the thing that happens if you take no action. If you don't go to the grocery store and buy milk, the default option is generally that you won't have any milk in your refrigerator. If an ambulance team finds you in the street in a cardiac arrest, their default orders are to try to resuscitate you. You can overcome these default actions by taking action: you can drive to the store and buy some milk, or you can tattoo the letters *DNR* on your chest. (Sadly, simply signing a living will won't do the trick, unless someone is around to tell the ambulance team about your wishes.)

Default options are pervasive and powerful. If you don't claim any withholding on your income tax, the IRS won't withhold anything. That's the default procedure for the U.S. Treasury, and as a result many people don't claim enough withholding on their income taxes. When doctors write prescriptions, pharmacists are often free to substitute generic equivalents, unless the doctor checks a box on the prescription pad specifically forbidding such substitutions. The default practice is to give pharmacists this leeway.[4]

Many of these default options could be changed. Indeed, a couple of decades ago, pharmacists wouldn't have dreamed of monkeying with the doctor's order. The default procedure back then was to do what the doctor ordered and only switch to a generic with the doctor's permission. Flip-flopping this default has enabled millions of patients to receive generic drugs, saving billions of dollars.

Which brings us back to 401(k) plans. Dick Thaler and his University of Chicago colleague Cass Sunstein recognized that 401(k) plans were a perfect example of the new brand of paternalism they were hoping to spread, which they called *libertarian paternalism*.[5] You see, the current default position for most employee retirement plans is $0. If you don't fill out any paperwork, your employer will assume that you don't want to put any money into your retirement plan. But some employers have flipped defaults, so that those employees who take no action will automatically have the maximum amount of their paychecks placed into 401(k) plans, along with the matching contribution from their employer. These companies have discovered that it doesn't take five years for employees to shift toward this wise investment. Instead, it happens immediately.

Two important things have happened here. First, a simple flip of a default option has dramatically increased the number of people who invest in their 401(k) plans, people who are eventually going to figure out that this is what they wanted to do. Second, and most important to Sunstein and Thaler, it hasn't limited people's freedom even half of an iota. People are free to invest as much or as little as they want in their retirement plan. They simply need to write the number in the correct part of their benefits paperwork.

Suppose we want to encourage people to wear seat belts but don't want to restrict their liberty. We won't support seat belt laws. But what if we could convince automobile manufacturers to make automatic seat belts the norm—you know, those seat belts that slide over your shoulder when you enter the car. Rather than buckling up, in other words, people would have to decide whether to *unbuckle*. This would increase seat belt wearing while still preserving people's ability to drive without strapping in. (Unfortunately, automatic seat belts didn't work as well as people hoped. They didn't include automatic waist restraints and thus led to many injuries, even some broken necks. But other than this little problem, they worked great!)

It's Nobody's Default but Their Own

Eric Johnson, at Columbia University, was one of the first people to establish just how powerfully defaults influence real-world behavior. While a professor at the University of Pennsylvania, he followed the local news closely and noticed that both New Jersey (his native state) and Pennsylvania had recently passed tort reform laws to reduce the costs of automobile accidents. The basic idea was the same in both states. Citizens could choose to pay one amount of money for full tort coverage and thereby reserve the right to sue people who rear-ended them on the turnpike. Or they could pay less money for no-fault insurance but would then give up the right to sue. While these two choices were essentially the same in these two states, one thing was different: the default option. In New Jersey, the default was no-fault; in Pennsylvania it was full tort. Consequently, 20 percent of people in New Jersey chose full tort coverage versus a whopping 75 percent in Pennsylvania.

It is worth reminding ourselves, right now, that standard economic theory has no good explanation for this dramatic difference in insurance choice. According to the standard economic view, this difference could only be explained either by there being significantly different insurance prices across the two states (which wasn't true) or by the existence of different preferences—with people in New Jersey having dramatically different insurance preferences than people in Pennsylvania. Behavioral economists, by allowing for irrational decisions, simply attribute these insurance choices to default option biases. People stick with the default option, neglecting to weigh the pros and cons of the two kinds of insurance.[6]

Johnson has also shown that defaults can powerfully influence organ donation decisions. If we assume that families don't want to donate their loved one's organs, then transplant experts need to convince them to donate, a task that is often quite difficult.[7] After all, the families of potential donors are caught up in tremendous grief, making for very challenging conversations about sensitive topics like organ donation. In many European countries, however, the law holds that newly deceased people are assumed to be willing to have their organs donated, unless families raise specific objections. In other words, the default procedure is to recover organs from newly deceased people, unless the family puts up resistance. Not surprisingly, organ donation rates are significantly higher in countries with these policies.[8]

We basically have a theme here, with little variation. By changing defaults, we can strongly influence people's behavior without in any way restricting their liberty.

Big Winners, Small Losers

Behavioral economists have begun looking for situations in which tiny restrictions on liberty can have powerful benefits for consumers. One place they have looked is at rent-to-own practices, consumer "bargains" that I have discovered, through personal experience, are frequently not such bargains.

I learned this lesson when I moved to Rochester, Minnesota, in 1988 to begin residency training. Excited about receiving my first real paycheck, I decided to rent a piano, since I didn't have the money to buy one. (You don't graduate from medical school with much money in the bank.) The company I rented from offered to let me put my rental money toward purchase of the piano, if I decided to buy it at a later date. I loved this idea at the time, as I didn't have to go deeper into debt in order to buy the piano, nor did I have to watch all that rental money go down the drain, leaving me with no instrument when I stopped paying.

The rent-to-own deal that I entered into at the time is an increasingly common tool that companies use to attract customers. But who is attracted to these deals? Generally, people who are strapped for cash, as I was in 1988. But we members of the rent-to-own crowd have one other thing in common: most of us are making stupid decisions. Take me, for example. I eventually bought the piano, convinced that I had been brilliant by making sure that part of my rent money had counted toward its purchase. Yet if I had simply started off in 1988 by taking out a loan and buying the piano, I would have gotten it for almost 50 percent less money. You see, the typical rent-to-own deal ends up costing as much money as taking out a loan with an annual interest rate of 100 percent or greater. What was I thinking?

Colin Camerer and several behavioral economics colleagues contend that rent-to-own deals are an example of a market transaction that harms people and that should therefore be more stringently regulated. Coming out of economics backgrounds, Camerer and his colleagues recognized that most economists would not take too kindly to this idea. Still they convinced themselves that they had found an example of regulation that even a conservative would love, what they call *asymmetrical paternalism*, a kind of paternalism that has very little downside to most people but is extremely beneficial to a small number of people who would otherwise be prey to their own decision-making follies.[9]

Suppose the government required rent-to-own companies to prominently display the interest rate people would pay if they rented something long enough to own it. Camerer and colleagues say that this kind of regulation would benefit people like me a lot. If this regulation had existed in 1988, for example, I would have never wasted so much money renting my piano. Nor would the regulation have had any ill effects on savvier consumers, who would have already figured out the true costs of this rent-to-own "bargain." Certainly, such a regulation would hurt the rent-to-own companies. But it would benefit banks willing to give people reasonably priced loans. And who could be against a regulation that more efficiently rewards companies that serve consumers' best interests?

We've seen two kinds of gentle paternalism now, offered by behavioral economists to nudge libertarians away from their extreme worldview. Sunstein and Thaler endorse a costless paternalism, involving subtle changes to the world that help people make better choices without restricting their freedom. Camerer and his colleagues endorse an only slightly costlier version, one in which the benefits far outweigh the costs. Neither of these groups is eager to stray far from the traditions of their economic tribe, wisely recognizing that if they want to pull economists away from libertarianism, they should start with small, persuasive steps.

Not a Member of the Tribe

Because I am a physician, not an economist, I don't have any strong libertarian traditions to buck. On the contrary, in medicine there is a long (and ignoble) history of paternalism. Several decades ago, doctors routinely refused to tell patients that they had cancer, out of concern that patients would become distraught and overly emotional.[10] Instead, physicians would vaguely mention that the patient had a shadow on her lungs or an infection visible on her X-ray, and then prescribe very strong medicines, presumably to chase away the shadow or cure the infection.

This extreme paternalism has gone by the wayside. Doctors rarely withhold diagnoses from patients anymore. Even so, they frequently feel justified in shaping the information they give patients in order to convince them to do what they think the patients *ought* to do. In other words, people trained in medicine today rarely view their profession in strictly libertarian terms.

I am significantly more of a libertarian in my medical practice than are most physicians. I work hard to understand what patients care about, and strive to involve them in important medical decisions. But because of my training in behavioral economics and decision sciences, I am also much more aware than most physicians of the reasons that patients, left to their own devices, will not pursue their best interests.[11] So, I'd love to see how much we can accomplish with soft forms of paternalism. But I'm worried that people like John Howard, ex–track star and current diabetic, will suffer unless we take more aggressive steps. John is well invested in a sensible retirement plan. He has listed himself as an organ donor on his driver's license. He wears seat belts, monitors his spending habits, and happily uses generic drugs when possible. But he also continues to cram two desserts into his belly most nights and hasn't exercised enough to produce a hard sweat in more than a decade. I can't help but wonder whether we can do more as a society to change the market in ways that will improve John's life.

In the next part of this book, I want to revisit the obesity epidemic and consider the irrational and unconscious forces that contribute to our waistlines. I'll show you why I am skeptical that a problem like the obesity epidemic can be addressed with a simple nudge.

PART III

Unconscious Appetites and

Expanding Waistlines

CHAPTER SIX

Irrational Tastes and
Bottomless Soup Bowls

GOOD SCIENCE REQUIRES GOOD DATA. Indeed, on many occasions, scientific progress has temporarily stalled while scientists waited for (and often spent their time developing) better instruments for measuring natural phenomena. Microscopes and telescopes, for instance, helped scientists see objects that, before these instruments existed, were too small or too far away to observe.

But as important as data is to good science, this data would be useless without scientific theories. If you look up into a telescope without a theory, you will see lots of lights shining in the sky and much more darkness, but you won't know how to make sense out of what you see.

Scientific theories help scientists analyze the data they collect. Give me a hard drive crammed with data on automobile sales—on the price of cars, the make and the models, et cetera—and I won't be able to tell you what's going on. Give me a theory of supply and demand, and I can start constructing a story for why a given model sold more units this year than last.

Theories not only help scientists make sense of the data they collect; they even play a crucial role in helping scientists decide what data *to* collect. Without Einstein's Theory of Relativity, physicists would not have thought of looking for evidence that light can be bent by gravity.

Theories are a crucial part of scientific progress. When some people criticize evolution for simply being "a theory," they are only demonstrating their misunderstanding of how science works.

I bring up the importance of scientific theories because theories have played such a large role in how people have come to understand the obesity epidemic. In chapter 2, we learned about people who have theorized that obesity is a consequence primarily of rational choice. The way science works, theories often precede the collection and analysis of data. That means that the people who study rational obesity didn't collect data, look at it with complete objectivity, and then realize (eureka!) that obesity was caused by rational decision making. Instead, like all good scientists, they started with their theory—in this case, a theory of humans being largely rational. Then they collected the kind of data by which they could test this theory. If obesity is rational, they surmised, then the price of food might explain the obesity epidemic—if food is cheaper than it used to be, it will be easier for people to eat more of it. Similarly, people with a rational view of obesity might look at how the time cost of food preparation has changed over time to see whether that explains the epidemic. Guided by their theory, these scientists have shown that their theory is consistent with what the data show.

Coming from a medical background, I have been exposed to other scientific theories that attempt to explain obesity. Given that physicians like me are immersed in biological sciences, not social sciences, we doctors have, not surprisingly, looked for biological explanations for obesity. We chase down molecules, like leptin, which we link to severe obesity.[1] We point our finger at microorganisms that alter people's metabolism.[2] We look for hormonal or genetic or physiologic causes of obesity. And we collect the kind of data that will test our theories of obesity, and find that they often prove our theories to be true.

The consequences of such scientific theorizing are profound. Medical theories lead toward medical solutions to obesity. Medical doctors and biotechnology companies look for pills that will alter people's metabolisms. Food companies develop molecules that will interfere with fat absorption. Surgeons even developed operations that limit the amount of food that people can stuff into their bellies.

Rational choice theories point toward different kinds of solutions. At an extreme, the one argued for by Philipson and Posner, rational choice theory calls "overweight" a misnomer and contends that no solution is needed for the obesity problem because obesity . . . is not a problem.[3]

But Philipson and Posner's approach is not the only one available to those who have sought out rational explanations for the obesity epidemic. Rational choice theories also point toward potential interventions to reduce obesity—interventions that would increase the cost of obesity (or increase the cost of eating) or interventions that would reduce the cost of healthy eating (or the cost of exercising).

I will return to some of these interventions near the end of this book. But before we start looking at potential interventions to reduce obesity, we really ought to broaden our theoretical framework. Because, you see, a theory can be true without being *entirely* true. Rational behavior really *does* explain the obesity epidemic: food and food preparation really have gotten cheaper; and the costs of exercise really have increased in recent years for many people. But rationality, alone, does not explain the obesity epidemic.

Suppose I measure the skin color of one hundred Irish men after an unusually sunny Dublin afternoon. I discover that twenty-five are sunburned. I theorize that sun exposure causes sunburn, measure how much time each person spent in the sun that day, and discover that being outside in the sun strongly predicts whether a specific man got sunburned. All twenty-five men who have bright red skin spent substantial time in the sun. My theory is proved correct with great statistical significance.

But imagine that another scientist looks at my data and notices that twenty-five of the seventy-five nonsunburned men also spent substantial time in the sun that afternoon. This scientist then develops an additional theory. She speculates that some sun worshippers slathered a strange cream on their skin before going outside and that this cream protected them from sun damage. And voilà: the data back her up.

Rational choice theory helps explain the obesity epidemic. But our scientific understanding of obesity will be more accurate if we supplement this theory with a broader vision of human nature. We will know more about why people become obese if we also look for irrational or unconscious forces that influence people's eating habits.

"Deciding" What to Eat

It is only natural to think of the food we eat as ending up in our stomachs because of deliberate choices we make. At home, we decide whether to cook pasta or pork chops. At the restaurant, we vacillate between the chef's special and the rib eye steak. At the grocery store, we carefully compare the prices of refried bean alternatives and squeeze the loaves of bread to find the variety that suits our tastes. And in making all these choices, we draw on vast experience, knowing full well what our tastes are and what we are looking for from our food.

And yet it turns out that our eating behavior is far less deliberate than we think. I first became aware of this phenomenon when our oldest boy began attending day care. Before having any kids, my wife and I had been quite confident in our ability to establish healthy eating habits in our household.

The week we had gotten married, in fact, my wife and I had gone out to dinner with some friends who had an eighteen-month-old boy, Max. We went to a diner and ordered burgers and turkey sandwiches, when Max piped up that he wanted "Thai food." Paula and I were quite impressed with the boy's advanced palate, until we learned that he had recently gone out with his parents to a Thai restaurant and, unwilling to eat any of the strange food there, had been given a hot dog from a restaurant down the street. He now assumed that hot dogs were Thai food. As we laughed at Max's culinary confusion, Paula and I muttered to each other that when *we* had kids, we'd get them to eat *real* Thai food.

A handful of years later, with our own toddler in tow, we thought we had succeeded in shaping his taste buds. He would inhale nonspicy Indian food, Mexican food . . . practically anything we put in front of him. But our victory was short lived. In day care, he'd sit around the eating table, locked in place with five other kids in built-in seats, his little hands wandering toward the other kids' food: Goldfish, saltines, and graham crackers . . . oh my. Food from home quickly lost its luster. He had tasted from the forbidden— well, not the forbidden *fruit*, but from the forbidden processed food—and he was hooked.

Processed foods are so immediately gratifying, they quickly dampen desire for more complex foods, especially on young palates. Influenced by his social environment, my boy's tastes had changed. His days of Indian and Thai food, indeed of food with discernable flavor at all, quickly came to an end. No doubt, I could have done a better job of parenting him—if I hadn't caved in to his demands for junk food at home, maybe he would have maintained a broader palate. After all, kids in India eat Indian food.

But many of us are unconsciously influenced by social forces. Our specific eating habits are much less individualistic than we think. In fact, studies of social networks have shown that obesity is, metaphorically speaking, "contagious"—if I become overweight, then my current friends are more likely to become overweight.[4] So is smoking behavior.[5]

In the case of smoking, social contagion isn't quite so surprising. When I talk with my patients about quitting smoking, I have long made the point of discussing the smoking habits of their closest friends and their spouse. If they quit, and their spouse continues to smoke, odds are high that my patients will relapse. Too much temptation. If they quit, and their friends at the bar keep smoking, they will face an uphill battle on even steeper terrain.

Eating habits appear to be similarly influenced by social interactions. It is hard to "go vegan" if you hang out with people like, say, Roger Clemens, who says he doesn't know what a vegan is. It is difficult to implement healthy eating habits if your spouse, your in-laws, and your neighbors continue to serve you unhealthy foods.

In fact, social context has an even subtler and more surprising influence on our eating habits that goes beyond mere exposure to other people's foods. It turns out that the sheer quantity of food people eat is unconsciously influenced by the social setting of their meals. Research experiments have proved that when people eat in groups, they put away significantly more calories than when they eat alone. For example, one group of researchers set themselves up at a day care and convinced the day care workers to vary the number of children that they placed around the snack table each day. They observed the children and discovered that as the number of kids around the table increased, so too did their snack consumption.[6] Studies of adults reveal the same finding.[7] When in large groups, people not only eat faster, but hang out at the dinner table longer, too, discussing sports and politics and such. The result is that the number of calories people consume at any given meal is not determined solely by their appetites or their caloric needs, but is also influenced, however unconsciously, by the social context of their meals.

Had you realized that you were stuffing in an extra 100 calories every time you ate in a large group? Probably not. The extra calories people consume in social gatherings are largely taken in unconsciously. People don't *decide* to eat more in such settings; they just get so energized by their environment that they consume accordingly. After all, almost no one consciously calculates the number of calories they ingest in any given meal (setting aside people in Weight Watchers or similar programs). Therefore, the amount of food people eat is influenced by a gaggle of unconscious forces.

Brian Wansink, a behavioral scientist at Cornell, has conducted a host of clever studies that reveal the subtle factors that influence the way we eat. More accurately, I should say he's hosted a bunch of clever studies, because much of his research (described in hilarious detail in his book *Mindless Eating*) takes place in real restaurants and cafeterias, where he experiments on customers to test his theories about the factors that influence how much food people will eat.[8] In perhaps my favorite study, he rigged up a bowl of soup that he could refill from underneath through hidden tubes, without being detected by diners. This study helped confirm his theory that people often rely on visual cues, like the emptying of a soup bowl, to tell their stomachs when to stop eating. Such visual cues are so important that one person in Wansink's study consumed a quart of soup, without even questioning how so much had fit into his bowl. In another study of visual cues, Wansink studied people dining at a Buffalo wings restaurant. At half the tables, he arranged for the waitresses to remove chicken bones from the tables as soon as the bones began to accumulate. At the remaining tables, he asked the waitresses to let the bones pile up in the discard bowls. Patrons whose bones accumulated, left with a visual reminder of their gluttony, ate significantly fewer wings.

Fascinating studies, no doubt, but a bit reminiscent of Kahneman and Tversky's early research on cognitive illusions. Wansink seems to be employing visual illusions, like bottomless soup bowls, to reveal the workings of our appetites. So even though his results are indisputable, what can we say about their practicality? People don't encounter bottomless soup bowls in regular life, after all.

But Wansink's studies are very relevant to normal life, because he has shown that visual cues influence many realistic eating situations. For example, in my own house, we have two sets of dinner plates, one with a diameter of 9½ inches and the other a bit over

11 inches. When we invite more than eight guests over for dinner, we are forced to pull out both plate sizes. Unbeknownst to me until I encountered Wansink's research, the amount of food each of my guests typically eats is being influenced by whichever plate ends up in their dinner setting. For Wansink, you see, has run experiments where he randomly assigns people to receive either small or large plates, and has discovered that plate size has a significant impact on people's eating habits. If you are handed a large plate, you will not only put more food on your plate than you would have with a smaller one, but you will also end up eating more food.

Suppose you fill a ceramic jar with peanuts and place it on your desk while working. You will probably reach into the jar, on occasion, and snack on some of the nuts, occasionally doing so without even thinking. You probably won't calculate how many calories you are consuming with each handful of food. And if you are like me, you'll often snack on nuts when you're not particularly hungry.

Hard to believe that such behavior is a result of rational calculation. But the irrationality underlying such behavior is even stronger than we think. For if you had placed the nuts in a glass jar, one that (unlike its ceramic counterpart) makes it easy to see the nuts resting inside the container, you would snack on substantially more nuts. The visual reminder of the food would influence you to snack more often.

When people put food into containers or onto countertops, they rarely contemplate the influence that the observability of the food will exert on their consumption habits. In an ideal world, our bodies would know how many calories we need to consume to maintain a healthy body weight, and make us feel satiated by our food once we've consumed that many calories. Our bodies might even make us averse to food once we reach our daily limit. But unfortunately, our bodies don't police us very well, leaving us victim to mindless munching behavior.

Consider all the eating that takes place away from our dinner plates. How many nuts did you snack on before dinner? How many of the rolls placed on the table by your waiter? How many M&Ms did you eat from the bowl on Nancy's desk at work? Did you actually make deliberate decisions about what to eat and how much to eat in those situations? Or did you simply tuck some food into your mouth, mindlessly munching on a few hundred calories?

Irrational Tastes

Some market enthusiasts, as we have seen, contend that obesity is a lifestyle choice and that, therefore, society should leave people alone to determine their optimal waistlines. But our food "choices" are much less chosen than we'd like to think. The amount of food we consume is not solely a consequence of our rational preferences. Indeed, even our preference for Fritos over fruit may not be as deliberate as we think. The very labeling of a food as being unhealthy can enhance its perceived desirability.

This finding was demonstrated by a group of marketing researchers who invited people into their research offices purportedly to test several kinds of crackers to see which were most flavorsome. The researchers portrayed one brand as having 11 grams of good fat and 2 grams of bad fat. They described the other brand as having 2 grams of good fat and 11 of bad. No matter which cracker they labeled as being high in good fat (and they varied which cracker was described as "healthy"), people described that healthy cracker as being less tasty.[9] The lead researcher, Rajagopal Raghunathan, repeated this experiment at a dinner party at his house, telling some people that the mango lassi he was serving them was "considered very healthy" in India, while telling other guests that it was "considered unhealthy." I don't need to tell you which guests enjoyed the lassi more.

As Raghunathan so sneakily demonstrated, the way food tastes is not just a function of which taste buds it stimulates, but also a result of our expectations. We expect unhealthy food to taste good, and therefore it does. So we roll through the grocery store, deciding what to buy. We grab the foods that look tastiest, unaware of how our tastiness predictions have been skewed by our misconceptions of healthy and unhealthy foods.

No one should be confident that food ends up in their stomach primarily as a result of deliberate choice. Instead, the food we put on our dinner plates, the snacks we mindlessly munch on between meals, the packages we place into our grocery carts . . . all of these foods end up in our stomachs not simply from conscious decisions we make, but also as a result of unconscious forces.

The Limits of Education

It might seem obvious that visible food will cause us to eat more than concealed food. It might even appear apparent that big plates will influence us to consume more than smaller plates. Nevertheless, we are often influenced by those matters without recognizing we've been influenced.

In his book, Wansink describes the great confidence his students exhibit when faced with his research results. They chuckle at the gullible people who gulped from the bottomless soup bowl, certain that they wouldn't fall prey to the same tricks. Then, Professor Wansink invites them to an end-of-semester party and secretly runs an experiment. Maybe he varies their plate size. Perhaps he messes with the shape of their drinking glasses (people often underestimate the amount of fluid in short, wide containers) or the color of their M&Ms (people eat more M&Ms out of a multicolored collection than out of one with a single color, even though the color of M&Ms has no influence on the flavor). Invariably, his students fall for the same tricks they have just finished learning about in his class.

Some of Wansink's findings can be used by individual people to improve their eating habits. People can put their junk food out of sight. They can trade in their dinnerware for smaller plates. But the wealth of things that unconsciously influence our eating habits is simply too much for us to control.

Market Failure

Nineteenth-century economists like Jevons developed the theory of rational decision making by pondering the psychology of food choice: how does the relative utility a person places on apples versus oranges determine the quantity of fruit that she will purchase at any given price? Jevons's generation could not possibly have imagined what a modern grocery store would look like—how many thousands of food choices would be stocked in its aisles or how many PhDs would be lurking in the corners figuring out how to draw us away from the produce section to the more lucrative processed food section. Indeed, I cannot imagine that Jevons would have used apples and oranges to develop his theory of utility maximization if he'd spent an hour at Kroger.

Then again, it's hard for me to believe that anyone can witness the obesity epidemic and assume that people are rationally choosing to be fat. Even ignoring the health consequences of obesity—the sleep apnea and the worn-out joints, the heart disease and diabetes—consider the economic and social consequences. People who are overweight make less money than those who aren't.[10] Obese people also report high levels of unhappiness and mental health problems.[11] Most people who are overweight, in fact, wish they could lose weight. I have personally witnessed dozens of marital squabbles in my clinic office, with husband and wife battling each other over which one of them is too lazy to lose weight.

The obesity epidemic is not a result of our genes, but of our genes interacting with modern markets. It is a consequence of our rational and irrational behaviors. The free market will never solve the epidemic on its own.

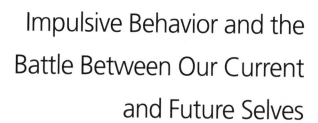

CHAPTER SEVEN

Impulsive Behavior and the Battle Between Our Current and Future Selves

YOU COULD SEE THE WHEELS turning as Taylor contemplated the choice I'd given him. Poke his big brother one more time, and he'd lose TV privileges for a week. Meanwhile, Jordan sat on the other side of the van, contemplating the same choice. Each boy felt a strange urge to reach across and gain some measure of retribution, convinced that the playful tussle they had begun several minutes ago had only escalated because the *other* kid had gotten out of control. Taylor had crossed the line, Jordan shouted, by whacking him in his privates. No, it was Jordan who had crossed the line, Taylor argued, having *almost* whacked his privates a moment earlier.

Who would cross the line next? Or would my threat deter further contact? The boys were caught between competing impulses: a strong pull for immediate gratification and a more measured influence, a steady tug toward self-control, with a distant reward awaiting them: a chance to watch TV when they woke up on Saturday morning.

It's amazing how frequently we are faced with choices like this one, choices between immediate and delayed gratification. When the amount of gratification is equal across time periods, the choice is usually easy. If your spouse offers to have, um, relations with you either tonight or tomorrow night, then anyone in the mood for sex right now (i.e., any male) would choose tonight. Who knows: by tomorrow, your spouse might have lost interest.

But in many domains of life, the choice between now and later is a real trade-off, between having a little bit now or significantly more later. A high school student chooses nightly between the short-term joys of relaxing (watching TV, IM'ing friends, or "like, whatever") and the long-term benefits of working hard now (better grades, acceptance to a better college, and, eventually, a more satisfying job). A dieter chooses between the short-term joys of a cupcake and the long-term benefits of dropping those last 5 pounds. A young couple decides between the immediate gratification of splurging on an expensive trip or the delayed benefits of investing in a retirement fund.

Many of these choices have much less predictable consequences than the choice Jordan and Taylor were contemplating that day. Because Jordan and Taylor *knew* that their Saturday-morning TV time was on the line; Dad doesn't make empty threats. Whereas the high school student has no reason to expect that his algebra grade will depend on one night's homework or that admission to Stanford and gainful employment are on the line right now; good grades, college acceptances, and fulfilling jobs, after all, are the results of thousands of such choices. The same reasoning applies to cupcakes and investments—waistlines and retirement accounts don't typically depend on a single decision but, rather, depend on thousands of small decisions.

Pity the people who have never splurged in their lives. At some point, after all, we must taste life's joys. But we must also reserve pity for the people who never defer gratification, who can't tolerate any short-term pain even when they stand to yield large long-term gains: the addict whose life is destroyed by the pursuit of immediate pleasure; the partially paralyzed motor vehicle accident victim who, prior to his accident, chose to splurge on material possessions instead of investing in disability insurance; the former big man on campus who blew off his studies and now watches the nerds climb past him on the corporate ladder, with their master's degrees and useful skills.

Do such people deserve our pity? They made their choices, after all, and are living with the consequences. They chose now over later. Is there anything wrong with that? More relevant to the topic of this book: Are such preferences for now over later rational or irrational? Should people be left alone to make such choices, or should society direct people toward "wiser" long-term behaviors?

A Matter of Rational Preference

Imagine you have just won a small lottery and must choose between receiving a $10,000 prize now or waiting one year and receiving $11,000. I expect some readers of this book will opt for the immediate prize, seeking to address an immediate financial need or, perhaps, hoping to celebrate their good news with a big purchase. Other readers will imagine waiting one year for the bigger prize, concluding that a 10 percent increase in their winnings is more than could have been expected if they'd invested the money now.

Is there a "rational" decision here? The short answer is no. Instead, the rational choice depends on a given person's preferences. If, for example, I posed readers with a choice between strawberry or raspberry yogurt, I would not expect a unanimous choice of one flavor over the other. The right choice would depend on which flavor a given reader likes best. In the case of the yogurt choice, market libertarians would say that the utility of strawberry yogurt is greater than raspberry for some people, and vice versa for others; hence, the optimal thing to do is let people choose what flavor to consume.

In the same way that preferences for yogurt differ across people, so do preferences for time. Economists call these preferences *discount rates*. To grasp the idea of discount rates, consider a choice between $10,000 now or $10,000 in ten years. Almost everyone will choose the immediate cash, aware that they may not be alive in ten years, and that they could invest the $10,000 now and it would appreciate in value over those ten years. It is rational to value the present more than the future in this kind of situation.

But how much more should we value now over then? Should I prefer $10,000 now over $100,000 in ten years? Over $1 million? The short answer, preferred by most traditional economists, is that there is no "correct" discount rate, just as there's no correct flavor of yogurt.

That means that believers in rationality think it is OK that different people have different discount rates. And thus it is also OK that as a result of these different time preferences, people make different choices in life. One college kid decides to become a heart surgeon, well aware that he won't achieve this goal for more than a decade. His roommate opts, instead, for the more rapid gratification of a consulting job right after graduation. It is possible that either student has made the wrong decision. Maybe the life of a heart surgeon won't be as fulfilling as the first student thought, and maybe the consulting lifestyle won't suit the other student. But it is also quite possible that both students know enough about their own preferences that they've each made the right decision.

As we have seen, then, some people are much more focused on short-term gains than others: they base their decisions on higher discount rates than other people. But is it ever irrational to have a high discount rate—to care too little about the future?

Consider addiction. Studies have shown that heroin addicts have higher discount rates than nonaddicts.[1] So do alcohol abusers, smokers, and compulsive gamblers.[2] But if a person has a strong enough preference for immediate over delayed gratification, could it not be seen as rational for that person to shoot up and enjoy the rush of heroin in his veins without worrying about the future?

In strict neoclassical economics, there are no such things as irrational preferences. In holding this open-minded view, in fact, economists have harked back to Adam Smith's friend David Hume, who famously wrote, "'Tis not contrary to reason to prefer the destruction of the whole world to the scratching of my finger."[3] Less eloquent shades of this view can be seen in Gary Becker and Kevin Murphy's theory of rational addiction, where they wrote, "This paper relies on a weak concept of rationality that does not rule out strong discounts of future events." To their credit, Becker and Murphy don't seem completely sold on Hume's notion that all preferences are rational, asking at one point, "Should someone who entirely or largely neglects future consequences of his actions be called rational?"[4] But they don't answer this question.

And who can blame them? After all, it is not easy to know when a preference for immediate gratification shifts from being a mere preference to being an irrational, even pathological, myopia. Is it irrational for me to prefer an immediate $10,000 over $20,000 one year from now? How about over $50,000? Or $1 million? Unless I'm starving and need immediate cash, or in debt to the mob and hoping not to be fitted for some very heavy shoes, I would be stupid not to take the $1 million. So somewhere along this continuum, between low and high discount rates, a person's preferences shift from rational to irrational, from curious to pathological. And since the place where this shift occurs is impossible to identify, many theorists have chosen, like Becker and Murphy, to remain agnostic.

I don't think it's necessary, however, to figure out exactly when preferences for now over later shift from rational to irrational, from defensible to indefensible. Because, you see, people's attitudes toward time—their discount rates, so to speak—are messed up in much more serious ways than I've described so far, ways that cause people to overeat and underexercise, overindulge and underinvest;

ways that are intimately connected to the battle within all of us to control our harmful impulses.

Tomorrow Is Always One Day Away

The alarm went off at 5 a.m. Work didn't start until 8:30 a.m., and the kids wouldn't rise until 7 a.m. So why the early alarm? I wanted to get an hour of exercise in, and that was increasingly difficult to do with all of my family responsibilities. But upon hearing the beginning of *Morning Edition* on my radio, I couldn't muster any enthusiasm for a workout. So I reached over, turned off the alarm, and went back to sleep.

I faced a simple choice between the pleasures of sleep and the benefits of exercise, and because of how I felt about those activities that morning, I chose to snooze. No one could call this choice irrational. Indeed, given my preferences that morning, it was obvious that the utility of sleep loomed much larger to me than the utility of, ugh, a morning run.

Only one problem with this story: at bedtime that previous night, I held an equally strong preference for exercise over sleep. Why else do you think I set the alarm for 5 a.m.? What's more, when I finally woke at 6:30 a.m., I told myself I'd get up the *next* morning at 5 a.m. and get in that run.

The world is full of people eating desserts, smoking cigarettes, reading trashy novels, watching bad Hollywood sequels, and splurging on unnecessary expenditures, all of whom vow, tomorrow, to eat more healthily, kick the habit, start catching up on their Dickens, check out that new foreign flick, and put some money away for Junior's college fund. The problem is that when tomorrow arrives, it has become today, and their desire for immediate gratification once again wins out.

Becker and Murphy were not prepared to conclude that, along a continuum of discount rates, some people's preferences for immediate gain were irrational. But how can they remain agnostic about the rationality of people who vacillate between one discount rate and another—between setting the alarm and turning it off?

Imagine you are choosing between receiving $100 in one year or $110 in one year and one day. If you are like most people, you'll choose the larger sum of money, figuring that a 10 percent increase is a nice reward for waiting just one day. Now consider a different choice: between receiving $100 today and $110 tomorrow. In this situation, the majority of people choose the *smaller* sum of money. In the distant future, most people are willing to wait one day to make $10, but they aren't willing to do that today. They have a high discount rate in the short run and a low one in the long run.[5] Which of these discount rates reflects their true preferences? Can we even talk about rational discount rates when people are so inconsistent?

Nobel laureate Thomas Schelling has written brilliantly about the multiple selves battling within us all, whose preferences vie for domination in our lives.[6] My long-term self wants to invest in a safe retirement account, while my short-term self wants to throw money at a high-risk start-up company. One of my selves wants to wake up at 5 a.m., and the other wants to hit the snooze button.

As we contemplate whether society should try to help people behave more rationally in market settings, we need to think about which of these selves people should listen to. Whose utilities should the market be maximizing? Libertarians argue that it is not society's job to answer this question. We should let people decide how to live their lives, and if they are conflicted about what to do, then, as grown-ups, they should figure things out and act accordingly.

Proponents of free markets think it is intrusive for governments or any external force to tell people how to choose between short- and long-term gains. If people have multiple selves, the free marketers say, it is for them to decide which self to obey at which time. It is for them as individuals to chart their course through life. Some people will make wiser decisions than others. Some people, who would have been better off in the long run if they'd stayed in college, will drop out. But who are we, as outsiders, to tell them what to do?

As Glen Whitman writes in a Cato Institute publication, "Adopting policies *solely* on the grounds that they advance the interest of the long-run self would be inappropriate" (Whitman's italics).[7]

And indeed, as Schelling has pointed out, people come up with clever strategies to help one of their selves win out over the other. You want to wake up at 5 a.m.? Set the alarm clock for that hour and place the clock across the room. Want to save more money? Get part of your paycheck directly deposited to a bank account where you will be penalized severely for withdrawing the money prematurely. If you want to keep from cutting your afternoon run short, don't run on a treadmill, where it's too easy to stop. Instead, run straight away from your house for, say, three miles, and you'll be forced to put in a six-mile run. Convince yourself you have to follow hard-and-fast rules to control your dieting or your spending. Find ways to punish yourself if you don't obey these rules. You should be able to master self-control.

Consider former Arkansas governor and presidential candidate Mike Huckabee, a Baptist minister who has also proselytized for the wonders of exercise and dieting. Through sheer determination and willpower, Huckabee has lost more than 100 pounds and has managed to keep that weight off. Shouldn't other overweight people be able to do the same?

But these strategies don't work if people don't employ them. Which means we still need to consider which self deserves prominence when we, as a society, are thinking about how to structure the free market.

The March 1 Problem

If you ask me on January 1 what I hope to do on March 1, I'll tell you I hope to exercise, eat well, be patient with my kids, be efficient at work, and watch no more than thirty minutes of TV. If you ask me the same question on January 2, or February 3, or February 15, I will give you the same answer. I have strong feelings about how I want to behave on March 1, and those feelings exist every day of the year. Until March 1 arrives, and I blow off exercise, stuff down a triple cheeseburger, snap at my kids, surf the Web at work instead of rewriting this chapter, and zone out in front of an NBA matchup between two teams I don't even care about. By March 2, I not only regret what I did on March 1, but I plan tomorrow and the next day and indeed next year on March 1 to behave better.

Which self deserves priority? The one that reigns 1 day a year, on March 1, or the one that states its preferences the other 364 days? Ted O'Donoghue and Matthew Rabin, a pair of behavioral economists from Cornell and UC Berkeley, respectively, pose the March 1 story as a way of refuting libertarians like Whitman. Whitman claims that there are no grounds for choosing long-term selves over short-term ones. O'Donoghue and Rabin believe that their March 1 example shows that short-term preferences are errors, not preferences that deserve respect when making policies. Indeed, they think people regularly harm themselves by abandoning their long-term preferences, buying more, smoking more, eating more, and exercising less than they should.

As evidence of harm, they point to the growing burden of credit card debt in many industrialized countries.[8] The majority of Americans do not pay off their credit card bills on time and therefore end up borrowing money at exorbitant rates, often exceeding 19 percent annually. On rare occasions, this high interest rate is justifiable, when people really need to purchase an expensive product immediately and cannot qualify for a lower-interest loan. But most consumers are simply throwing money away by paying such high interest rates. Indeed, if their goal were to maximize short-run consumption, then these people would be better off to exhibit just enough self-control to pay off their credit card bill on time, a practice that would spare them the cost of the 19 percent loans and, therefore, leave them with more money to purchase what they desire.

Similarly, almost 10 percent of Americans take out payday loans, forking over a whopping 18 percent interest in as little as two weeks in order to get an advance on their paycheck. "No matter how bad their situation," O'Donoghue and Rabin contend, "to repeatedly borrow at exorbitant rates puts people in worse situations." Everyone, that is, except the lenders.

Market evangelists would caution us against regulating credit card companies or payday loan operations. After all, these companies compete in the marketplace for customers, many of whom purchase their services multiple times. These customers, they argue, would clearly take their business elsewhere if they found the company's products to be unsatisfying. Believers in near-total rationality figure that if people really wanted to save more money, they would do so.

Most of us trained in behavioral economics no longer buy these arguments, and we'd like to explore gentle regulations that will help people avoid the March 1 problem. We don't see short-term decisions as being driven solely by discount rates, but understand them, instead, as being hijacked by the limited energy people can draw on to regulate their own behavior. People, it turns out, are too exhausted to control their short-term impulses. Don't believe me? Watch what happens when researchers force people to eat radishes while sitting next to a plate of freshly baked chocolate chip cookies.

Self-Control: A Valuable and Depletable Resource

You have just been placed in a room suffused with the odor of freshly baked chocolate chip cookies. But the research assistant informs you, with a shrug, that the cookies sitting in front of you are off limits, because you have randomly been chosen for "the radish condition." The study you are participating in, you see, is purportedly about taste perception. That's why the researchers asked you to skip a meal before coming to the lab.

It is not easy for you to refrain from pilfering one of the cookies. It takes willpower. But you refrain from indulging in the cookies and dutifully munch on radishes.

If you were a little kid, you might not have shown such restraint. Most little kids have not developed the willpower to fight off such a strong temptation. In fact, some of the most profound research on self-control has involved toddlers given various challenges, like leaving a pile of toys alone until the researchers return to the room. If you give toddlers such a challenge, some will give in right away and others will show more restraint. How long it takes to start playing with the toys is a strong predictor of these toddlers' futures. Those who exhibit the greatest restraint will be more likely to score high on the SAT, stay out of jail, avoid teenage pregnancy, and live to old age.[9] Self-control is, after all, a very valuable resource. The myopic preferences that people show for short-term consumption, when taken to an extreme, are no recipe for a fulfilled life.

But when the researchers placed you in front of their cookies, they were not testing the level of restraint you would exhibit. Instead, they were studying whether such restraint would exhaust your willpower. So after torturing you with these forbidden cookies, the research assistant returns to the room, asks you to fill out a quick mood questionnaire, and then says that you need to wait around while the radish taste fades from your mouth. To help kill time, he asks you to conduct a problem-solving test. He shows you a simple figure, say, a square, and asks you to trace it without lifting the pen off the paper and without retracing any of the lines. The first couple of figures are easy, and the next couple are a bit trickier. Then the research assistant hands you a more complex figure and says you should do your best to trace it. He even gives you multiple copies of the figure, because this one looks as if it's going to be tough. He tells you to ring the bell either when you've succeeded in tracing the figure or when you've given up.

What the research assistant hasn't told you is that the figure cannot be traced without retracing at least one line. You'll never solve this problem, and so you'll eventually have to give up. The researchers gave you this figure because they want to discover whether the self-control you just exerted, resisting the temptation of eating the cookies, has exhausted your supply of self-control sufficiently that you'll give up on this second task sooner than other people.

You struggle with the figure and finally, after a little more than eight minutes, ring the bell in defeat, twenty copies of the figure lying in front of you covered in your unsuccessful scribbles. Would it surprise you to discover that if you hadn't been tempted by the cookies, you would have spent more than twice as long trying to solve the problem?[10]

Studies like this have led many psychologists to conclude that self-control is finite. When people have exerted self-control for a while in one situation, they inevitably have less willpower to draw on in the next situation.

This is a profound finding and presents many challenges for people hoping to behave rationally within the free market. For instance, I have a strange pattern of buying too many fruits and vegetables at the grocery store—I buy so much that some of the food invariably rots before my family can eat it. Why do I consistently make this mistake? It's because I mispredict my self-control. When buying fresh veggies at the grocery store on Sunday, I envision all the healthy meals I'll cook for my family throughout the week. Then I come home at dinnertime on Monday, tired from a day of work, my lower back aching from too much time at my desk, my emotional resources spent. Pretty easy at that point in time to push aside the veggies and zap something less healthy in the microwave.

I'm not alone. Consider a stay-at-home mom who has just spent the day caring for two toddlers, a veritable marathon of self-control. She had planned to go to the fitness center when her husband got home, but by the time he arrives, a glass of wine and ten minutes with *People* magazine feel awfully tempting. Is it any wonder that the vast majority of people who join fitness centers use them so infrequently? Their long-term selves want to go to the center four times a week, to shape those abs. But their short-term selves cannot haul their sorry abs over to the club often enough to make the monthly fee worthwhile. There are simply too many days of the week where the demands of family or work drain them of the energy to exercise.

Social psychologists who study self-control have described it as "one of the most precious endowments of the human self," pointing out that problems like depression, aggression, teenage pregnancy, obesity, gambling debts, and poor school performance are a result of poor self-control.[11]

In fact, you might have noticed that many of the problems that result from lack of self-control strike especially hard at people with low incomes. For example, obesity rates among low-income women are 25 percent higher than they are among high-income women of the same age.[12] Supporters of free markets, often also being strong proponents of personal responsibility, may respond to these statistics with a call for people to get their acts together. Fox News commentator Radley Balko bemoans any efforts to "shift responsibility for individual health away from individual Americans," writing that the only solution to the obesity epidemic is to compel people to take ownership of their own health.[13]

Now I am a big believer in personal responsibility. And I think the world would be a better place if more people exerted better self-control. But I also recognize that it is easier for me, a wealthy doctor, to exert control over my own health than it is for a single mother working a low-wage job. I remember how exhausted I was when my kids were younger. I can't imagine how much more exhausted I would have been if I had also had to contend with financial problems at the same time, or if I'd been stressed out by neighborhood crimes or by a bad work environment.

Being poor depletes people's reserves of self-control. Indeed, obesity rates around the world are rising fastest in some of the poorest areas. This has created what at first appears to be a paradox— researchers in Africa and Asia have noted that some of the most dramatic weight gains are occurring in areas that also have the highest rates of malnutrition.[14] But this paradox can partly be resolved by understanding the kinds of self-control problems facing people in those same regions. To resolve more of this paradox, we need to move beyond what social scientists have learned about self-control in the past twenty years, to understand what the past few million years of evolution have done to thwart people's attempts to control the size of their waistlines.

Choosing to Lose Weight

In theory, losing weight should be simple. Just burn more calories than you consume, and you will lose weight. Seriously. That's all it takes. If you are overweight and can't shed excess poundage, that must mean either you don't want to lose weight (perhaps you chose, rationally, to remain obese) or you don't have enough willpower to regain your ideal body mass. Consider what dieters have been told by their doctors, or what they've heard on *Oprah*, about the tiny changes that influence how much people weigh. Weight gain, they've been told, can result from a handful of extra crackers a day, those 50 extra calories adding up over the years to thousands of calories.[15] If this is true, they are told, then the flip side should hold: if they simply cut out a few crackers a day, they will lose weight. So they eliminate crackers, but nothing happens. They cut out snacks, but lose nary a pound. They drop one of their three daily meals, and they still don't seem to lose any weight. They report their efforts to their doctors and are met with incredulity, their doctors noting that they must be cheating on their diets. Their spouses leap on these words, pointing out the dessert they had just last weekend at their friend's house. The poor dieters don't know what to think. This calorie-in/calorie-out theory doesn't seem to fit their experience. The calories do a great job of coming in but not such a good job of departing.

So why is it that only 5 percent of people who try to lose weight manage to do so in a sustained manner?[16] This low success rate is a result of what happens when you mix the modern food industry with age-old forces of evolution.

In considering how evolution has conspired against diet success, let's hark back briefly to our time as hunter and gatherers, out on the tundra living in constant threat of starvation.[17] In times of plenty, our ancestors would gorge themselves on the kill, storing the meat in their own fat cells and glycogen stores rather than letting it rot on the bone. In between successful hunts, however, it was important to stave off starvation.[18] Consequently, evolution favored those individuals who could conserve energy and thereby hold on to the calories they'd already consumed. Dieters will recognize the unfortunate result of these evolutionary pressures. When they diet, they don't seem to lose as much weight as they are supposed to.

Dieters have every right to bemoan their caloric struggles, because evolutionary pressures have made human beings into prolific hoarders of calories. When we diet, our bodies respond as they did back on the tundra when our seasonal food supplies would dwindle. They go into starvation mode. To cope with this seeming starvation, our evolutionary programming kicks in to slow down our metabolism. We might drop our calorie intake by 10 percent and still not lose any weight, or plateau after dropping just a few pounds.

To lose substantial weight, then, requires an even bigger drop in consumption. That will take incredible willpower, however, because our evolutionary programming—which, remember, thinks we are starving—has also tweaked our brain chemistry to fixate our attention on finding food. This programming was quite helpful in our tundra days, of course. But it backfires when you are forced to walk by Nancy's candy bowl at work each day. As a result of this programming, dieters obsess about food. They even experience a shift in their dietary preferences. A sugary meal that before their diet would have struck them as cloying will now taste great.[19] When we were evolving on the tundra, no survival advantages accrued to people who were good at losing weight. We didn't evolve to be successful dieters. On the contrary, as psychologists Janet Polivy and Peter Herman put it, "Dieting is precisely the sort of threat that we have evolved to combat."[20]

Oh, and there's a final bit of cruelty built into this evolutionary framework. After depriving ourselves of thousands of calories, we splurge on, say, 750. Our metabolisms slowed to a crawl, our brains fixated on food, we succumb in a moment of weakness to the temptations of a Big Mac. But with our metabolic rates now down to a crawl and our bodies on starvation duty, those 750 calories—no matter that they fall well below our previous normal calorie intake—will probably lead to weight *gain*.

Clearly, life did not evolve to be fair. In the best of circumstances, dieting takes tremendous willpower, surrounded as most of us are by enticing snacks and delicious meals. To make matters worse, those people in society who face the greatest stresses—job insecurity and poverty chief among them—find themselves with fewer reserves of self-control to draw on to avoid these foods. Finally, the kind of stress such people face induces their bodies to hoard whatever calories they consume.

Which brings us back to the idea that obesity is solely due to personal weakness. Does any credible person actually believe that *regional* variations in obesity are caused by some regional weakness of character?

As I stress throughout this book, human beings behave in both rational and irrational ways. Their decisions are influenced by both conscious and unconscious forces. In a similar way that people are only partially rational, they are also only partially responsible for their behaviors.

In caring for veterans, I urge many of my patients to take more responsibility for their health. I try to help them quit smoking and start exercising. I am often not as successful as I'd like to be. And my patients deserve some of the blame for their erratic lifestyles.

On the other hand, if I had been exposed to the trauma of military battle at a young age; if I had been having violent nightmares for several decades; if I had come back from the military with a disability that prevented me from returning to my old job and with disability checks that barely lifted me above the poverty line—what would I weigh now and how many packs of cigarettes would I be inhaling each day?

It would be arrogant for me to conclude that I'd have enough self-control, enough strength of character, to emerge from this experience unscathed.

Internalities

Economists have long recognized that the free market cannot, on its own, deal with what are called *externalities*. Externalities are costs and benefits that are borne by third parties. For instance, if a factory emits a great deal of smog, the cost of these emissions is borne by those people who will be inhaling that smog. The factory, therefore, has little incentive to reduce its smog.

Drawing on the long history of work in such externalities, behavioral economists have begun referring to self-control problems as *internalities*.[21] If an obese person with diabetes decides to devour a pint of ice cream, then his short-term self is harming his long-term self. His short-term self gets all the benefits (the pleasures of a full belly and of a tasty dessert), while the long-term self bears all the harmful consequences (the clogged arteries and the failed kidneys).

In situations involving externalities, most people think that government regulation or intrusion is justified. The government can tax companies for polluting, to give them an incentive to reduce pollution. Or the government can regulate the quantity of particles companies can emit from any given chimney.

For the same reason that the government is justified in intruding to reduce externalities, some behavioral economists believe the government should act to reduce internalities. The free market, on its own, won't necessarily protect people's long-term interests. A government program that can help people save for retirement, or eat healthier foods, or spend more time in school will better the interests of people's long-term selves.

And when the people most harmed by internalities are the poorest among us, when they include the veterans I care for, whose supply of self-control is being exhausted by the challenge of coping with disabilities and post-traumatic stress disorder, shouldn't our government look for appropriate ways of reducing these harmful internalities?

Helping People Help Themselves

Dick Thaler's economic colleagues thanked him when he removed the tempting bowl of cashews from their field of vision, for they recognized that their powers of self-control were limited, and welcomed the helping hand of their host. As Thaler discovered that night, when the existence of such choices will leave people susceptible to their own lack of self-control, constraining people's choices can increase their overall well-being.

Dan Ariely recounts a startling example of this phenomenon in his book, *Predictably Irrational*.[22] He describes a time when he assigned three term papers to a class and told them they could hand the papers in any days they wanted, spacing the papers out evenly across the semester if they preferred, or waiting until the last day to submit all three, or any strategy in between. Not surprisingly, many of the students procrastinated and handed in mediocre rush jobs at the last possible minute.

Ariely took another strategy with a different class, forcing them to hand in the three papers at evenly spaced intervals across the semester. This class of students, their choices constrained, wrote much better papers. The first class could have chosen to impose evenly spaced deadlines on themselves, or could have chosen other deadlines that fit better with their class schedules. Yet with this freedom came the freedom to fail.

Most people lack the willpower to lose weight and keep that weight off. And this failure is completely understandable. Many people fail to save enough money for retirement, too, tempted as they are by the wealth of consumer goods available to them and by our easy-credit economy. Frankly, I have more pity for dieters than for most big spenders, but I try to understand both groups and to think about what a humane society should do to help both groups control their impulses.

Is it any wonder that there is such strong public support for Social Security in the United States or for similar programs in other countries? People recognize that they need help helping themselves. Much as people love the idea of freedom, most of them don't want *complete* freedom. Certainly, they don't want to squander all the resources of their youth on material goods, at the cost of being bankrupt on retirement. A humane government, then—a government that takes account of human nature— will find ways to get its citizens to save money for retirement. In doing so, it might stick exclusively with a government retirement program, or it might take advantage of private savings mechanisms. But it won't leave people prey to their own worst instincts.

Freedom is a wonderful thing, but not so wonderful that it should exist, unrestrained, at the expense of people's well-being. I expect most people, like Dick Thaler's guests, would be happy to give up some amount of their liberty to increase the chance of acting in their long-term best interests. People recognize that they need help with self-control.

Food Stamps and Human Nature

We are not done with the topic of self-control in this book. It will bubble up to the surface elsewhere. But for now, it is worth considering an example of the policy relevance of the ideas that I have laid out in this chapter. Let's consider how self-control should influence the way society distributes food stamps.

The food stamp program was created to make sure that poor people didn't face malnutrition or starvation. It has been criticized by market libertarians since its inception. If you believe that people generally make rational decisions, programs like food stamps won't make much sense to you. As Milton Friedman pointed out, if people were fully rational, then it would be better to give them money and let them decide whether they want to use it to purchase food or something else.[23] Food stamps, the argument goes, simply narrow people's choices and thereby reduce their ability to maximize their own best interest.

Opponents of food stamps have new arguments now to make, to criticize these programs. They can point out, as I did earlier in this chapter, that poor people these days are more likely to experience obesity than starvation. Add that to the problems of high bureaucratic costs, fraud, and a black market for food stamps, and the critics have a strong case for eradicating the program.

But the science of self-control raises another way of using food stamps to promote people's best interests. Imagine a family that relies on food stamps to support its grocery bills. The money comes in at the beginning of each month, and for two or maybe three weeks, the family is able to go to the grocery store and purchase whatever it needs. However, by the end of the month, they are tight on money and find themselves having to skip meals. The food stamp program has set this family up for the same cycle of starvation and plenty that ancient humans experienced on the tundra. Now we know that evolution has programmed us to combat this cycle by storing food as fat when times are plentiful. In other words, monthly allotments of food stamps may make families more susceptible to obesity.

If, instead, the government distributed food stamps not each month, but each week, this cycle could potentially be broken. The food stamp program could add money to a credit card account each week and require the money to be spent within a specific time period. As with the students in Ariely's class who were forced to hand in term papers at evenly spaced intervals, such a spacing of food stamps might lead to healthier eating habits. In addition, it might even be possible to limit the kinds of foods people could buy with food stamps, to make sure that such money is not used to purchase unhealthy processed foods.

I don't know whether this kind of program is feasible currently. All government solutions come with their own costs, and all need to be tested in the real world, to look for unintended consequences.

Nevertheless, if we want to help people live the kind of lives they want to live, we should invest government resources to develop and evaluate innovative ways of making up for market failures.

We ought to develop and test programs informed by an understanding of humanity and its rich mixture of rationality and irrationality. Indeed, before looking at any other potential market reforms, we should explore other domains of our lives, beyond our waistlines, in which our irrational impulses keep us from acting consistently in our own rational best interests.

PART IV

Irrationality at Home, Office,

and Hospital

CHAPTER EIGHT

Spacious Lawns and Long Commutes

DAVID AND TERRY were successful lawyers in Minneapolis who lived close to downtown in a modest three-bedroom home. They were happy in their house, enjoying the easy access to downtown, the short commute to work, and the diverse neighborhood community. But as they whittled away at their student loans and began to reap the rewards of their first real law jobs, they yearned for something better. They couldn't reconcile their impressive jobs with their tiny kitchen, and they lusted after the spacious lawns gracing the properties of their more senior colleagues. So they bought a house in a growing community on the edge of the Minneapolis suburbs. They now have to drive forty-five minutes to work each morning, if there are no delays. In winter snow, this commute exceeds an hour each way, meaning they have increased their car time—time away from each other, time away from Rollerblading and cross-country skiing—by more than eight hours per week.

When they bought their new house, they were convinced that the unpleasantness of their long commutes would be more than made up for by returning home each night to a living space that suits their lifestyles, and to a spacious lawn that, once they have children, would easily accommodate a two-on-two soccer game. As far as David and Terry were concerned, they would be much happier in their new house.

If you believe in the pervasiveness of rational choices, you would be inclined to conclude that David and Terry have improved their lot in life, have increased their utility, by buying a house in the exurbs. After all, they thought about this move for a long time. They visited dozens of houses and waited until they found one with all the features they were looking for. They meticulously jotted down a list of the pros and cons of moving. They even investigated the main con, the long commute, by driving out to the house in the early morning so they could test the commuting traffic and see just how long it would take them to reach their respective law offices. If ever the world has seen a rational decision, surely this was it.

Did David and Terry make the correct decision, when they bought this new house? As we've now learned, people aren't always as good at making decisions as they'd like to be. Their decisions are biased by all the psychological weaknesses, the heuristics and computing errors, that Kahneman and Tversky made so famous. Many of these heuristics and biases reflect our misjudgments of the likelihood of certain things occurring, or reflect strange ways that we incorporate probability information into our decisions, overemphasizing things like certainty. But David and Terry's decision did not hinge on probabilities. Availability biases and representativeness heuristics were not at play.

Nevertheless, Daniel Kahneman worries that people like David and Terry are making bad decisions for another reason. He suspects they aren't doing a good job of predicting what will make themselves happy. Or to put it into terms of neoclassical economics—he thinks they are mispredicting their future utility.

When economists make theories about maximizing people's utilities, they are practicing what is known in the field as *welfare economics*. When used this way, *welfare* doesn't refer to a government program for poor people but, rather, to overall human well-being. It is a field of economics that tries to figure out what makes people better off. Daniel Kahneman, as we have seen, is deeply concerned about the way economists have settled on utility maximization as a measure of well-being. He is concerned that neoclassical economists have gotten caught in the middle of a false tautology. They believe that people are rational, and that rational people make choices based on what would maximize their utility the most; and, therefore, that if you want to know what maximizes people's utility, you should observe their choices.[1] Kahneman has shown some of the cognitive processes that interfere with rational decision making. From that work, alone, he is convinced that people's choices don't always maximize their utility. But for a long time, he was quiet in his criticism of welfare economics because he did not have an alternative measure of welfare to offer, to replace the observable utility that economists had come to depend on.

Then he had a flash of inspiration. He reflected on the philosophical works he had read on utility, as utility was defined before economists got a hold of the idea. Specifically, he thought about the ideas of Jeremy Bentham, widely considered as the father of utilitarianism, and wondered whether economic theory would be improved if economists went, as he put it, "back to Bentham."[2]

The Pleasures and Pains of Jeremy Bentham

If people can be described, at least in part, as rational utility maximizers—their decisions based largely on their idea of what will benefit themselves the most—then neoclassical economics can be characterized as the science of utility maximization, a discipline that demonstrates how a society or an economy can maximize the well-being of its citizens or consumers.

But what is this "utility" stuff that all these people are trying to maximize? Before Jevons wrote about apples and oranges, Jeremy

Bentham came up with an answer to this question. Bentham was born in London in 1748, several days' journey from where the twenty-five-year-old Adam Smith was living at the time. Bentham was a child prodigy, mastering Latin grammar by age four, enrolling at Queens College to study law at age twelve, and turning down a job as a lawyer at the advanced age of sixteen, having much greater ambitions even at that early age. In school, you see, he had been appalled by the intellectual flaccidity of the legal code, where things like prison terms were being determined by emotion or whimsy rather than by any rational procedure.

So instead of embarking on a lucrative career of putting criminals in prison, he began developing a philosophical system that would determine how long specific criminals ought to spend in prison. And by the time he had finished developing his system, he was convinced that he had found a way not only to reform the legal system but also to improve virtually *all* policy decisions. Bentham had convinced himself that if you want to know what to do with your tax code, your school system, your penal code, or your welfare laws, you simply need to assess which policy options will maximize people's utility.

To put some more meat on the bones of this theory, let's return to the penal system that had so thoroughly infuriated the young Bentham. Jurists of the day had a hard time figuring out whether, for instance, a horse thief deserved more punishment than an embezzler. And although everyone agreed that a murderer deserved more punishment than a vandal, few agreed on how *much* more punishment. Bentham told people that these challenges could be met by an appeal to utility, by which he meant anything that tends to "augment or diminish the happiness of the party whose interest is in question: or, what is the same thing in other words, to promote or to oppose that happiness."[3] Bentham's view of utility was hedonistic, emphasizing pleasure and pain. As Bentham saw it, if you want to figure out how much worse armed robbery is than vandalism, you simply need to figure out how much more the former reduces people's happiness than the latter. In pondering the haphazard British penal system, Bentham came upon the idea of basing criminal punishment, indeed of basing all "morals and legislation," on the principle of utility. The goal of any policy, for Bentham, was to maximize how much pleasure people experience while minimizing their pain.

Bentham's view of utility was completely and explicitly hedonistic. He was concerned with how people felt—whether they were happy or unhappy, in pain or not in pain. If we are going to punish people, we should pay attention to how much unhappiness their crimes have created. Greater unhappiness deserves greater punishment. Indeed, the goal of all public policy, for Bentham, should be to maximize the happiness and minimize the pain of the populace, as a whole. Thus, if you want to compare two policy alternatives, say, two ways of designing a public education system, you should "sum up all the values of all the *pleasures* on the one side, and those of all the pain on the other."

Bentham's View of Human Nature

Bentham believed that policies should focus on pleasure and pain not simply because he believed that pain and pleasure are morally important, but also because he believed that a focus on pain and pleasure fit well with human nature. In Bentham's view, "nature has placed mankind under the governance of two sovereign masters, pain and pleasure. It is for them alone to point out what we ought to do, as well as to determine what we shall do." To Bentham's credit, he was no hedonist extremist. He didn't glorify Las Vegas–style debauchery. And while recognizing that people are motivated to pursue pleasures, he hardly proposed that all pursuits are equally laudable. Pursuing sexual pleasure, he wrote, is not always the immoral pursuit that the ascetics would have us believe. Bentham didn't think men should feel guilty for enjoying sex with their wives (phew!). But he did believe that virgin ravishing, though also driven by the pursuit of sexual pleasure, was morally wrong.

Why? Because for Bentham, moral behavior, like policy decisions, should be guided by the balance of pleasures and pain that *all people* will experience as a result of a particular action (or policy). People should not pursue their own pleasures regardless of how such pursuits affect other people. Indeed, of all the motives that drive human behavior, "the dictates of good-will are the surest of coinciding with those of utility."

Bentham was a political radical, whose moral treatises called for the reform of British society. A lifelong bachelor, he spent his free time organizing political groups and intellectual societies, even founding the University College of London, where, in accordance with his will, his body has been preserved in a glass case with a wax head affixed to his shoulders, so that he can still attend important faculty meetings. (We Ann Arborites wouldn't tolerate such a strange request from anyone less than a successful football coach!)

Bentham looked forward to a time when pleasure and pain could be quantified, so that policies could be guided by science and data. But scientists were not soon up to this formidable task. Indeed, economists abandoned Bentham's hedonistic view of utility in large part because it was so difficult to quantify.

Kahneman proposed a return to Bentham for two reasons. First, as we'll see later in this book, he was convinced that science had reached the point where it could achieve Bentham's goals of measuring pleasures and pains. Second, as we'll see in this chapter, he felt that people's decisions often failed to promote their own happiness, and believed that the removal of hedonism from economics was causing many social scientists to overlook or underemphasize the importance of people's emotional lives.

Indeed, social scientists have discovered in the last couple of decades that people's decisions are often biased by an inability to predict what will make themselves happy. For example, people assume that money will significantly increase their happiness, when, in fact, a middle-class person is almost as likely to be happy as someone who's wealthy.[4] Similarly, people assume that chronic illness or disability will make them miserable, when instead the best data suggest that people are highly resilient in the face of adversity.[5] Mispredictions are rampant. People think they will get used to highway noise, and they don't.[6] They believe they will attain long-lasting happiness if they get a nicer car, but their joyous moods rarely linger longer than the new-car smell.

If people can be wrong about money and disability, how accurately will they predict the effect of commuting on their well-being?

Rush Hour

Most people recognize that long commutes are typically unpleasant experiences, putting a strain on the lower back and reducing the time they have for exercise, play, or cooking interesting dinners. David and Terry could have kept their short commute by staying in their small Minneapolis home. Now that they've moved, they could reduce their commute by looking for new jobs out in the burbs. But the pay is abysmal at suburban firms, so they have kept their old jobs, confident that, despite their long commutes, they've found the best possible combination of neighborhood and work.

Standard economic theory holds that if commuting is a source of unhappiness, then people like David and Terry will choose long commutes if they believe such commutes will raise their happiness in some other ways, like by bringing them higher pay or better living conditions. If this economic theory is true, then when you ask people how happy they are with their lives, those with long commutes should be just as happy as those with short ones. Rational people should be able to find the proper balance between property value, work life, and time on the roads.

Yet when the economists Alois Stutzer and Bruno Frey studied the German populace, they found that the longer people commuted each day, the less satisfied they were with their overall lives.[7] According to their data, Stutzer and Frey estimate that experiencing a long commute is 20 percent as bad as being unemployed. Daniel Kahneman and his colleagues confirmed this finding in the United States. In their study, they even linked the specific activity of commuting with a measurable decline in moment-to-moment mood.[8]

These findings should concern us all, because commuting is taking up an increasing amount of people's time. In Germany, where Stutzer and Frey conducted their study, people commute an average of forty-two minutes per day. This is solidly exceeded in the United States, where the average person spends forty-nine minutes per day on the road. In fact, one out of six Americans spends more than ninety minutes driving back and forth to work each day. Things are even worse in parts of Asia. In Bangkok, for example, the average person spends two hours a day commuting.[9] Two hours!

What could compel people to spend so much time driving? A good guess is that this behavior results from a desire to work in the city, where salaries are higher and job opportunities are greater, while living outside the city, where properties are larger and taxes are lower. Markets, in other words, drive the driving.

Good decisions require accurate predictions. Many people are convinced that the happiness they derive from making more money will make up for their longer commutes. Indeed, when Kahneman and several colleagues asked people to predict what would make themselves happy or unhappy, they found that people held strong beliefs about money and happiness. People assume that someone making $100,000 per year will be significantly happier than someone making $50,000 per year.[10] But scads of studies have shown a surprisingly small relationship between money and happiness, once people make enough money to meet basic living needs.[11]

I fear that we've been seduced by the lure of larger salaries into a less fulfilling life. A salary of $100,000 sounds much better than one of $50,000. If such a salary requires a longer commute, then that seems a small price to pay. But sometimes measurable things like salaries have too much influence on our decisions, causing us to pay too little attention to other factors that have an even greater impact on our lives. Chris Hsee, from the University of Chicago, demonstrated this problem in a brilliant experiment. He and his colleagues asked people to work for ice cream. They recruited people who preferred vanilla ice cream over pistachio ice cream, and gave them a choice between performing a little work for vanilla ice cream or a lot of work for pistachio. Not surprisingly, everyone chose to do the easy task to receive vanilla ice cream. Less work, greater reward. People are often irrational, but they're rarely complete idiots!

But Hsee altered the situation for another group of vanilla lovers. In this version of the study, he gave people a choice between performing an easy task for 60 points or a harder task for 100. He then gave them an opportunity to exchange these points, like money, to purchase ice cream, with vanilla ice cream costing 60 points and pistachio 100. In this situation, most people chose to do the harder task and ended up buying pistachio ice cream. What happened in this experiment? People were seduced by their intuition that more must mean better, and ended up worse off as a result. We all know that 100 points is better than 60 points, just as we know that a $100,000 salary is better than a $50,000 one. This intuition drives people to pursue higher-paying jobs, even if that means spending more time commuting.[12]

By no means am I implying that people mispredict everything all the time. Indeed, I expect that few people seek out long commutes for the anticipated pleasure of congested roads. I expect that most people correctly guess that a longer commute will be a less happy one. But it's the *other* things in life that people are often wrong about. They mistakenly believe that the emotional benefits of bigger salaries and larger lawns—which, alas, are often transient—will make up for the misery of commuting.

What about David and Terry? Did they make the wrong decision? Ask them this question, and they'll vehemently defend their move. They'll acknowledge that commuting isn't fun, but will tell you that they enjoy listening to public radio while they drive, and love having space for all that kitchenware they received as wedding presents.

But here's the rub: I'm not sure we can trust David and Terry when they tell us they are happier than ever. We should be suspicious of their reported "happiness" not because they are dishonest, but instead because they are human beings who, like the rest of us, don't keep running tabs on their moods from year to year. To show you what I mean, let's take a quick detour, to explore people's perceptions of how happiness typically changes across their adult life spans.

A Whole Lot of Misremembering Going On

Research has shown that as people age, they become less bothered by little nuisances, having learned how to avoid people they find irritating, how to shrug off small nuisances, and how to direct more of their waking hours to pursuits that they find meaningful and rewarding.[13] In short, people become happier as they age, with the typical seventy-year-old being significantly happier than the typical twenty- or thirty-year-old.[14]

But are people aware of the joys that come with age? When my colleagues and I asked a group of younger and older people to tell us how happy they were, we confirmed that the seventy-year-olds were happier than the thirty-year-olds. But when we asked the thirty-year-olds to predict how happiness changes across the life span, they assumed incorrectly that happiness declines with age.[15] They can be forgiven for this view. They haven't experienced the joys of aging. When imagining old age, they probably thought about wrinkles and arthritis. Did they conjure up images of one of my heroes, Jack LaLanne, who, in his nineties, can bench-press more weight than most thirty-year-olds and brags that he still has sex almost every day: almost Monday, almost Tuesday, almost Wednesday . . .!

Young people can be forgiven for mispredicting how happiness changes with age, having not experienced how wisdom influences our emotional states. But what about those people who *have* experienced the joys of aging? As it turns out, when we asked seventy-year-olds to tell us how happiness changes across the life span, they *too* believed that it declines with age. They have lived in both young and old shoes, have experienced life pre– and post–arch supports, if you will. But they don't realize that they've gained more than enough wisdom to make up for their aching joints.

This study illustrates an important truth: that misremembering is driven by the same forces that lead to mispredictions.[16] We all carry around theories about what makes us happy and unhappy. But we rarely keep a running tab of our moment-to-moment moods. Therefore, when asked to predict how, say, kidney failure would affect our moods, we're certain that it will make us miserable, even though the best available data suggest that people adapt, emotionally, to this serious illness.[17] To make matters worse, once a person has experienced kidney failure, he'll largely be unaware of how much he has adapted. He'll misremember how happy he was before he had kidney failure, "remembering" the constant bliss that was once his life.

When my research team followed a group of people waiting for kidney transplants (note to readers: we didn't literally follow them around; we surveyed them several times over the course of a year), we discovered that once they received a transplant, they began misremembering what their life had been like prior to the transplant. The further removed they were from their old dialysis days, the more miserable they remembered being.[18]

If you ask David and Terry about life in their new home, they will tell you they are happier than ever. But given what researchers have learned about people's mispredictions and misrememberings of happiness, they may not be right. There is, in fact, good reason to believe that people would be happier if they sacrificed part of their salary, or settled for a smaller lawn, in order to have a shorter commute.

David and Terry were free to choose where to buy a home, and might well have made a poor decision by moving to the exurbs. Their moment-to-moment moods have certainly suffered, since the couple has discovered the hard way that commuting is one of those things that people rarely adapt to. Meanwhile, they have largely adapted to their new home, emotionally speaking, and are no longer thrilled at the mere sight of their stately lawn.

Society could react to the Davids and Terrys of the world in many ways. It could take a libertarian position and let them choose where to live, for better or worse. But in truth, I haven't found a place in the world that is fully libertarian in this sense. Zoning laws, after all, strongly influence housing price and density in the cities and exurbs, and thereby influence people's housing choices. Highway appropriations and oil company subsidies make it easier for people to move farther from the city, where they can find the kind of acreage they seek. Tax laws make it easy for people like David and Terry to pay low property taxes in the exurbs while still enjoying the cultural benefits of living near a thriving metropolitan area.

Governments need to look for ways to reduce commuting. Commuting harms the environment, an externality that the market won't address on its own. Long commutes also reduce the quality of people's lives, an internality that should also be of great concern.

The government doesn't need to outlaw hour-long commutes in order to reduce such behavior. Gasoline taxes, for example, not only encourage people to buy fuel-efficient cars, but also entice them to find ways to drive less. The government could also make commuting more pleasant, by supporting high-quality public transportation in areas with adequate population density.

It is easy to view commuting as part of American culture. We love cars and wide-open spaces. We don't share the European love of trains and tiny yards. But we should recognize that our culture not only shapes our policies, but is in return shaped by them. The city of Portland, Oregon, for example, has tightly regulated the density of suburban and urban neighborhoods in that metropolitan area, trying to battle the sprawl that has affected so many U.S. cities. No doubt such aggressive zoning regulations were easier to implement in Portland than they would have been in Houston. People in Oregon have different attitudes toward the government than do most people in Texas. Nevertheless, the citizens of Oregon have, in turn, been influenced by these same laws. They have settled in different kinds of neighborhoods than their Houstonian counterparts. They've spent different proportions of their lives commuting than have people in Chicago or Atlanta.

The market alone won't necessarily give us the commutes, and the neighborhoods, that we deserve.

CHAPTER NINE

Risky Feelings and
Cigarette Breaks

AS SHE APPROACHED her obstetrician's office, Marta had made up her mind not to have an amniocentesis. Making use of her training as an academic physician, she had poured over data on the risks and benefits of amniocentesis, calculating and recalculating the odds that her fetus would have a serious genetic abnormality. She had spoken with her husband, also a physician, at length about the pros and cons of the procedure and had definitively concluded not to risk the health of her unborn child by undergoing the test.

Feeling confident in her decision, she took a seat in the waiting room. Across from her, she saw a mother nursing her newborn. To her left, a very pregnant woman looked after what appeared to be a two-year-old. To her right, a mother was struggling to calm down her baby. The mother looked healthy and happy, but the baby . . . the baby looked as if it had a serious chromosomal abnormality. Marta found herself wondering what this mother's life would be like, and the baby's life, too. She saw the mother smiling and cuddling the baby, but could not imagine smiling under similar circumstances. What she saw that day—a happy mother cuddling a restless baby—filled her with horror.

The nurse called her name and led her down the hall to the examining room. The obstetrician came into the room and asked her whether she had given more thought to whether she wanted an amniocentesis. "Yes, I've given it plenty of thought," she heard herself say, "and I've decided I want to have the test."

Animal Brains

Without a doubt, humans are quantum leaps beyond any other animals in their ability to reason. Consider the enormous evolutionary programming that enables you to scan this piece of paper and effortlessly (if I'm doing my job well) glean meaning from the scattering of ink dots spread across the page. It is this tremendous cognitive ability that inspired the ancient Greeks to settle on rationality as the distinguishing characteristic of humans.[1] Unlike other animals, humans can engage in abstract thought, pondering and occasionally even solving mysteries of how the world works. The Greeks undoubtedly underestimated the neurological capabilities of other animals. Humans are not the only animals that make music, use language, solve problems, or even create tools. We are not the only animals that educate our young or that transmit learning through culture. Still, no other animal can compose a symphony, write a sonnet, or develop calculus. The Greeks were right to identify our cognitive abilities as being our distinguishing attribute: we might differ from other primates in being a naked ape; we might differ from most other mammals in walking upright and in having opposable thumbs; but the true characteristic that separates us from other animals is our brain. Humans are brainiacs.

Marta didn't feel like a brainiac when she came home from the obstetrician's office that day. She tried to explain her decision to her husband, telling him that in choosing an amniocentesis, she hadn't undergone a shift in thought so much as a change of heart. Her gut, her heart, her reptilian brain—some kind of deep-seated instincts—these felt like the source of her conversion, not her cerebral cortex. He looked back at her blankly, his confusion about her decision only increasing the more she tried to explain it to him.

Perhaps Charles Darwin could have explained things more clearly. You see, Darwin was profoundly aware that many human emotions are also shared by other mammals. In *The Expression of the Emotions in Man and Animals*, he had even catalogued the overlapping facial expressions and body postures that humans share with other mammals when experiencing fear, disgust, hunger, and anger.[2] He realized that when humans evolved from animals, they had not lost their old reptilian and mammalian brain structures but, rather, had added new layers of brain on *top*. And so, if we hope to understand how people behave—how they think and feel their way through life—we need to pay attention not only to the cerebrations of our brain's cortex but also to the primitive brain structures lying underneath.

Which of Our Brains Decides to Smoke?

Jean Connor's friends had told her that her cigarette habit was a dangerous one. She had started smoking Winstons at age fifteen and smoked steadily for the next twenty-seven years. For twenty-two of those years, her cigarette of choice was manufactured by the R. J. Reynolds Tobacco Company. So when she was diagnosed with lung cancer while still in her forties, she decided to sue R. J. Reynolds. When she died at age forty-nine, leaving behind two children, her family chose to continue the litigation.

The trial that followed did not hinge on whether tobacco killed Jean Connor. Despite testimony from an R. J. Reynolds scientist that he "didn't know if cigarette smoking causes cancer," the jury was convinced that smoking *had* caused Jean's cancer.[3] Nor did the trial turn on whether tobacco manufactured by R. J. Reynolds had caused her death. All parties recognized that she was consistent in her preference for Winston and Salem for the first twenty-two years of her smoking life. Instead, the lawsuit revolved around a single contentious issue: was Jean duped into smoking, or did she pick up the habit in full awareness of the potential dangers she faced?

The year was 1997, and Jean's lawyer, Norwood Wilner, had recently won a $750,000 settlement on behalf of another lung cancer victim. He confidently resurrected his successful arguments: "This is a simple and straight-forward case," Wilner said in an interview. "The company made a defective product that killed people, and failed to make feasible modifications to the product. And they didn't tell the truth about it. And now the jury will be able to punish the plaintiff."[4] The cigarette company's lawyer adamantly disagreed: "Jean Connor was exposed to 27 years worth of warnings, and chose to ignore them."[5]

Indeed, Jean was well aware that, as the surgeon general of the United States puts it, "smoking causes lung cancer, heart disease, emphysema, and may complicate pregnancy," having run her eyes over that warning thousands of times in her life. She knew, too, that tobacco could be addictive, having met plenty of people who tried unsuccessfully to kick the habit. By the time she became a regular smoker, tobacco was one of the most heavily regulated consumer products in the world, regularly vilified by the government, health professionals—even Brooke Shields.

But did her reptilian brain know how risky cigarettes could be? Did it have any idea that she might die of lung cancer before her fiftieth birthday? More to the point, were her feelings telling her the same thing about her smoking risks that her centers of reasoning might have been?

The Pros and Cons of Smoking

Kip Viscusi, a preeminent economist who has taught at Harvard and Duke universities, is convinced that smokers are making rational decisions to smoke, decisions in which they accept the risks of tobacco in order to enjoy its benefits—its flavor, its soothing effect on the nerves, its ability to suppress the appetite, and its social value. As Viscusi wrote in his book *Smoking: Making the Risky Decision*, "Individuals make a consumption decision about whether they will engage in smoking that is not entirely different from deciding on one's diet or new car purchase."[6]

Viscusi recognizes that not all people, of course, are perfectly informed about the risks of smoking. In fact, in a 1985 study, Viscusi asked over three thousand people across the United States to estimate the odds that lifelong smokers will develop lung cancer. By 1985, experts had estimated that lifelong smokers faced a 5–10 percent chance of developing lung cancer. This risk is nothing to sneeze (or cough) at. But it paled in comparison with the risk perceptions of the people responding to Viscusi's survey. On average, Viscusi's respondents, many of whom were adolescents, as Jean Conner was when she began smoking, thought that lifelong smokers faced almost a 50 percent chance of developing lung cancer.[7]

In fact, being a big believer that cigarette smoking is a result of a rational contemplation, Viscusi has concluded that too *few* kids are smoking these days. If these kids realized that they faced only a one-in-ten chance of developing lung cancer, surely more of them would choose to light up and enjoy the pleasures of a good smoke!

At this point in the book, we have discovered all kinds of reasons to challenge Viscusi's hyperrational view of cigarette smoking. We've seen that people are prey to all kinds of cognitive biases and are often caught in losing battles between their short-term and long-term interests. But the existence of irrationality and frailty surely doesn't force us to conclude that all the risks we take in our lives are signs of either stupidity or weakness. As I'm sure Viscusi would be quick to point out, people make all kinds of risky decisions in their lives. Rock climbers and white-water rafters, for example, enjoy these activities *because* of the risks. News reports of rock-climbing fatalities inevitably quote grieving family members who console themselves with the thought that their loved ones knew it might end this way. Other risks are worth taking not because of the thrill of the risk, but despite the risk. Every time I bike across Ann Arbor, I accept a tiny risk of injury or death, a risk outweighed by the benefit of getting to work or picking my boys up from school.

So we all accept the idea that taking risks is often the rational thing to do. But can we talk about rational decision making—about logically weighing risks and benefits—in the context of, say, addictive drugs? Doesn't the whole nature of addiction preclude rational choice? Think of all those smokers out there, trying but failing to quit. They don't want to smoke, nor do they choose to smoke. They just can't, physiologically or psychologically, muster the strength to quit. Having weighed the risks and benefits of smoking, they have decided that they should quit, but simply can't follow through.

The difficulty people have in kicking the habit doesn't interfere with Viscusi's view of the situation: "The fact that many smokers profess a desire to quit smoking should not necessarily be treated as an index of market failure. Almost half of the residents of Los Angeles indicate a desire to move out of the city, but do not do so."[8]

Viscusi is not the only brilliant economist who holds these kinds of views. Consider Gary Becker and Kevin Murphy again, and their theory of rational addiction. Becker and Murphy are convinced that if we place addictive behaviors out of the reach of rational choice theory, we will be forced to exclude a wide range of behaviors from economic study: "People get addicted not only to alcohol, cocaine, and cigarettes but also to work, eating, music, television, their standard of living, other people, religion, and many other activities. Therefore, much behavior would be excluded from the rational choice framework if addictions have to be explained in another way."[9] Addicted to music and their standard of living? Yes, according to Becker and Murphy, who define addiction as happening when the past consumption of a good raises the utility of consuming the good again. In other words, once you get a taste of Mozart, the next Mozart symphony you hear is even more enjoyable than the previous one, spurring you on to consume more and more of his symphonies. (Truth be told, I mainlined Mozart while revising this chapter.)

In his book *The Logic of Life*, the economist Tim Harford tries to explain why smoking and gambling are a result of rational decision making, following logically from basic concepts like supply and demand, or risk and reward.[10] In backing up this view, he glowingly refers to the theory of rational addiction. He points out that the use of addictive substances like tobacco fluctuates with its price, going down as you'd rationally expect it to do when the price rises. Indeed, cigarette use dropped by more than one-third after the surgeon general's first report on its harms in 1964, just as we'd logically expect.

As a physician, however, I have a hard time accepting this definition of addiction. I understand that this definition allows economists to use their analytic tools to study the factors that influence, say, the supply of cocaine or the elasticity of people's demand for heroin. I recognize that we need to grasp the market forces that influence drug (and Mozart) consumption. But I also think we need to account for the very different kind of "addictions" people experience.

I have cared for many patients who, when trying to quit drinking alcohol, have experienced what are known as withdrawal seizures. I've never seen the withdrawal of string quartets lead to such a violent physiologic reaction. I held the hands of a forty-year-old man recently—his belly swollen like he was pregnant with triplets, his skin the color of a faded dandelion—while he cried about his inability to stop drinking beer. In fact, we recently had a patient in our hospital who was so addicted to alcohol that he swallowed three dispensers' worth of Purell Hand Sanitizer and collapsed in his hospital room with a blood-alcohol level three times the legal limit. And to return to cigarette smoking, I witnessed dozens of patients, their voice boxes removed because of throat cancer, who, despite having a chance of avoiding a cancer recurrence, still insisted on smoking through their tracheotomies.

I cannot equate people who continue smoking with people who can't get out of L.A.

Apparently, the jury in Jean Connor's trial was more convinced by Becker, Murphy, and Viscusi than by me, concluding that R. J. Reynolds bore no responsibility for her death. As the jury forewoman put it to reporters, "Connor knew the risks."[11] But what does it mean to know a risk? And does knowledge of risks necessarily lead to rational decisions about whether to take on such risks? It is time to look at how risks look and feel to people whose decisions depend on an accurate understanding of those risks.

The Hazards of Guessing

Most doctors recommend that women over the age of fifty receive yearly mammograms, to look for signs of treatable breast cancer. Yet many women refuse to receive mammograms or conveniently miss their scheduled appointments. Mammograms are a bother, taking up scarce free time. They can be scary, leading to follow-up tests and even biopsies. And they are often quite painful. As a female friend once asked me, "Would you like someone to put your testicles into a Vise-Grip?" And what is there to counterbalance these negative aspects of mammography? A vague, unspecified risk of breast cancer, a risk most women probably don't want to think about. Can you blame anyone for skipping the occasional mammogram?

Caryn Lerman, a cancer researcher at the University of Pennsylvania, didn't like the idea that women would miss out on this important test. So she took it on herself to educate women about their breast cancer risks so that they would be able to make a better decision about mammography. She began by asking women to estimate their lifetime risk of being diagnosed with breast cancer. As it turns out, the women were in need of substantial education. The typical woman faces a 13 percent chance of being diagnosed with breast cancer in her lifetime.[12] But the women in Lerman's study estimated their risk as being threefold higher than this, on average, reminiscent of Viscusi's research participants who greatly overestimated smokers' risks of developing lung cancer.

So Lerman educated the women, successfully in fact, with most holding far more accurate beliefs about their risks of breast cancer after meeting with Lerman's educators. But after contemplating their risk of contracting breast cancer—a risk that was much lower than they had guessed it to be moments earlier—many of Lerman's research participants . . . lost interest in mammography![13]

It would be easy to view Lerman's study through the lens of rational choice theory. In deciding whether to receive a mammogram, women balance the costs of a mammogram (the inconvenience, the pain, etc.) with its benefits—its ability to diagnose a treatable breast cancer. If they think their risk of breast cancer is extremely high, then women will be more inclined to tolerate a mammogram. Once they are aware that the risk isn't as high as they thought, the balance of costs and benefits will shift away from mammography. This is the only rational way for people to have responded to Lerman's educational intervention.

I prefer to view Lerman's study through a different lens, however, a lens that will reveal people's risk perceptions as being not just about the numbers—whether their lifetime risk of breast cancer is 13 percent or 33 percent—but also about the way people intuitively and emotionally process such risk information. As I will show you, Lerman's preeducational test of women's perceptions, her seemingly benign query of what they think their lifetime risk of breast cancer is, was *itself* a powerful intervention that dramatically influenced the way women responded to her educational intervention.

To uncover what had happened to Lerman's women, my colleagues and I conducted a simple study. Like Lerman, we asked a group of women to estimate the lifetime risk of breast cancer, and then presented these women with the actual figure, the 13 percent risk number I mentioned above. We then asked them what they thought about this information: how did that risk make them feel, and did it strike them as a high or low risk. Unlike Lerman, however, we randomly excluded half of our participants from the guessing game, providing these participants with the 13 percent number up front, without asking them first what they thought that risk would be. As you will see in a short while, this random exclusion played a crucial role in demonstrating the subtle forces that influence how people respond to risk information.

But first, let's look at those women who, like the participants in Lerman's study, were first asked to estimate the lifetime risk of being diagnosed with breast cancer. Like Lerman's participants, these women dramatically overestimated the risk of breast cancer. On average, they believed that 41 percent of women would receive such a diagnosis in their lifetime, more than three times the actual risk.

With so much information in the media about breast cancer, and with the "one in eight" number bandied about so often in the press, how could women have been so misinformed? For starters, we should consider the 50 percent problem. In studies of risk perceptions, you see, it is common for people to guess that a given risk has a 50 percent chance of occurring. Now to many readers of this book, I expect that 50 percent means 50 out of 100. But to many people, the number means "I don't know"—a flip of the coin. People might get breast cancer, they might not, so . . . it's a fifty-fifty prospect.[14]

When mathematically literate people like Viscusi ask members of the general public to make risk estimates, they assume that their respondents use basic numerical concepts the way that they, the researchers, use them. But this assumption overlooks rampant innumeracy plaguing the general public.

Let's take a quick test of your numeracy. Suppose I hold a fair coin in my hand and flip it 1,000 times. How many times do you think it will come up heads?

Did you guess 500? Great. I would have accepted any number between 450 and 550 as a correct answer. And yet, even with such a forgiving grading scheme, about a quarter of people will get this type of question wrong.[15]

OK, let's try another question. Suppose there's a population of 1,000 people, 10 percent of whom suffer from a dreaded illness—let's call it chronic hotchocolitis. How many of these people have this disease? This is not a trick question. The answer is 100, and once again about a quarter of people answering this question will get it wrong. Indeed, if I ask one more question that's about as difficult as these two, about half of the general public will get at least one question wrong. Almost half! Many members of the general public, in other words, no longer retain the mathematical skills of an average high school graduate.

When defending his research, Viscusi likes to boast about the large number of people he has surveyed, over 3,000 people in one study, and over 1,000 in another.[16] He questions how a smaller study could ever refute the truth revealed in his massive surveys. What Viscusi overlooks is the reality that if you ask 4,000 people to answer a question, and half of them don't understand the question, all you have gained with the enormous size of your survey population is a large pile of useless answers. You can't fix bad data by simply collecting more of it.

Returning to our breast cancer study: as I told you earlier, women estimated, on average, that the lifetime risk of being diagnosed with breast cancer was greater than 40 percent, even though the true number is closer to 13 percent. These overestimates were not the exception, but the rule. More than 90 percent of the women we surveyed guessed that the risk was 5 percentage points or more greater than the true number. The misestimates, in other words, weren't simply provided by those women who were having difficulty understanding things like percentages.

Where did women come up with this unbelievably inaccurate risk perception? Well, to figure out the answer to that question, let us turn our attention to the other half of our respondents, the group that we didn't ask to guess this lifetime risk number. On the first page of these women's surveys, we presented them with the 13 percent figure and asked them an innocent question: "If we had asked you to guess this risk, would you have guessed a number that was higher, lower, or about the same as this 13 percent figure?" Now remember, among the random half of women who *did* make this guess, more than 90 percent significantly overestimated the risk. Yet among nonguessers, only one-third told us they would have guessed a higher number. Another one-third, in fact, said they would have guessed a *lower* number, and the remainder said that that 13 percent figure is pretty much what they would have guessed.

The nonguessers demonstrated a phenomenon that psychologist Baruch Fischoff calls *hindsight bias*.[17] Once people know the answer to a question or the outcome of a situation, the answer and the outcome seem obvious. Why did the Nazi war effort get bogged down in Russia? Well, it's obvious—Hitler didn't have enough troops; the weather was bad. How could John Kerry have lost to George W. Bush in the 2004 election? Again . . . duh: the exurban, values voters would never favor a Massachusetts Democrat over a Texas Republican.

Our nonguessers, by demonstrating such profound hindsight bias, have also demonstrated that the 41 percent figure was not already in their heads. Most women didn't hold strong prior beliefs about the lifetime risk of breast cancer. Instead, when we asked them to give us a number, they pulled it out of . . . I don't know, out of thin air, I guess. Some wrote down 50 percent, because they had no idea. Some guessed 30 percent or 40 percent, because they knew that breast cancer was a common disease, and so they figured it must be a big number.

And then we told them the *real* number, and the guessers responded practically with an audible sigh. The 13 percent figure relieved them of their worries and struck them as a low risk. Not surprising, really. If you thought you faced a 41 percent chance of an awful illness, wouldn't you be relieved to learn that the risk was only 13 percent? By contrast, the nonguessers weren't so relieved. They hadn't been forced to pull the number out of thin air, so when they saw the 13 percent number, they were alarmed by it: it made them anxious, and it felt, to them, like a high risk.[18]

I present this study because it illustrates an important way that people process risk information. On the one hand, a 13 percent risk has a very specific meaning: a 13-out-of-100 chance of something bad happening. But is a 13 percent risk something to be worried about? Is it high enough that a person should do something to avoid this risk? Well, that is a matter for the other hand, so to speak. Because when people process information about risk, they don't simply absorb the numerical data—they *interpret* the risk too, as being high or low, alarming or relieving; their mathematical brains take in the information, but so, too, do the emotional centers in their brains.[19] And as different parts of their brain battle to sort out this information, strange things can happen.

Back to the Reptilian Brain

Neuroscientists have long known that the brain houses emotional centers that need not announce themselves to the conscious brain. An early hint of these emotional centers was discovered by an early twentieth-century French physician named Edouard Claparede, who became fascinated by the condition of a woman with severe amnesia and began visiting her regularly. On each visit, because of her memory problem, he would be forced to reintroduce himself to her. Indeed, if he left the room briefly during a visit, he would need to reintroduce himself when he returned, forced to go through the same handshakes and hellos that he had gone through just minutes before.

Upon meeting her one day, he shook her hand (as he always did), causing her to pull back her hand in pain. The doctor was experimenting with her and had slipped a thumbtack into his hand. She quickly forgot about this injury, and the rest of that visit went on like any other. By the next time they met, she not only had forgotten about the thumbtack but, once again, had forgotten that she had ever met him. They started going through their normal introduction ritual, he telling her his name, and she telling him hers. But when he reached out to shake her hand, she pulled back in fear. She couldn't explain her reluctance, but she felt wrong about reaching out for his hand.

Her higher brain, the evolutionarily newer cerebral cortex, had no memory of the thumbtack episode. But somewhere else in her brain, in locations like the amygdala and the hippocampus, she had stored this memory, an unconscious one, and this memory had prevented her from shaking the young doctor's hand again. If her cerebral cortex had not been damaged, her conscious memories would also have warned her off. But it is key to recognize that her older brain would *still* have been part of the warning signal, creating a wave of fear in her even before her conscious brain told her to stay away from his handshake.[20]

In the 1960s and 1970s, a University of Michigan psychologist, Robert Zajonc, made a name for himself with a series of groundbreaking studies that revealed the primacy of unconscious brain systems in people's judgments about things they encounter in the world. Zajonc (pronounced to rhyme, appropriately enough, with science) began by establishing that, in many circumstances, familiarity breeds not contempt but, instead, approval. If I show you a series of, say, one hundred Chinese ideographs, and you have no knowledge of written Chinese, you will have a hard time telling whether you have seen a particular ideograph before. On round seventy-three, in other words, I might show you a brand-new ideograph or one that I have shown you five times before, and you won't be able to tell me whether this is a new or an old ideograph. But if instead of asking you whether you recognize the ideograph, I simply ask you whether you *like* it, then you will report being significantly more pleased with the familiar ideographs than unfamiliar ones. The more often you have seen an ideograph, the more pleasing and attractive you will find it, regardless of whether you remember seeing it before. The same goes for exposures to unfamiliar musical melodies. You will like the familiar melodies more than the unfamiliar ones. (This puts some of popular culture into perspective, doesn't it? The *American Idol* judges have a hard time relating to contestants until they can categorize them: "Your singing is like a cross between Tina Turner and Bonnie Raitt—I love your stuff!")

When nineteenth-century economists were developing their theory of human nature, they viewed human judgments largely as top-down processes. They assumed that when people decide whether to purchase a pair of boots, they inspect the boots, examining how well constructed they are, how comfortable they feel to wear, and, of course, thinking about how much they cost compared with other boots. Such cognitive ponderings were seen as leading to judgments—that the boots are cheap or ugly or overpriced. However, this top-down view has now been turned upside down. As Zajonc puts it, "Preferences need no inferences."[21]

People often have gut feelings about things (where by gut, of course, I'm talking about primitive brain structures). But this notion that preferences come from our cogitations? That notion is an illusion.[22]

The emotional centers of our brain influence the way we think about the world. Feeling, in other words, often precedes thinking. Consider a patient who experiences a complication after undergoing a surgical procedure. Does he sue the doctor? Rationally speaking, he should sue the doctor if the doctor was sloppy, or if the doctor failed to explain the risks and benefits of the procedure. But as it turns out, decisions to sue doctors have almost nothing to do with these matters. Instead, the strongest predictor of malpractice suits is whether people *feel* good about the way their doctors communicated with them. Researchers uncovered this by recruiting a random set of physicians and another set of physicians who had been sued at least two times in their career, and tape-recording their conversations with new patients. They then analyzed the communication styles of the two groups of physicians. In one analysis of these tape recordings, the researchers filtered the audio recordings so that it was impossible to understand what the doctors were saying. With this filter slapped on over the recording, the physicians all sounded like Charlie Brown's teacher—sounds with pitch and volume but no words. Thus, the people listening to the tape had nothing to go on except the tone of voice expressed by the physicians. The researchers were able to identify which doctors had been sued with high precision, just by analyzing the tone of these voices.[23] The physicians who had been sued expressed less empathy and compassion.

When patients experience bad outcomes, they don't simply cogitate about whether the accident was avoidable. They don't think back to whether they had been specifically warned about this specific complication. Instead, they respond to how much they liked the physicians. And these feelings, these attitudes toward their physicians, come from the same affective centers of the brain that respond to the physician's tone of voice. As Zajonc puts it, "One cannot be introduced to a person without experiencing some immediate feeling of attraction or repulsion."[24] Our brains make rapid-fire judgments that rarely await the considered reflections of our higher reasoning powers.

Knowing Versus Doing

In videotape testimony taken shortly before her death, Jean Connor admitted that she "knew smoking was hazardous" to her health. She never tried to quit smoking, however, until a plastic surgeon told her she'd have to do so if she wanted a tummy tuck.[25] She didn't live long enough after that time for us to know whether she would have relapsed into her old habit. But does it matter? If she knew smoking was bad, why hadn't she tried to quit earlier?

I can't answer that question. No doubt, a part of Jean's brain simply didn't think, or feel, that the risks of smoking were serious enough to change her ways. She might also have lacked willpower; who knows? And given her desire for a tummy tuck, it is not a stretch to think that she smoked, in part, to keep from gaining more weight. In any event, Viscusi is right that she consciously considered the pros and cons of smoking, largely aware of the risks she was facing. The strength of this rational view of human behavior is that it is partly correct. Some people *do* quit smoking when the costs rise, when cigarette taxes get too high or when their habit stands in the way of a tummy tuck. That's why if you read *The Logic of Life*, you'll be shown that wherever you look, even at what seems to be the strangest behavior, an economist will show you the underlying logic. Teenagers have more oral sex, now, because regular sex has become more risky. Juvenile crime declined in location X because the local government decided to treat seventeen-year-olds as adults. You see? Kids only commit crimes when it's rational to do so!

But the danger in this hyperrational worldview is that it precludes any policy that would help keep people from engaging in risky behaviors, like cigarette smoking. For if we believe, à la Becker and Murphy, that smoking is a utility-maximizing behavior for those people who chose to smoke, then we will only regulate tobacco in order to reduce the harms of secondhand smoke, or to make sure that people have accurate information about the risks and benefits of smoking so they can decide what's in their own best interests.

If we only look for the logic underlying people's behavior, we will miss the illogical forces that influence people's emotional reactions to risk. For example, people are significantly more concerned about experiencing a 120-in-1,000 risk of a stroke than a 12-in-100 risk. Both risks, of course, are the same, amounting to a 12 percent chance. But the 120-in-1,000 risk somehow feels larger, because more people are described as having a stroke. Similarly, women with a 6 percent risk of breast cancer over the next five years are significantly more worried about this risk if they are told that the average five-year risk is 3 percent rather than 12 percent. The same 6 percent risk has much more emotional salience if women believe it is an above-average risk.[26]

Consider a mother deciding whether to undergo an amniocentesis to determine whether her fetus has a severe chromosomal abnormality. Suppose that the amniocentesis has a 5-in-1,000 chance of harming the fetus and that, on the basis of a blood test, there's a 5-in-1,000 chance that her fetus has one of these chromosomal problems. The likelihood that this woman will choose to get an amniocentesis depends in large part on whether the blood test result, which helped determine the 5-in-1,000 risk, is described as "normal" or "abnormal." A 5-in-1,000 chance of chromosomal problems feels more worrisome if it is the result of an abnormal blood test, prompting many more women to say they would opt for amniocentesis.[27]

People like Viscusi understand that 6 percent is 6 percent is 6 percent; that the decision to get an amniocentesis should be based on the risk that your fetus has a chromosomal abnormality, and not on whether that risk is derived from a normal or an abnormal blood test. But what people should rationally do and what people *actually* do are not always the same thing, a fact Viscusi seems to forget. He thinks that when people say lifelong cigarette smoking carries a 40 percent risk of lung cancer, they not only know what 40 percent means, but also feel this risk in a real enough manner to motivate their behavior.

People like Viscusi are undoubtedly quite good at math. But that doesn't mean they understand the way most people make most decisions. I'm reminded of what my mother says about her college experience. She went to MIT at a time when few women attended that prestigious school, making her quite popular with the guys on campus. But she did not always welcome the attention from them, telling me that "the odds were good, but the goods were odd." Now I have never met Kip Viscusi, and he may be a very normal guy in many ways. But isn't it likely, with all his training in mathematics and economics, that he makes decisions in a way different from most other people?

People simply don't *think* about risks so much as they *feel* the risks. How else can you explain the power of terrorism? The chance of any American's dying from a terrorist attack is, of course, minuscule, and indeed would have remained minuscule even if we hadn't pursued new antiterrorist tactics after 9/11. The average American is far more likely to die in an auto accident or as the result of a bee sting than from a terrorist attack. But terrorism works through emotion—fear, uncertainty, and the like—not through probabilities.[28]

The same goes for fear of flying. The traumatic violence of any plane crash and the gravity-defying strangeness of flight, to begin with, make air travel feel much scarier for people than automobile travel feels, even though, mile for mile, automobiles are much more dangerous. Is it any wonder that terrorists have targeted airplanes for so many of their attacks?

Consider the way many of us feel about seat belts and bicycle helmets. If I bicycle without a helmet, I feel extremely vulnerable, worrying about every bump in the road. If I drive without a seat belt, I feel almost naked. Our feelings about bicycle helmets and seat belts are almost completely divorced from the actual risks and benefits of these safety devices. I was presented with a dramatic example of this phenomenon a couple of years ago when staying at my parents' house in Minnesota. My older brother Andy had dropped by with his kids and picked my boys up to take them back to his house, all of one-half mile away. When my wife came outside and found out that Taylor and Jordan had left in Andy's car, she vaporized me with her "evil eyes of death" glare, incensed that I had allowed them inside his minivan without being strapped into a car seat. (Unbeknownst to her, he had brought along extra car seats.) My wife is an extremely rational woman, having studied economics at Cornell and business at the University of Chicago. But she had become totally freaked out by an infinitesimal risk. Why? Because the probabilities weren't the issue. It was a feeling—that a mother ought to do everything within her power to protect her kids, and that when it comes to automobile behavior, there aren't high-probability and low-probability risks, simply acceptable and unacceptable risks. And letting your kids ride without a car seat— that's, well, unacceptable!

Market enthusiasts argue that governments should stay out of people's affairs. If a person wants to smoke cigarettes, he should be allowed to do so, and the government shouldn't try to coerce him—whether through taxes or laws—to kick the habit. And for gosh sakes, the argument continues, if people choose to smoke despite dramatically overestimating the risk of smoking, then we shouldn't penalize tobacco companies by awarding money to the "victims."

I hope you will now see that these views don't necessarily follow from the kind of evidence that Viscusi has collected about people's perceptions of cigarette smoking. Jean Connor knew the risks of smoking, but those risks didn't feel overwhelming at the time. What's more, the tobacco industry had systematically manipulated the amount of nicotine in its products in order to maximize the chance that those people who start smoking won't stop.[29] Although Connor undoubtedly deserved some of the blame for her unhealthy habit, the tobacco company should not have gotten off scot-free.

The rational choice model of decision making assumes that as people get more information about any decision—for example, about the risks and benefits of smoking—the quality of their decision improves. They believe that knowledge and freedom lead to optimal choice. Now I'm a big fan of knowledge, and I hope this book imparts knowledge on gaggles of unsuspecting people. But we cannot ignore what scientists have discovered about decision making: they've learned that knowledge doesn't always lead to optimal decisions, and that when people *know* what a risk is, they still may base their decision on how the risk *feels*.

I hope that knowledge doesn't scare you too much.

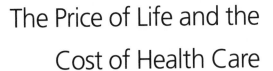

CHAPTER TEN

The Price of Life and the Cost of Health Care

I WON'T SAY that your life is hanging by a thread. I don't know you well enough to know whether that is true. But I can say, with confidence, that your life depends on three tiny structures, each no bigger around than the hole in the middle of a spool of thread. These structures are the three arteries that convey blood from the heart to . . . the heart.

Your heart depends on these three vessels to deliver blood back into its own muscles. If one of these arteries gets blocked, you will have a heart attack. If your right coronary artery is blocked at its distal tip, you might have a tiny heart attack, perhaps even a silent one, one you won't even be aware of. If your left anterior descending (LAD) artery is blocked near its origin, however, you are in big trouble. That artery feeds critical parts of your heart. A *proximal LAD lesion*, as cardiologists call it, can kill you. And if it doesn't kill you, it can cripple you, weakening your heart muscle so much that you will get short of breath walking to the bathroom.

Unless, that is, you get to the hospital quickly enough for someone to open up your artery. Sometimes doctors will open up patients' arteries by infusing them with clot-dissolving drugs. But with increasing frequency, they now rely on balloons to do this life-saving work. Cardiologists snake catheters up through people's legs right up to their LAD, say, and identify the source of a heart attack. They then open up the artery, with a balloon that pushes out, from the inside, on the walls of the obstructed artery. Through these catheters, in fact, cardiologists have learned to place stents in people's coronary arteries—tiny wire devices that spring open within the artery, squishing arterial plaques outward to keep the artery open.

In 2003, a general internist whom I will call Dr. Holmes arrived in his local emergency room with crushing chest pain and ECG changes consistent with a life-threatening heart attack. The cardiologists told him that they wanted to bring him up to the catheterization lab and stent his blocked arteries. "Are you going to use drug-eluting stents?" he asked them. The cardiologists were caught off guard. They explained that they were stocked with traditional stents up in the cath lab, which they had been using successfully for years. But Dr. Holmes was insistent on receiving the brand-new, highly touted drug-eluting stents. He knew that standard stents sometimes got overgrown by plaque in the long run, leaving people at risk for a renarrowing of their arteries down the line, while the newer, drug-eluting stents were suffused with chemicals that prevented such plaque formation.

The cardiologists told Dr. Holmes that it might take an hour or two to get hold of these newer stents; they'd have to call a nearby hospital and have the stents delivered. Meanwhile, they told him with great concern, his heart attack would advance. They told him that the new stents were not likely to be enough of an improvement over the old stents to justify the wait. (At the time, there were no clinical trials available to determine whether the new stents were actually an improvement over the standard ones, but even in a best-case scenario, the cardiologists could not imagine that the new stents would be so much better that they'd make up for all the time, the heart-attack-in-progress time, that it would take to obtain the drug-eluting stents.) Holmes, in mid–heart attack, remained unconvinced and told the cardiologists he'd wait.

How could these unproven stents have been so attractive to this physician that he was willing to suffer a longer heart attack in order to receive them? The answer to this question lies in the psychology by which people judge the quality of consumer goods, a psychology that often defies logic. As we'll see, a broad array of consumer decisions are influenced by strange beliefs people hold about what makes one product better than another. These beliefs interfere with our ability, as consumers, to use our purchasing power to make markets more efficient at delivering to us high-quality goods. And most importantly, these beliefs doom efforts to control the rapidly rising health-care expenses that are overwhelming so many people.

Demanding Efficiency

For a market to work efficiently, consumers need good information about the cost and quality of the goods they are thinking of buying. With this information, in fact, consumers should bring discipline to the market. If a company makes a shoddy product, for instance, word should get around, causing people to either avoid the product or wait until its price comes down enough to make it worth purchasing. Consumers will bring especially strong discipline to those parts of the market they interact with most frequently. The more experience consumers have with any specific product, the better they should become at judging whether the product is worth its price.

We have already seen that consumers are not always as savvy as fans of the free market have told us they should be. Many people fail to exert enough self-control, others behave irrationally in contemplating the risks and benefits of products like cigarettes, and yet others neglect hidden hotel costs, thereby becoming burdened with the inflated price of local phone calls or Snickers from the minibar. All of us make bad purchasing decisions in our lives because we aren't as informed as we should be or because we are being unknowingly influenced by our all-too-human irrationality.

But almost none of us are irrational all of the time, or even the majority of the time. And we often become quite knowledgeable about those consumer goods we are most interested in. We are so savvy, in fact, that the market has responded by producing an explosion of well-designed, useful products that are amazingly affordable. Look how inexpensive computers have become, over the years, through consumer pressure. Or take a gander at the amazing produce available twelve months a year at your local grocery store, and compare it with what was available in your childhood. Were you even able to buy cilantro then? And at what cost?

Consumer pressure has even worked its magic in the health-care industry, forcing doctors and medical companies to improve their services while lowering their prices. I'm thinking right now about a specific part of the health-care industry—about laser surgery for nearsightedness. In 1999, if you wanted to rid yourself of eyeglasses, you would be forced to fork over $2,100 to your ophthalmologist so she could zap your eyes into shape. By 2005, that same laser procedure would cost you less than $1,700, and if you wanted a newer, improved laser procedure, you'd still be able to get it for that same 1999 price of $2,100.

Wall Street Journal editorialists point to such laser surgery as an example of what would happen if people were more accountable for their health-care expenses. If the health-care market were more like a free market, health care would be better and cheaper: "If so many people are willing to ante-up for optional procedures like Lasik," they opine, "surely they'll be able to get used to more direct spending on urgent medical needs as well."[1] George W. Bush agrees, bemoaning the fact that "people are able to shop based upon price and quality in almost every aspect of our life [sic], with the exception of healthcare."[2] His chief economic adviser, Allan

Hubbard, expanded on this sentiment in a *New York Times* editorial: "By enabling consumers and doctors to make healthcare decisions that are right for them, we can greatly improve the effectiveness, affordability, and value of our healthcare spending . . . And no consumer is better than the American consumer at driving prices down and quality up."[3]

But are consumers really that good at wringing inefficiency out of the market? Consider Dr. Holmes, waiting for that new stent. He was a pretty savvy consumer, much savvier, in fact, than the typical patient, given all his medical training and experience. But just how great were those new stents he insisted on receiving? Since 2003, we have learned much more about the risks and benefits of these new drug-eluting stents. As promised, they have reduced the number of arteries that get clogged with arterial plaque. But this benefit comes with a substantial downside: drug-eluting stents lead to more clots than the old stents, clots that can only be avoided by taking expensive blood-thinning medicines.[4] I have taken care of a number of patients who have experienced life-threatening bleeding as a result of these blood thinners. What's the balance of these risks and benefits? The new stents are a little bit better than the old ones at preventing new heart attacks, but there's no evidence, to date, that they have saved any additional lives. They have, however, definitely added additional costs, upward of $2,000 per stent.

Health-care expenses have been rising faster than inflation in virtually every industrialized country for the past several decades, regardless of whether that country has national health insurance, like Canada, or a larger market presence, like the United States.[5] This inflation is deeply troubling, making it increasingly difficult for people to afford health insurance.[6] Market advocates like George W. Bush argue that the solution to health-care inflation resides in the power of markets. If health-care markets were more competitive, the thinking goes, then health-care quality would increase at the same time that health-care prices go down, as it has for laser surgery.

I completely agree with President Bush that health-care costs would be significantly lower if people had to pay out of pocket for all their health-care services. But I don't share his rosy view of the kind of health-care system that would result from his free market approach. Because unbeknownst to President Bush, when people evaluate health-care interventions, they often rely on psychological shortcuts that impede good decision making. As you will see, these shortcuts are hardly limited to health-care domains. But within such domains, these shortcuts are especially troublesome, because life and death is often on the line. To deepen our understanding of market failures, we need to dig deeper into the brains of people, like the stent-demanding physician, to see how factors—like scarcity, novelty, and price—influence their perceptions of the quality of the goods they purchase.

If It's Scarce, I Want It

Few things are more attractive than those that are unavailable. Tell me I can't have something, and I will be much more likely to desire it. Indeed, if you place a child in a room that has two toys in it, and place one toy on the other side of a tall Plexiglas wall, the child will immediately walk around to grab the toy behind the wall, ignoring the toy that would have been easier to reach. Make that wall short enough, however, and the more distant toy will lose its appeal.[7] When Dr. Holmes discovered that the hospital did not have drug-eluting stents, he felt like a child on the wrong side of a Plexiglas wall. He became doubly convinced that he *had* to have one of those scarce stents. Indeed, he was not alone in feeling this way. At the time of his heart attack, drug-eluting stents were hard to come by. They were brand-new and in such demand that manufacturers could not make them fast enough. The scarcity resulting from this imbalance between supply and demand only fueled people's desires for such stents.

We have all seen how scarcity works in the marketplace. Toy companies are often slow to release their new Tickle-Me-Whatchamacallits in October, in hopes of generating news images of people lining up to buy the toy, knowing that this pent-up demand will pay off in December.[8] In his book *Influence*, Robert Cialdini describes a trick his brother employed to sell used cars that relied on the psychological power of scarcity.[9] He would place an ad in the paper, inviting people to set up a time to look at the car. When the first person would call, he would set up a time to meet, say, one o'clock on the following Saturday. When the second person would call, he would set up another meeting at *exactly the same time*. The first customer would arrive and start looking at the car, skeptically kicking its tires, pointing out its flaws, working hard to ratchet down the price. Then, inevitably, the second customer would arrive mid–tire kick, and Cialdini's brother would tell him to "wait just a few minutes," the other customer had first dibs on the car. Cialdini's brother had brilliantly manipulated the situation to make the car look popular and to ramp up people's competitive juices.

Not convinced that this works? Well, my research team conducted an experiment to try to increase the number of people responding to our invitation to fill out an Internet survey. Half of the people we e-mailed received our standard invitation, promising that the survey would be fascinating and that they would receive a small amount of money as a token of our appreciation. But for the remaining invitees, we added a sentence letting them know that "only the first five hundred respondents" would be allowed to complete our questionnaire. We had a significantly higher response rate from that group. We had made our survey more attractive by making it more scarce!

Scarcity not only increases our desires, but also augments the pleasure we receive on fulfilling our desires. For example, in a clever experiment, a group of psychologists asked people to sample a chocolate chip cookie. They presented half of the participants with a jar full of cookies and had them each pull out a single cookie. They presented the other half of participants with a jar that contained only two cookies. This latter group experienced significantly more pleasure from the cookie.[10]

New and Improved: A Redundancy?

I expect Dr. Holmes was adamant about receiving a drug-eluting stent not only because it was scarce, but also because he relied on the simple rule of thumb that newer means better. Although it is not always true that newer products are better than older ones, if you know nothing else about two competing products other than the date that each product came to market, odds are good that the more recent addition is the better product. After all, industry spends billions and billions of dollars on research every year: the pharmaceutical industry tests new drugs, targeting the molecular basis of one disease or another; electronics companies look for ways to cram even more memory into even smaller computer chips, while developing longer-lasting batteries to run our phones or computers on; automobile manufacturers develop new safety features, enabling us to survive crashes that a decade ago would have been deadly. Consequently, when advertisers put words like *new* into their sales pitches, they sell more products.[11]

Of course, sometimes companies develop new products that are meant to be inferior to existing products, bringing them to market as an inexpensive alternative to the existing goods. When a company produces a knockoff of a popular shoe, for example, most customers recognize that the knockoff won't be as durable as the high-priced shoe. But in health-care markets, there is not much precedent for bringing a product to market that is known, from the start, to be worse than existing products. For starters, health-care consumers, whether patients, physicians, or medical groups, aren't generally shopping around for bargains. The name of the game in health care is excellence, not thrift. When proven products like medications become less expensive by losing patent protection, many health-care consumers will flock to the new generic product, largely confident that they are getting an equally good product at a lower cost. But when it comes to bringing new products to market, it generally doesn't pay to bring a lower-quality product to market.

Consequently, new health-care products generally come in one of two flavors: a "me-too" variety or a "new and improved" variety. Me-too products are common in the pharmaceutical industry. When Pfizer began making billions off of Viagra, for instance, other companies had a huge incentive to develop equally good pills, to grab part of the market, knowing that the new pills didn't have to be better than Viagra to siphon away business.

Drug-eluting stents were an example of the second category of new health-care products—brought to market in the belief that they would be dramatically superior to older stents. So superior, in fact, that when they first came to market, they were thousands of dollars more expensive than the old stents. This pricing partly reflected the cost of producing these new stents. But it also reflected a brilliant marketing ploy. If you want people to perceive your product as being superior to a competitor's product, simply raise your price.

Standard economic theory holds that consumers independently evaluate the quality of a product and its price in order to make trade-offs between quality and price. According to this theory, people will be willing to pay more for product A than B if they perceive that A is better than B. But consider the following experiment, in which Baba Shiv and colleagues gave 125 people a beverage that claims to increase mental acuity, and then asked them to solve a series of word-jumble puzzles.[12] They informed people that the regular price of the beverage was $1.89. However, they sold the drink at a discounted price of $0.89 to half the participants, selected randomly. Shiv found that people in the discounted-price group not only reported lower expectations of the drink than those in the full-price group, but also performed significantly worse on the puzzle task, solving only 7.7 puzzles correctly, as compared to 9.5.

People believe that they get what they pay for and that a bargain may not be a bargain after all. In fact, consumers frequently use price to infer the quality of products. This psychological phenomenon explains the business strategy of Ursinus College, a small liberal arts institution in rural Pennsylvania that in 1999 was faced with declining enrollment. Rather than lower tuition, to encourage more applicants, the president of Ursinus *raised* tuition, almost 20 percent, in fact. And in response to this price increase, the freshman class swelled 35 percent. By becoming an "expensive liberal arts college," Ursinus was signaling to prospective customers that it was an elite one, too.[13]

A classic example of this phenomenon occurred in the early 1980s, when a little-known pharmaceutical company called Glaxo introduced its new ulcer pill, Zantac. At the time of Zantac's release, Tagamet was already available as prescription therapy for patients with ulcer disease. Tagamet was arguably the first blockbuster drug, making billions of dollars for its manufacturer and revitalizing the pharmaceutical industry's approach to growing its business. Zantac was a me-too drug, designed to siphon away market share from the blockbuster that preceded it. Prior to Zantac's release, most pharmaceutical companies priced me-too drugs slightly below the existing product already on the market, to entice people away from the predecessor. This pricing practice conforms with standard economic theory, which holds that competition should lower prices.

But Glaxo took another approach. In an unconventional move, it decided to price Zantac at a 30 percent premium *above* the price of Tagamet. Zantac rapidly surpassed Tagamet in sales and went on to become one of the best-selling drugs of all time.[14] Although Zantac did have some small advantages over Tagamet, which undoubtedly helped it commandeer market share, the psychological phenomenon demonstrated in the word-jumble example also played a substantial role in Zantac's overnight success. Zantac's high price made some physicians and patients believe that it was substantially better than Tagamet. I'm quite cognizant of the

Zantac case because I was one of the physicians enthusiastically prescribing it at the time. Marketing studies have shown that people intuitively respond to price information when evaluating product quality.[15] When Zantac came out, I was aware of its higher price. I don't remember whether I consciously equated that price with its quality. But in retrospect, I now realize that Zantac was one of the few medications whose price I was aware of. Looking back now, I see that the company worked hard to make doctors like me aware of its higher price. The company understood my prescribing behavior better than I did.

In fact, higher prices might even augment the *effect* of some drugs. As the word-jumble example illustrates, higher prices create higher expectations, which can actually make some products work better.[16] This phenomenon probably contributed to the blockbuster success of expensive pain relievers like Vioxx and Celebrex. Clinical trials had shown COX-2 inhibitors like Vioxx to be no better at relieving pain than less expensive pills, like Motrin or even Tylenol. Yet many patients were adamant that Vioxx and Celebrex were much more effective, demanding that their doctors prescribe these new and expensive medicines. No doubt, many patients benefited from them at least in part because they figured that such an expensive pill simply *had* to be better than an old generic medication.

Dr. Holmes, in the midst of his heart attack, was facing a triple whammy. As he lay there with what seemed like an elephant sitting on his chest, he wanted to receive the best possible medical care. And those drug-eluting stents, well, they were newer, more expensive, and scarcer than the old stents. He simply *had* to have one!

When Probability Means Hope

The gunman places the tip of his revolver on your forehead, cocks the trigger, and asks you a simple question: how much money will you give him to spare your life? If you are like me, you will give him everything you can get your hands on, including whatever you can get through begging, borrowing, or stealing. I have too much to live for to let money stand in my way.

Many people with potentially terminal illnesses feel as if *they've* got a gun aimed at their heads. Desperate to live, they aren't about to haggle over the price of their health care. They simply want the best available medical care, whatever treatment their doctors think will give them the best chance to survive.

Under less desperate circumstances, consumers of medical care or other goods and services often look carefully at the costs of the goods they're considering purchasing and the likelihood that these goods will benefit them. A cell phone comes with a GPS locator, and a consumer thinks about how likely she is to need such a feature and whether the feature is worth the cost. A man is told by his dentist that for $50 more, he can receive a filling that is more durable than the standard filling. Sounds good. But if that man is seventy years old, he is going to think about the odds that such durability will matter.

But when their lives are on the line, most people have only one way of viewing the odds of success: they want to know what increases those odds the most. And unless that best-chance therapy comes with horrible side effects, they will typically desire it. Not surprisingly, then, medical care in industrialized countries is heavily invested in lifesaving therapies. Hospitals own one or two and sometimes even three helicopters that they can send around to rescue desperately ill patients. They sport brand-spankin'-new ICUs, stocked with all the latest technology. A large metropolitan area might have some six hospitals that offer heart transplantation services. And then the pharmaceutical industry joins in, spending millions and millions of dollars developing high-tech cancer drugs that might extend patients' lives by one or two months, and charging $50,000–100,000 for these treatments, well aware that the market for these drugs will easily bear these costs. Who, after all, is going to tell a grandmother with colon cancer that she won't get the newest and most effective treatment because it is too expensive?

Of course, it is not irrational to want to live. Nor is it irrational to desire the best possible medical care when the illness is threatening your quantity or quality of life. But in such situations, why should we expect the market to develop the most efficient ways of addressing our health-care needs? When I'm desperately ill, I can assure you I won't be haggling over the price of my transplant or my ICU bed.

To make matters worse, even if I were inclined to pay attention to the costs of my health care, I'm not personally responsible for paying most of the bill. My insurance company has been given that job. I might only see 10–20 percent of the cost. In response, if I were a cost-savvy health-care consumer, I would demand even more health-care goods than an unsavvy one.[17] Of course, if I demand expensive interventions, the insurance company will probably respond by raising premiums next year. But my premium will be influenced immeasurably by my own health-care expenses, and so it would be illogical for me to consider next year's premiums when thinking about this year's spending.

Unfortunately, everyone else in my insurance plan faces the same situation that I do. We all have an incentive to overspend on health care, because our fellow enrollees are picking up part of the tab. The consequence of all these incentives is rampant health-care purchasing, which makes next year's premiums much more expensive than this year's.

Free Market Medical Care

Every week, I care for patients and see the limited market savvy they bring to bear on their medical problems. And I recognize that even a physician like me is susceptible to the same psychological forces. We patients and physicians strive to use the latest and best technologies. And we work tirelessly to find hope in the midst of often desperate situations. It's hard for me to reconcile my hands-on view of health care with the pronouncements of libertarians who are so confident that we can best control health-care costs by ramping up the free market.

Karl Rove confidently proclaims in the *Wall Street Journal* that "increasing competition will ensure greater access, lower costs and more innovation."[18] A win-win combination! Allan Hubbard, an economic advisor to George Bush, proclaims the wonders of the private system of medicine in the United States, which "taps into the efficiency and flexibility of competition and markets."[19] Efficiency, huh? How would he explain the fact that the United States, which has one of the more market-oriented health-care systems in the world, dwarfs all other systems when it comes to the cost of medical care and, arguably, with no better health outcomes than those other systems?[20]

Unfortunately, when pressed to answer a question like this, some market-oriented pundits raise the haunting specter of, you guessed it, "socialized medicine." Karl Rove, for example, warns us that "socialized medicine inevitably leads to poor quality, inefficiency, rising taxes and rationing."[21]

John Stossel, writing in the *Wall Street Journal*, asserts that "when government is in charge of health care, people get less of the care that is absolutely necessary."[22] Interestingly, he published his article on the same day that the *Journal* reported a front-page story of a woman who could not receive timely treatment for her breast cancer because she didn't qualify for government assistance.[23] Would government-subsidized health care have been in her worst interests?

I could quote a dozen more *Wall Street Journal* editorials that restate these same platitudes. But I will drag out just one other example, since we are on the topic of cancer. Early in the presidential primary campaign in 2007, Betsy McCaughey pulled out a common argument trotted out about the wonders of market medicine in the United States: that it saves the lives of cancer patients. You see, she pointed out, cancer patients in the United States have "the highest survival rates in the world."[24] In other words, if you are diagnosed with cancer in the United States, you stand a better chance of being alive five years from now than if you are diagnosed in any other country.

You have to admit that's a pretty decisive statistic. Who can argue that surviving cancer is a bad thing?

Well, I can. Because, you see, surviving cancer requires being *diagnosed* with cancer, and what this statistic really demonstrates is the aggressiveness with which U.S. physicians seek out potential cancer diagnoses in their patients. They do so, of course, with the best of motives. They really believe their aggressive screening tests will save people's lives. But these tests often lead to debatable treatments. Men above a certain age are encouraged to get PSA blood tests, to look for prostate cancers. When the result is at all abnormal, urologists biopsy their prostates (not a pleasant procedure, if you think about it). And when they find a tiny focus of cancer within the prostate, they offer to remove it surgically, a procedure that often leads to impotence and incontinence. Now, mind you, they do all of this aggressive and expensive stuff even though there is still *no* evidence that we can save lives by addressing the kind of cancers that are visible only with the PSA.[25]

"Wait a minute," you say. "I thought you just agreed with the *Wall Street Journal* that patients *do* survive longer with cancer in the United States." Well, not exactly. They survive longer with cancer diagnoses, but for all we know, those men with tiny cancers would have died of old age or heart attacks, while those tiny cancers smoldered away. We don't know yet whether finding and removing a tiny, tiny prostate cancer or a precancerous breast lesion called a *ductal carcinoma in situ* actually saves people's lives. What we do know, however, is that the fee-for-service system in the United States rewards doctors for being aggressive in biopsying and operating on these precancers. It's possible that we will learn someday that all this aggressive care has saved some lives. I certainly hope it has. Because we already know that it has caused tens of thousands of patients to worry about cancer and to suffer the complications of our cancer treatments.

Unsavvy Consumers

If you are looking for a place where the free market most efficiently delivers goods and services to consumers, you'd do well to avoid health care. The beneficiaries of health-care interventions, the patients, are often not very savvy about the pros and cons of their health-care alternatives. Nor are they subject to the full price of most of the care they receive, things like Lasik surgery being more the exception than the rule. (Lasik surgery is basically a cosmetic procedure and therefore is not covered by insurance.)

The medical market is never going to achieve the powerful combination of better and cheaper that we have become used to in so many other high-tech industries, like computer electronics and even bicycle manufacturing (where semiserious athletes can now get hold of carbon-alloy bicycles that only professionals could have afforded a decade ago). Consumers simply aren't savvy enough to drive down medical prices. For instance, I have witnessed hundreds of patients who come to the VA because they can no longer afford their medications. After reviewing their medical histories, I look over their medications with them, almost always discovering that they are on the newest and latest pills for whatever ails them. Sometimes they've been paying hundreds of dollars per month out of pocket for these new wonder drugs, though in many cases these pills are no better than the generic alternatives; in some cases the pills are actually worse. If they want me to prescribe medicines for their hypertension or diabetes, I tell them, they will have to switch to different pills. This disturbs them because they have faith in their previous physicians, whom they trust to know what is best for them. Often they will have suffered from huge prescription bills without even asking their doctors whether a less expensive alternative is available. Meanwhile, their doctors, just as influenced by the psychology of "newer is better" as their patients are, often feel strongly that the VA alternatives are simply not acceptable.

When people buy stereos or automobiles, they think hard about the trade-off between the cost and quality of available products. And by pondering these trade-offs, they pressure manufacturers to compete on both cost and quality. But when thinking about sending their kids to college or paying for Mom's funeral or undergoing bypass surgery, people don't feel as if it's time to pinch pennies.

In medical settings, people's unwillingness to pinch pennies is aggravated by their difficulty in evaluating the cost and quality of their health-care alternatives. What is the better medicine for your blood pressure: a beta-blocker or an ARB? Most patients can't be expected to know the answer to this question, so they rely on their doctor. That means that the ultimate consumer of the product, the patient, is not the person who actually chooses the product. This job goes to the physician, who won't bear the financial costs of the medication; and who, if she is like most doctors, is uncomfortable talking about money with her patients; and who, moreover, probably has a belly full of food provided to her by a pharmaceutical sales representative.[26]

Without a doubt, the medical marketplace needs to be designed in a way that makes consumers—both doctors and patients—more aware of the trade-off between cost and quality of various health-care interventions. But given people's psychological predilections to believe in the value of new and expensive products, it would be naive to think that a free market solution, on its own, would lead to a health-care market that resembles the computer industry, with people receiving ever-cheaper products without trading off any of their health.

But that doesn't mean we need to fear the world of socialized medicine. For the alternative to a totally free medical market is not a completely socialized one. Indeed, when market enthusiasts drag out the term *socialized medicine*, they are purposely obfuscating the issue. Is Medicare socialized medicine? Then how do you explain the ability of Medicare patients to receive care at the Mayo Clinic or

Johns Hopkins or M. D. Anderson? Are *all* of these institutions government-run health-care centers?

The fact is, government can insert itself into the health-care market in lots of ways without kicking private companies out of the insurance business, or private hospitals out of the hospital business. It can set standards for what insurers ought to cover or to whom they ought to offer coverage. It can become an insurance company itself, as it has for older Americans with Medicare in the United States. It doesn't have to take over hospitals, as it has in the United Kingdom. "Socialized medicine" comes in many flavors. There are many very different ways for the government to involve itself in the health-care system. To taint them all with the derogative label of *socialism* is a disservice to those of us in the general public who care about finding the best ways to make up for the many ways that the free market fails to operate efficiently in health-care settings.

Being a third-way kind of guy, I'm not eager for the government to take over the entire health-care industry. I certainly recognize the value of the VA system and have seen that this relatively well-run government agency has become a leader in health-care quality.[27] For example, we clinicians in the VA have one of the best electronic medical records systems in the world, a system that helps us monitor our patients' health more efficiently, communicate with other clinicians more effectively, and offer more appropriate care to our patients. The system warns us when a new medication might harm a patient by interacting harmfully with another pill they are already taking. I have seen, in other words, that a government-run health-care system doesn't *have* to be a failure.

But I also recognize that the VA system is an anomaly, in many ways. It garners strong political support from the right and the left, because politicians don't want to be seen as abandoning soldiers who lost limbs for their country. Patients within the VA system can choose to receive care outside of the system if they desire to, an option that many pursue. At the same time, the VA system serves as a safety net for desperately poor veterans, who put up with some of the long waits inherent to the system because they have no other choice. And, as recent news reports have shown, the system can be overwhelmed when the country is at war and the number of new veterans in need of health-care services rises quickly. I don't think Americans would tolerate a VA system applied universally to the population.

The best health-care system will undoubtedly sit somewhere, uncomfortably, between the extremes of a free market and the extremes of a completely socialized one, disappointing zealots on the right and on the left. In early 2008, left-leaning legislators cried foul when President Bush presented a plan to control Medicare costs by charging wealthier people more money for their prescriptions. "Dead on arrival," pronounced Ted Kennedy.[28] Kennedy and his colleagues are wrong to reflexively reject any type of market discipline in medicine. But right-leaning legislators are also wrong to think that the market on its own will solve all of our health-care problems.

I don't pretend to have a simple recipe of market and nonmarket mechanisms—a pinch of co-pay, a dash of electronic medical records—that will ensure affordable and effective health care to everyone who needs it. Instead, I have tried to shake your faith in markets, to help move us, as consumers of health care, toward a more nuanced debate, one that will consider the psychology by which people make purchasing decisions. Even in mundane situations, people frequently allow unconscious psychological forces to distort their purchasing decisions. We let anchoring heuristics, or a belief that "newer" means "better," to influence our willingness to shell out cash for the latest gizmo. Sometimes, as a result, we buy things we shouldn't buy or at a price we shouldn't buy them at.

I've focused on health-care settings in this chapter to drive home the point that such decisions can have very important consequences. I've also discussed health-care decision making because market enthusiasts are so, well, enthusiastic about the ability of free market discipline to painlessly control health-care costs.

To be perfectly honest, that point of view makes me sick.

CHAPTER ELEVEN

Marketing and the Science
of Persuasion

TWO DAYS AFTER a call night during my residency, feeling almost as if I were back in the proper time zone, I remember catching word that some pharmaceutical representatives had put together a bagel and donut display in the hotel across the street from Rochester Methodist Hospital. Figuring I wouldn't have to pay for lunch that day, I decided to check it out. When I arrived, I slathered a bagel with cream cheese and chatted with a few of the sales representatives. One sales rep gave me a pocket card with a quick mnemonic device for diagnosing patients with eosinophilia. Another rep, an attractive woman, was nice enough to give me a new penlight to replace my old one, its batteries having given out while I was examining a patient's sore throat. I was surprised that none of the sales reps pushed any products off on me. I don't believe, in fact, that I talked about any of their medicines with them. Most were just chatting me up, asking me where I went to medical school and how I was adjusting to residency. One even told me about a great running trail stretching out behind the hospital. The bagel break turned out to be a nice little diversion from the patients on 5 West.

Back in my residency days, I was confident that the sales reps were not influencing my prescribing habits. I was not alone in feeling impervious to marketing influences. Most physicians I've spoken with report that pharmaceutical marketing has far less influence on their prescribing habits than do more respectable sources of influence—like medical journals, grand rounds lectures, or colleagues' recommendations. Many of us physicians recognize, of course, that pharmaceutical companies wouldn't spend billions of dollars marketing to physicians unless it was effective marketing.[1] But we persist in the belief that it is *other* physicians who are susceptible to these influences, not us.[2] We even find ways of justifying our interactions with sales reps. We tell ourselves that most sales reps are merely promoting "me-too" drugs. So if that gorgeous Pfizer rep somehow sways us toward the Pfizer cholesterol pill rather than the Merck one, does it really matter? Moreover, we console ourselves with the thought that the sales representatives are providing us with some truly useful information.[3] When reps tell us that one of their products has just come out in a once-a-day formulation, isn't that a good thing to know?

Even as an exhausted resident, I felt uncomfortable with these justifications. I felt guilty about accepting penlights and reflex hammers from the sales reps—why are they being nice to me, I wondered? What do they want in return? And yet, I recognized the value of what they were doing. After all, the *New England Journal of Medicine* doesn't publish articles telling me when a drug like, say, Cardizem comes out with a new once-a-day formulation; that isn't deemed to be important science. So I had no way of knowing about these new products unless I spoke with someone whose job it was to sell Cardizem.

I had never struggled with the marketing industry before. I didn't have any reason to feel guilty when Miller Lite supported my ability to watch *Cheers* episodes for free. I didn't worry that I was being "bought" when I would see the advertising banners draped around the Metrodome at a Twins game. These advertising subsidies, which effectively lowered my entertainment costs, didn't feel as unseemly to me as that little Post-it notepad that the Glaxo representative gave me.

But I began to wonder whether such marketing was promoting the well-being of my patients or whether, at times, it was violating their best interests. Indeed, we need to ask ourselves this question much more broadly. We live in a capitalist society that is increasingly inundating us with advertising. We exist in a world where many of the best psychology and neuroscience graduates are being hired by marketing firms or marketing departments within large corporations. These marketers are becoming increasingly sophisticated at targeting and persuading us consumers. And to what end? When are they promoting our best interests, and when are they harming us?

Selling Good Goods

Marketing is a crucial grease in the gears of capitalism. New products won't succeed unless people learn about them. Consider the book you are reading right now, one I hope will improve thousands (millions?) of lives. When I was looking for a publisher, I sought out one that would market it aggressively, having discovered the hard way that a good book won't sell itself. Without effective marketing, a good product that can improve people's lives won't have a chance to do so. In this information age, marketing cuts through the clutter and grabs people's attention. In an era where consumers face so many choices—dozens of minivans, hundreds of shampoos, and thousands of DVDs—marketing helps consumers learn which minivan has OnStar capabilities, which shampoos fight dandruff, and which Adam Sandler movie features him playing a lovable, down-to-earth guy.

In fact, many experts believe that advertising and marketing serve the interests of the general public, "a powerful force for good," in the words of Mary Azcuenaga, commissioner of the Federal Trade

Commission under Bill Clinton, because it is "a means of improving the ability of consumers to make informed purchasing choices."[4] This informational theory of advertising fits quite nicely with the rational choice strain of libertarianism that I have been exploring in this book. Indeed, only when ads are fraudulent does Azcuenaga see a role for the government to restrain advertisers.

I hope that most of you, by this point in my book, will be skeptical of the informational view, recognizing its naivety; people don't simply absorb new information like a computer, weighing it rationally and updating their data files when they learn about a new brand of light beer. And even if they could make rational use of the information they receive through advertising, how much of advertising can really qualify as useful information? What does that duck ("Aflac!") tell us about . . . about insurance, I think? How is our knowledge of underwear increased by seeing Michael Jordan stride around in Hanes? What does a bikini model on top of a car tell us about the car's performance, other than that the hood can support 101 pounds?

I guess you could defend the informational view of advertising by claiming that these irrelevant images don't inform us about products, but instead make us more aware of the products so we can inform ourselves about them. A teenage boy seeing that bikini model on the hood of a sports car may soon be able to tell you what's underneath that same hood. (How else did Bruce Springstein know it was a '69 Chevy with a 396, Fuelie heads and whatever it was on the floor?)

But there's a more plausible view of advertising that springs forth from the rational choice tradition, developed by Gary Becker and Kevin Murphy, of rational addiction fame. Their theory sees advertising not only as information, but also as a consumable good in its own right.[5] Part of the popularity of the Super Bowl, for instance, results from its clever commercials. So, regardless of whether the "Whazzup" guys taught us anything about beer (if I remember correctly), they raised our utility by entertaining us.

Becker and Murphy also point out that advertisements can increase people's enjoyment of products, complementing the products the way ketchup and hot dogs complement each other. In economics, a complementary good raises the utility of a companion good. A spoonful of lonely ketchup, you see, is a delicacy only to people like my youngest son, and not something most discriminating consumers enjoy on its own. Nor is an isolated hot dog all that appetizing to most people. But put the hot dog and ketchup together, in the middle of a tasty bun, and these ingredients are far better than the sum of their parts. By the same token, I guess, Hanes briefs are simply more comfortable (?), enjoyable (?), and sexy even (?), now that we believe that Michael Jordan wears them too. The bikini model raises the utility of the sports car by associating the car with sex, thereby increasing the car's sexiness. When I wore Tom Cruise–style Ray-Bans back in the day, it made me sexier. Not sexier than Tom Cruise, of course, but sexier than the Ray-Ban-less me (which, truth be told, is a pretty low bar).

The power of this utility-maximizing view of advertising resides in its truth. Marketing often *does* provide people with useful information. It really *is* a crucial part of an efficient market. And even when it doesn't provide much information, it can provide entertainment, or it can create powerful images that spill over onto products, making them more enjoyable. The same power holds for the rational decision-making theory underlying libertarianism. This theory is powerful because it is in many ways true. People really *do* consider the pros and cons of alternatives they face when making decisions. And they often do have a much better idea of what will make themselves happy than their elected representatives.

But these hyperrational worldviews are also dangerous, because they are only partially true and capture people's behaviors only incompletely. Marketing provides people with information, but it also influences consumers in many other ways that have nothing to do with information. Rationality influences our day-to-day decisions, but so do many other forces, unconscious ones and often irrational ones. To understand how marketing works, therefore, we need to move beyond this rational model. Only by recognizing the psychology of marketing will we begin to grasp what Madison Avenue has done to Adam Smith's invisible hand.

The Psychology of Reciprocity

If you glance at the hands of a young physician while he's writing a prescription, you might see a pen emblazoned with the name of a new antibiotic, anxiety pill, or antidepressant. The pen was a gift from a pharmaceutical sales rep, probably tossed in as an extra thank-you on the day that the rep donated some sample medicines for the doctor to hand out to his patients for free. The pen works as a marketing tool on two distinct levels. On the surface, it is a simple informational device, reminding the physician of the name of the particular drug, perhaps even reinforcing one of its attributes with a catchy slogan. But the effectiveness of this 15¢ pen as a marketing tool lies in a much deeper psychological reality. This pen triggers the law of reciprocity.[6]

In a classic social psychology experiment, research participants were left in a waiting room with what psychologists like to call a *confederate*—a person pretending to be a research participant but who actually is in cahoots with the researchers. In this study, the confederate leaves the room to go to the bathroom and returns with two Cokes. "I saw them near the bathroom and asked if I could take one, and they said it was OK, so I brought one for you, too," the confederate says. A simple gesture, costing the confederate neither time nor money. A few minutes later, the confederate asks the research participant whether he would be willing to purchase a raffle ticket to raise money for his high school. Here's where that Coke pays off. It has triggered the law of reciprocity—you scratch my back, and I'll buy a raffle ticket. Those research participants who received a Coke from the confederate bought twice as many tickets as those who did not.[7]

How do you say no to someone who has just given you a nice gift? Physicians often pooh-pooh their interactions with sales representatives, pointing out that they can't be bought with a pen or a tote bag. And of course, if someone asked the physicians to do something in exchange for such a small gift, they'd get nowhere. These little gifts work, however, because they are gifts. No strings attached. And the lack of strings triggers reciprocity.

I am often forced to take advantage of the psychology of reciprocity when conducting research studies, because I operate on tight research budgets. For example, when surveying physicians by mail, some researchers put in checks for $100 or $200, to entice physicians to return the survey. Many physicians see these checks and throw them, and the surveys, away without feeling guilty (since they didn't cash the checks). In return, the researchers write checks for even larger sums of money. When I survey physicians, I keep things within budget by dismissing the $100 or $200 checks and placing a little old $5 bill inside each envelope. This small amount of money often works as well as much larger checks, because the money is already theirs whether or not they fill out the survey, and the doctors (who aren't about to throw a crisp $5 bill away) feel obligated to return the favor. It's difficult to slip a bill into your wallet at the same time that you toss my survey into the recycling bin.

Pharmaceutical sales departments understand the psychology of reciprocity much better than does the average physician, and therein lies their power to influence medical practice. Indeed, the power of the marketing industry resides in large part in its knowledge of psychology. The industry understands consumers better than consumers understand themselves.

Typecasting

If you watch the evening news with Charles Gibson, Brian Williams, or Katie Couric, you will see a flurry of pharmaceutical ads, promising to lower your cholesterol, reduce your arthritis pains, improve your sex life, and cure your restless legs. If you are watching these shows, there is also a decent chance that you suffer from one or more of these conditions. In fact, many of the companies airing these ads have a good idea of the proportion of viewers who are potential customers. They have seen the Nielsen data on the aging demographic of news watchers, they have even figured out how many Couric viewers have arthritis, and they target their ads accordingly.

Does this feel Big Brother-y to you? Are you bothered that some advertisers know so much about your aches and pains? Would it bother you to know that you've also been typecast according to where you live, what magazines you subscribe to, or any other number of habits you have?

Psychologists have famously divided people into personality types based on five broad characteristics, things like neuroticism and openness to experience.[8] Marketers have sliced and diced things even further. In the PRIZM system, they have segmented people into one of sixty-two neighborhood types. If you are a rural Caucasian working in a blue-collar job or on a farm, for instance, then you are part of neighborhood 41, "New Ecotopia." Marketers derived the sixty-two neighborhood types by analyzing people's consumption and looking for patterns in what people spend their money on. Marketers then use this neighborhood consumption data to target people who are likely to respond to their products. Hyundai, for example, bumped up its U.S. sales when it found ways to target two neighborhood types that it had learned were open to an affordable alternative to Japanese cars, people in the "kids and cul-de-sac" neighborhoods and in the "bohemian mixed" neighborhoods.[9]

Marketers have become increasingly sophisticated at matching their advertisements to potential customers, a process reaching new heights with the Internet. When people return to the Amazon.com Web site, they receive suggestions of new books they might enjoy. When I play a song from my iTunes library, Apple lets me know about new releases from the same artist. Some people find this kind of marketing creepy. And I must admit, it's strange that marketing professionals can learn so much about me that they often know my tastes better than I do. But from an informational view, such targeted marketing is often a great thing. When I am watching *The Colbert Report*, it is nice to be exposed to commercials for funny new movies rather than ones for treating constipation. I am glad that iTunes knows to inform me about Richard Thompson's new album. I am not disturbed that advertisers can target me, except for the sinking feeling I get when I recognize that I am not as unique as I once thought. Targeting consumers is an efficient way to get people information about the products they are most likely to care about.

What bothers me is not that I'm being targeted with useful information about new products; instead, I'm bothered that marketers, who know how old I am and what neighborhood I live in, are thereby creating ads that take advantage of the way my brain works.

Take Charlie Gibson's viewers, many of whom are retirement age. The seventy-year-old brain differs from the twenty-five-year-old brain in ways that are quite important to advertisers. By age seventy, even the healthiest people (those who have avoided strokes and Alzheimer's, for example) have begun to experience declines in important brain functions. Seventy-year-olds are slower to process new information, have less working memory, and have more difficulty consciously deliberating about decisions than the typical twenty-five-year-old.[10] Such declines, it should be noted, begin in the early thirties, a fact I am increasingly aware of as my elementary school boys begin to outpace me in games requiring rapid pattern recognition or short-term memory.

But despite the age-related declines I've just identified, retirees are neither stupid nor feeble. Indeed, their decision-making abilities often exceed those of younger folks. You see, what seventy-year-olds lack in processing speed capacity, they usually make up for in emotional intelligence. Indeed, as we saw in chapter 9, people's decisions typically result from the convergence of deliberative and emotional processes—people know something about Coke and Pepsi, but they also have *feelings* toward these two products, and their choice of one product over the other will often depend on those feelings.

Feelings often work like a mnemonic device, a shortcut to the truth. We meet someone and develop strong feelings about that person, even before we've analyzed the data from our encounter. Often, in fact, we reflect on our meeting to discover what it was about that person that made us suspicious or infatuated. These rapid emotional judgments are often quite efficient at informing our judgments and decisions. Our gut, so to speak, is often shrewder than our brains.

As people age, they base an increasing proportion of their decisions on emotion rather than on strict deliberation. And these emotions have been trained, over many years, to line up with what an informed deliberative judgment would have led them to conclude. It is this emotional training that enables older people, despite objective declines in brain processing power, to often make better decisions than younger people.

Marketers, who are becoming increasingly sophisticated in their knowledge of psychology and neuroscience, have responded to research on the aging brain by developing much more emotive ads for products aimed at older consumers or for television shows watched by older people. If seventy-year-olds base their decisions on emotions, then advertisers need to appeal to those emotions. Good advertisements don't need to bestow information on potential consumers as long as they create positive feelings toward the products: "I'd like to buy the world a Coke!"

The power of emotions is strongest for older consumers, but emotions influence everyone's decisions and often act as shortcuts to reduce people's cognitive workloads when making choices. Indeed, marketers have even discovered that much of the power of branding resides in the emotional benefits of making it easy for people to recognize and relate to their products. In a recent study, neuroscientists in Germany scanned the brains of people while exposing them to images of company logos. When they flashed the Volkswagen logo in front of people for three seconds, people's brains lit up in regions known for their role in positive emotions and in reward systems. When they flashed a lesser-known logo, a Spanish car manufacturer called SEAT, the centers of negative emotion fired, as well as memory centers. People were relatively unfamiliar with the brand, causing them to struggle to figure out what the logo stood for.[11] This kind of brain effort can induce negative emotions—when people have to work hard to remember something or understand something, their brows furrow and their moods decline. These negative emotions spill over to whatever it is that people are thinking about. One group of researchers, in fact, exposed people to marketing slogans, varying the legibility of the font across participants. All the ads were legible, and all the research participants were exposed to the same information about the product. But those who had fuzzier words to read had a harder time processing the ads and ended up with less positive attitudes toward the products.[12]

Brands are powerful marketing tools not only because they generate positive emotions but also because they generate high expectations, expectations that are often self-fulfilling prophecies.[13] More kids recognize Ronald McDonald than recognize Mickey Mouse.[14] Their positive attitude toward the McDonald's brand spills over onto their french fries. If a child tastes a french fry from a McDonald's bag, he will like it more than if he pulls an identical fry from an unmarked bag.[15]

One could argue that McDonald's has earned its reputation for delicious fries; if people have positive attitudes toward the McDonald's brand, that is simply the result of people absorbing their experience at McDonald's and translating that into the kind of emotional shortcuts that people create across all life domains. But this view doesn't explain why McDonald's fries taste better when pulled out of a McDonald's bag than an unmarked container. We think that our taste buds tell us what foods taste like, but Madison Avenue isn't content to cede control to our basic senses. Instead, it works to create expectations in consumers that influence how people experience their products.

Feelings toward brands aren't simply a passive response to brand quality. They actively contribute to how people perceive a brand and how they experience a product. Becker and Murphy's analysis of advertisements captures the real way branding works. The marketing of McDonald's actually improves the taste of its fries. The positive association people hold toward McDonald's—their love of Ronald McDonald, the reputation they hold for McDonald's fries— spills over onto the product like a splash of ketchup and, like the ketchup, enhances the flavor of the fries. That means when you eat McDonald's fries, you aren't simply consuming potatoes, salt, and oil. You are consuming bits and pieces of Ronald McDonald. (OK, that image probably won't improve the taste of your fries.) You are feasting on your memories and perceptions of the entire McDonald's brand. And consequently, if you are a fan of McDonald's, your enjoyment of those fries—the utility you gain from your meal—is increased.

They don't call it a Happy Meal for nothing.

"Think. Don't Smoke."

If I have convinced you of Becker and Murphy's views, then you now believe that good ads not only are enjoyable themselves, but can also increase the joy people get from consuming the advertised product. In accepting this view, you are acknowledging some of the irrational forces that influence free markets. But such is the nature, the all-too-human nature, of consumer experiences.

But what does this view of advertising imply about the answer to the question I posed at the beginning of this chapter? Does advertising promote people's well-being? To begin to answer this question, I invite you on a short tour of an unusual kind of advertisement, one designed purportedly to convince people *not* to consume the product.

In the closing months of 1998, the Philip Morris Companies launched a $100 million national campaign to inform teenagers about the dangers of smoking, emphasizing to kids that they don't have to smoke in order to fit in with others. The campaign trumpeted a positive message: "Think. Don't smoke." Not to be outdone, the Lorillard Tobacco Company (makers of Newport, Kent, Old Gold, and other tobacco products) launched its own campaign one year later, telling kids, "Tobacco is wacko if you're a teen." And yet, when researchers looked for a relationship between exposure to these ads and teen smoking rates, they couldn't find one. The campaigns had no effect on kids' behaviors.

But not all was lost, because the companies did not rely solely on their teen marketing campaigns. They also developed campaigns targeted at parents. Philip Morris's campaign carried the slogan "Talk. They'll listen." On its surface, this campaign looked exactly like the kind of public service announcement (PSA) you see from any noble government agency. But public health expert Melanie Wakefield studied the effectiveness of these campaigns and concluded that "the overt message of the parent-targeted campaign is that parents should talk to their children about smoking, but no reason beyond simply being a teenager is offered as to why youths should not smoke."[16]

I have not raised a teenager. But even in my preteen household, I know that kids are not satisfied with a simple "because" as an explanation for why they can't, say, play on the computer, eat a second dessert, or wrestle on top of their bunk beds. I can only imagine how poorly this kind of nonexplanation will work on a teenager.

It seems that some of the tobacco executives *have* raised teenagers. Because Wakefield discovered that the more exposure teens had had to the parent-targeted ads, the more interested they were in smoking cigarettes and the less concerned they were about tobacco's harms. It won't be news to many readers that teenagers are struggling to become independent from their parents. The brilliance of the tobacco campaigns is that, in the guise of a PSA, they managed to tap into this struggle and convince more teens to use their products.

Which returns us to a major theme of this chapter: marketing experts know more about how kids' brains work than do most parents. They watch kids interact, observe them playing with toys. They—shock of shocks—even talk to kids and find out how they think. These experts also know quite a bit about the dynamics of parent-child relationships, knowledge they use to find a way to create just the kind of parent-child tension that can only be relieved by purchasing their products. If you don't believe me, ask the mother of any Barbie-loving girl.

Not Diaper Dandies Anymore

Mattel first introduced Barbie to the American public in 1959, and her overt sexuality shocked many mothers.[17] Dolls prior to Barbie didn't have breasts, they had diapers. Concerned about parental reaction to its radical new doll, Mattel hired a former psychoanalyst, Ernest Dictor, to run focus groups of girls and mothers. Dictor discovered that parental disapproval of Barbie only fueled girls' delight with the new doll. That left Mattel with the job of making Barbie just acceptable enough for moms to fork over cash for her, while keeping Barbie just shocking enough to appeal to young girls. The parent-child relationship was viewed by Mattel as a wedge that it could exploit to sell its product.

Leading marketing textbooks highlight how this wedge operates, in effect teaching the next generation of marketers to exploit this same wedge.[18] Step 1: get the parents to disapprove of the product, thereby increasing children's desires for the product. Kids will then take care of step 2: nagging their parents to buy the doll, toy, or video game. Only very strong parental disapproval of a product can overcome the power of a whiny child. Which means parents will then take care of step 3: handing over cash to buy the product.

Pharmaceutical companies tap into a similar psychology when using direct-to-consumer advertisements. They realize that when patients ask physicians for specific medications, many doctors will accede to their request, even in the face of an equally good generic pill, or even if the requested medicine is of limited benefit to the patient. It takes time, you see, to talk a patient out of a medicine, time that many physicians don't feel they have. And those often uncomfortable conversations may cause patients to become disgruntled and take their business elsewhere. Most doctors want their patients to remain gruntled!

Marketing companies are not in the business of maximizing people's utility. They are professional persuaders, trying to convince people to buy products. Therefore, marketers can only promote people's well-being if they convince people to buy products that are in people's best interests. When they convince people to buy this book, then the world of course will be a much better place. When they convince people to buy Barbies, then reasonable people will probably disagree about whether the world is a better place, but I expect that few people will feel a need to impose regulations on the marketing of curvaceous dolls. When they promote McDonald's french fries to little kids, I expect many more people will join me in being disturbed. Does a children's television program really need to be accompanied by ads that persuade kids to consume junk food? Is it unreasonable to limit our children's exposure to these obesity-promoting commercials? And finally, when marketers find ways to persuade kids to take up cigarettes, I expect (and hope) that most readers by now will be convinced that this is not in people's best interests and that we need to find ways to protect kids from such influences.

A completely free market society would allow the Joe Camels of the world to insinuate themselves into our children's lives. I don't want to live in that kind of society.

How we think about Ronald McDonald and Joe Camel is extremely important, because we live in world where our youngest citizens are the targets of intense marketing. The average U.S. child encounters more than thirty thousand ads per year.[19] And these ads are often quite powerful influences on children, an influence magnified because young kids, those less than seven years old, often have a hard time distinguishing between TV ads and television shows. What's more, marketing experts have learned that they can make it even harder for kids to distinguish between shows and advertisements by placing the shows' characters into the ads; Fruity Pebbles cereal commercials are especially effective when plunked in the middle of a *Flintstones* episode. Even marketing gurus at PBS have tapped into this dynamic, employing Barney to help out with fund drives in the middle of *Barney and Friends* episodes, causing thousands of little children to beg their parents to send money to help the beleaguered purple dinosaur.[20]

By targeting children with so many ads, marketers hope to accomplish one of two goals. They want to take advantage of children's persuasive powers to convince adults to buy their products. Thus, even automobile companies target children with their advertisements. Get a kid excited about a Hummer, and he'll nag his parents to buy one. According to James McNeal, a child-marketing consultant, children less than fourteen years old influence almost half of household purchases.[21] And almost two-thirds of parents say their children "actively participate" in car-buying decisions.

But doling out Hummers in Happy Meals (yes, that has happened!) works not only by encouraging kids to nag their parents about buying a Hummer. It also works by generating long-term allegiance among the kids, who, after all, will someday become adults and buy cars for themselves. Children and young adults have a disproportionate influence on television programming because they are understood, by marketing experts, as being a much better investment than older consumers. If a TV show is watched by a lot of fourteen- to thirty-year-olds, then advertisers have a chance to influence decades of consumer behavior, so they will pay hand-somely to advertise on that show. Pity the higher-rated crime dramas that attract the older viewers, who have but ten or twenty years to purchase consumer goods and, moreover, who might be too set in their ways to switch to new products. Eighty-year-olds drive Buicks, not Hummers.

Does Marketing Improve People's Lives?

As we've now seen, marketing campaigns don't simply inform consumers about available products; they also use the tools of psychology to persuade people that specific products are in their best interests. Marketers know how to persuade five-year-olds to beg for Fruity Pebbles and sixteen-year-olds to take up smoking. They've learned how to convince parents to pick up KFC on the way home from work. God willing, they'll figure out how to cajole hundreds of thousands of people to purchase my books. Some of this advertising makes us happy. TV ads are often more entertaining than the programs they support. And when they aren't, they still pay the bills so that TV networks can offer us new entertainments. Moreover, people really do feel more attractive when they are wearing clothes that they have seen draped on gorgeous celebrities.

But does all this advertising-related happiness mean that marketing necessarily improves our lives? Hardly. As a physician, I will illustrate my concerns with a study showing how even subtle product placement can make young men want to smoke. Sonya Dal Cin and colleagues conducted an experiment using clips from the macho masterpiece *Die Hard*, in which a chiseled Bruce Willis rescues a building full of hostages, biceps a-flexing and, more importantly, lips a-puffin'. At one point in the movie, you see, Willis's character takes a deep drag on a cigarette. Dal Cin wondered whether the image of such a hero, midsmoke, would make male viewers want to emulate their hero. So she showed young men thirty-six minutes of this movie, scenes in which Willis's character, John McClane, dispatches the world of bad guys. She randomized viewers, however, so that some saw a clip that included John's smoking behavior, while others did not. The men who viewed the smoking clip ended up more interested in smoking than those who saw the smokeless clip. This desire to smoke even existed among lifelong nonsmokers.[22]

In the rational world of Becker and Murphy, all is good. Bruce Willis's charisma has simply oozed onto a product, cigarettes, causing people to get more joy out of smoking. In the world that I reside in, all is not so wonderful. In my world, I prescribe oxygen for people whose pack-a-day habit has turned their lungs into tissue paper; I admit patients to the hospital, to receive chemotherapy for their lung cancer, blood thinners for their strokes, and cardiac catheters for their heart attacks, problems directly related to their habit. That's why, in my world, advertising can both improve our lives and destroy them. As I see it, advertising is neither good nor bad on its own. It is the individual *products* that are good or bad and specific uses of products that are good or bad. Smoking is almost never good. Alcohol is good in moderation, but deadly in high doses.

If people were as rational as traditional economists once believed, then advertising would be a strong and consistent force for good. Advertising would make people aware of products, and in response people would accurately evaluate the products and consume only those products that improve their lives. By now, I hope I have successfully put the myth of near-total human rationality to rest and thereby shown why we have to be careful about how much freedom we give to advertisers.

When Harmless Foibles Become Marketing Opportunities

As we've seen throughout this book, humans are neither completely rational nor totally irrational. Some readers may wonder which side of human nature usually dominates our decisions. This is a fantastically difficult question to answer (I'm tempted to say, "42," and at least leave *Hitchhiker's Guide* fans satisfied). Undoubtedly, for every behavioral economics study that points out irrational behaviors, there are dozens of more traditional economics studies demonstrating rational behaviors.

But the relative number of each kind of study doesn't tell us which kind of behavior predominates. For starters, the number of behavioral economists, while growing rapidly, is still small. More importantly, the statistical tools for identifying rational behaviors are more plentiful and better honed than the ones for identifying illogical decisions. Every time the supply of a product dwindles and its price rises, an economist can show the rational side of the market. It is not as simple to know whether or not the product is, therefore, rationally priced or whether the people who purchase the product are acting in their best interests.

While it is impossible to figure out the relative prevalence of rational and irrational decisions, I'd venture to guess two things. First, as imperfect as our brains are, most consumers make considerably more logical decisions in their lives than illogical ones. We actually do a good job of figuring out which pasta sauce we like best and which way of spending our entertainment dollars will bring us the greatest joy.

But, and here's my second conjecture, the intense (and psychologically informed) marketing of products has shifted the balance of decision making toward irrationality. When Kahneman and Tversky created Linda, and exposed the flawed ways people make probability judgments, they posed no threat to free markets. Believers in human rationality argued that the flaws that Kahneman, Tversky, and their followers had exposed were rare phenomena, like visual illusions, that exist primarily in research labs, not in the real world. Such biases, critics contended, were the result of experimenters' creating artificial situations that point out the rare weaknesses in human logic.

Well, now, consider the rapid adoption of behavioral research findings by marketing experts. Marketing experts are paid to know how people think, decide, and behave. When Adam Smith envisioned the invisible hand, he could not have foreseen how marketing scientists would manipulate the movement of these hands, like a puppeteer working a marionette. When Stanley Jevons pondered the choices people make between apples and oranges, he could not have begun to imagine that, under the influence of cartoon characters, people would push these healthy, delicious foods aside for processed foods.

The free market, so beloved by Smith and Jevons and by many living people too, has enriched all of our lives. But this free market is not the perfect happiness-maximizer that some claim it to be. We humans are too easily manipulated by other humans. We are too easily seduced by our worst instincts. We are too often overwhelmed by the multitude of choices we face in our fast-moving market economies.

When consumer advocacy groups propose regulations to limit advertising to children or direct-to-consumer advertising of pharmaceuticals, market enthusiasts are quick to point out that such regulations interfere with free speech and thereby threaten the exchange of information that is so crucial to market efficiency. Having learned more about how advertisers exploit human foibles, I'm less impressed with those arguments than I used to be. When important human interests are at stake, we need to consider the costs *and benefits* of regulating advertisers.

How do we go about setting the proper balance between regulation and market liberty? I will try to convince you, in the next chapter, that if we are honest with ourselves, we'll see that there is no simple answer to this question. But there is real wisdom to be gained by recognizing the complex trade-offs that the world forces us to make.

CHAPTER TWELVE

Balancing Liberty and the Pursuit of Well-Being

WHEN I WAS trying to interest publishers in this book, I had a stimulating conversation with an editor whom I respect a great deal, and who has brought some very successful political books to market. He was pushing me to describe my bottom line, the thesis of the book. I launched an erudite summary of my thoughts, but he wasn't satisfied, so he rephrased his question: "Are you aiming for a nuanced argument?" he asked. "Yes," I replied, and explained how I planned to write a book that could be both nuanced and yet captured in a marketable sound bite. I believe I lost him at the word *yes*. Nuance was not what he was looking for.

We live in a culture that places great value on simplicity. We yearn for the "ten steps toward a healthier you" or the pithy prescription that will cure our political ills. We allow pundits to define important elections along the lines of flag pins and haircuts rather than on sustained discussion of the complicated challenges we face as a country. A politician who needs a paragraph to explain himself on a hot-button issue is in trouble. Almost as much trouble as an author striving for nuance.

The basic message of this book is quite simple: we humans are not as rational as some libertarians would have us believe, and therefore the free market puts us in a position to harm ourselves. To make matters worse, the free market often rewards those people who understand consumer behavior well enough to exploit our weaknesses. Because the free market fails to protect consumer interests, a good government should find appropriate ways to protect us from ourselves.

That's where the simplicity ends. If humans were largely rational, the world would be a simpler place. If I weren't so easily persuaded to do things I shouldn't do, if I weren't so prone to mistaken judgments and flawed decisions, then it would make sense for the government to maximize the freedom of our markets and leave me alone. In this simpler world, the government could limit itself to fighting fraud and combating monopolies, to protecting us from theft and vandalism and the like. In a world dominated by rational behavior indeed, the government could focus on externalities and leave us consumers alone to choose our way of life.

But once we acknowledge that humans aren't always rational, we are compelled to consider whether the government should take action to prevent us from harming ourselves—to dissuade us from smoking and overeating, to protect us from predatory lenders and uninformative advertisers. Aware of our foibles, we can no longer judge government policies solely by whether they increase the freedom of markets. Instead, we must tackle the more complex job of balancing competing goals. Specifically, we need to figure out how to balance our desire for liberty with our pursuit of happiness.

Maximization Begins with Measurement

Back in the nineteenth century, Jeremy Bentham urged politicians to design policies that maximized people's happiness, increasing their pleasures and reducing their pains.[1] Bentham's influence, although great, was constrained even in his day, in part because there were no good ways for scientists to measure people's hedonic well-being. His vision of utility, therefore, was abandoned by economists in the nineteenth century, in favor of preference-based utility measures that were more easily quantified.[2]

In recent years, Daniel Kahneman has tried to bring policy makers back to Bentham.[3] As we saw in chapter 8, Kahneman is keen on Bentham in part because of all the research that reveals people making decisions that reduce their happiness—people don't know what will make themselves happy or unhappy, and therefore don't always make optimal decisions. Kahneman is also excited about Bentham's political ideas because the scientific measurement of well-being has advanced significantly since Bentham's day. Researchers have developed taxonomies of mood, and have developed survey measures of mood that correlate (run together) with unconscious facial expressions, physiologic measures of stress, and even fMRI scans.[4] Kahneman even helped develop a new measure of mood that can be collected affordably enough to inform policy making.[5] Given these advances in measuring happiness and unhappiness, Kahneman believes we are finally ready to achieve Bentham's vision.

Other prominent psychologists have joined Kahneman, in promoting policy measures that aim to maximize people's happiness. Ed Diener and Martin Seligman have proposed that we develop national measures of well-being, akin to GDP measures. If money doesn't necessarily make people happy, after all, then why should we place so much emphasis on ramping up our GDP?[6] Barry Schwartz, psychologist and author of *The Paradox of Choice*, has taken this reasoning further, writing in the *New Republic* that happiness research has shown us that "we now *know* [Schwartz's italics] there is some significant subset of people likely to be made better off through heavier taxation, and that these people reside at the top end of the wealth distribution."[7]

Many economists have jumped on the bandwagon, too. Lord Richard Layard, from the prestigious London School of Economics, has put forth a series of policy proposals centered on the idea of promoting states of affairs that make people happy.[8] Robert Frank, a Cornell economist and a prolific author of popular books, has argued for the redistribution of wealth on the grounds that this would maximize societal happiness.[9]

Not surprisingly, this line of thinking is a great threat to libertarians. For it replaces an individualized version of well-being—with each person free to pursue his idea of the good life, as long as that pursuit doesn't have harmful consequences on other people—with what seems a very top-down approach. Rather than judge people's welfare by how free and informed they are when making decisions, it judges welfare by figuring out how happy people are. Consequently, the happiness approach opens the door to all kinds of government intrusions. Would that mean if commuters aren't happy, we need to prevent people from moving to the exurbs? Or if money doesn't make people happy, that the government needs to play Robin Hood and take money away from rich people to give to the poor? We'll return to these questions later.

But first, we need to ask ourselves whether happiness is the proper aim of our policies. Putting aside lingering concerns about whether we could really measure happiness as well as Bentham would like us to,[10] we need to think about whether policy makers should judge their policies in Benthamite terms—according to how the policies influence people's moment-to-moment moods. Before being swept away by the happiness proselytizers, we should return to Bentham's time, for even then his ideas were being criticized by people who did not share his view about what it really means to live a happy life, people who did not think that policy makers should concern themselves solely with people's moment-to-moment moods. And chief among these critics was a former child prodigy, John Stuart Mill, who himself was a protégé of Bentham's.

Bentham's Protégé

Having gained fame through his writings and his political activities, Jeremy Bentham befriended many young intellectuals, who worked closely with the great man to spread his ideas. One of these young men was a writer named James Mill, with whom Bentham coauthored a number of controversial pamphlets. Bentham and Mill not only held similar political beliefs, but also shared nearly identical views on human nature. Specifically, they both believed that when children are born, they are blank slates. They believed that the intellectual abilities and behavioral inclinations people demonstrate as adults are a direct result of their experience. In their view, nurture trumps nature every time.

On the basis of this theory, James Mill decided to homeschool his children with the help of Bentham.[11] That meant steeping his oldest child, John Stuart Mill, in lofty ideas from an early age while protecting him from lowly thoughts—the kind of tripe that, say, the presence of other people's children might add to the mixture. The Mill children were not allowed to have any friends outside of the family unit until they were well into their teens, and even at that age, when John excitedly spoke about a teenager he had met while traveling in France, Papa Mill was none too happy.

The level of control that Bentham and Mill exerted over the children's surroundings was astounding. They closely regulated how the children spent every waking moment, carefully monitoring the games they played and the books they read. They went so far as to banish fairy tales from the household. Bentham, you see, had been so scared by fairy tales as a child that he required a roommate for the rest of his life, someone who would spend the night in his bedroom and soothe him if he had nightmares. (This might explain why Bentham never married.)

In part due to this child-rearing experiment, young John became a phenomenal prodigy. At age three, he was reading Greek. At age six, he wrote a 1,500-word history of Rome.[12]

As part of the plan for raising the children, James Mill and Bentham withheld their utilitarian teachings from John until he had returned from his teenage travels in France. They then presented him with a copy of Bentham's book, in French of course, and John was transformed, writing later in his autobiography that the theory gave him a quasi-religious purpose in life.[13]

But over time, Mill's infatuation with Bentham's hedonistic theory would wane, and he'd question the shallow pleasures and pains that Bentham promoted. Mill's questions took hold over him in his early twenties, when he suffered from an episode of depression. He recovered from this episode through a series of insights that would inform his own theory of utilitarianism. Mill came to believe, around this time, that happiness is not found by seeking ordinary pleasure but, instead, by striving for loftier goals. He began to open himself up to emotional pursuits that he had been protected from as a child, things that Bentham and his father considered to be dangerous. Things like poetry and the arts. Having been forced to live a life of the mind, he was now experiencing a broader range of passions, all of which would inform his new views on what humans ought to strive for.

In short, Mill rethought utilitarianism and decided that Bentham, while correct in promoting the importance of utility in guiding moral and political behavior, was wrong in thinking that utility is simply a function of pleasure and pain, such that, in Bentham's words, "The quantity of pleasure being equal, pushpin [a child's game] is as good as poetry."[14]

As good as poetry, Mill asked? Not on your life!

Happy Pigs

Like Bentham, Mill thought the goal of moral and political action should be to maximize people's happiness. But happiness of the pushpin variety, he felt, was too lowly to qualify as the goal, or end, of all human strivings. Instead: "some *kinds* of pleasure are more desirable and more valuable than others [Mill's italics]."[15] He believed that policies and moral guidelines should aim to promote *higher* pleasures over lower ones, famously writing that "it is better to be a human being dissatisfied than a pig satisfied."

Mill never rejected utilitarianism but, rather, tried to make it compatible with a broader view of human nature than the lowly pleasure-seeking beasts who dominated Bentham's worldview. Mill's broader understanding of human nature may reflect his broader range of experiences. Mill famously described Bentham as espousing "the empiricism of one who has had little experience."

According to Mill, we can't judge a policy the way Bentham (or Kahneman) would have us do, by tabulating whether the policy raises or lowers people's average moods. Instead, when deciding on policies, we need to think about other goals.

Mill's ideas are especially relevant today, now that behavioral science has helped us better understand what kind of circumstances influence people's moment-to-moment moods. Emotions and moods (which are distinct concepts to experts in the field, but which I'll lump together here) aren't simply a function of people's circumstances. People don't feel the way they do simply because of what they are experiencing right now. Instead, people typically feel one way or another because of how their circumstances have recently changed. Moods alert people to changes in their environment, so they can address those changes. But when people's circumstances remain stable, their emotional response to those circumstances frequently diminishes over time. This is a phenomenon called *emotional adaptation* (which I wrote about in *You're Stronger Than You Think*).[16] When a man experiences a disabling injury following a motor vehicle accident, for example, he's likely to be miserable for a while. However, if he's like most people, his emotions will rebound over time, and he will regain a good portion of his earlier happiness.

But if people are able to achieve moment-to-moment happiness in the face of what objectively are horrible circumstances, what does that say for Bentham's world?

Nobel laureate Amartya Sen recognized this problem many years ago. Sen, who won a Nobel Prize in economics, is famous for promoting economic initiatives that reduce poverty.[17] One of the things he's recognized about poverty is that it often doesn't make people nearly as miserable as one would think it *ought* to. People adapt to circumstances, even oppressive circumstances, often because they've never known anything better. In philosophy this is referred to as the "happy slave" problem.[18] If a person has been a slave since birth and has known no other kind of life, should we accept his slavery on the basis of the knowledge that he is happy with his lot in life? Or is there something inherently wrong about slavery that we would want to address?

From what I've said so far, it would appear as if Sen is presenting a libertarian critique of Kahneman and Bentham's reliance on the idea of happiness: poor people and slaves—despite any happiness they feel—are being harmed because their liberties are restricted; so even if they are happy, we ought to do something about making them free. No doubt, Sen believes that freedom is important in its own right, regardless of whether it makes people happy. But Sen is not a strict libertarian. Freedom is only *one* of the things he thinks ought to guide policy decisions. He also thinks we need to promote what he calls "capabilities"; we need to maximize what people are capable of doing.[19]

If people are poor, their ability to make life choices is restricted because they are trapped in poverty. In addition, if people are unhealthy, their opportunities are automatically restricted. A person who can't walk or who can't see is unable to perform certain jobs because of these disabilities. If people are poorly educated, they also lose many capabilities, and the opportunities they have in their lives will be restricted. Unlike libertarians, then, Sen is an aggressive advocate for government intervention in health care and education, and in redistributing wealth to try to equalize opportunities across populations.

No Simple Answers

Bentham thought he had found a simple answer for figuring out how to make policy decisions: people want to be happy, so we should make policy decisions that maximize their happiness. Kahneman tried to resurrect Bentham's idea, having convinced himself that the science of happiness had advanced enough that we could finally achieve Bentham's goals. We could bring economics back to where it began, he thought, back to a place it had only abandoned because the science hadn't yet been up to the task.

But Kahneman's ideas aren't up to the task either. He's right to say that we need to understand more about what makes people happy and unhappy. He is totally correct in contending that people often make bad decisions, because they don't know what will make them happy or unhappy. And he's done the world a huge service by reminding people that we ought to care about people's happiness. But he's wrong to have ignored the things people care about in life beyond moment-to-moment mood.

What, then, should be the goal, the end, of our policies? There are no simple answers to this question. Libertarians think that freedom itself is all we need to maximize. But this book has already shown that when given complete freedom, people often make decisions that they live to regret: they make decisions that interfere with happiness, even when happiness has been their goal; and they make decisions that reduce their income, even when income maximization was precisely what they were trying to achieve.

Wise politicians have long recognized the complexity of determining what goals should guide our policies. Perhaps nowhere was this put more eloquently than at the University of Kansas in 1968, in a speech by Robert Kennedy. Kennedy points out the folly of capturing national well-being with a single measure like the GNP:

Too much and for too long, we seemed to have surrendered personal excellence and community values in the mere accumulation of material things. Our Gross National Product, now, is over $800 billion dollars a year, but that Gross National Product—if we judge the United States of America by that—that Gross National Product counts air pollution and cigarette advertising, and ambulances to clear our highways of carnage. It counts special locks for our doors and the jails for the people who break them. It counts the destruction of the redwood and the loss of our natural wonder in chaotic sprawl . . . And the television programs which glorify violence in order to sell toys to our children. Yet the Gross National Product does not allow for the health of our children, the quality of their education or the joy of their play. It does not include the beauty of our poetry or the strength of our marriages, the intelligence of our public debate or the integrity of our public officials. It measures neither our wit nor our courage nor our devotion to our country, it measures everything in short, except that which makes life worthwhile.[20]

As Kennedy's words make clear, when we make policy decisions, we need to set a balance between a number of competing objectives. Freedom is a good thing. Happiness is a wonderful thing, too. And being able to have good health and a decent education is likewise important. Indeed, often these things go together. People who are given more freedom are often happier than those with less freedom.[21] People with good educations are often healthier and happier and wealthier than people without good educations. But these wonderful things don't always run together. If people are free to smoke and choose to do so, they will suffer from poor health, they will have shorter life spans, and they'll very probably regret having smoked. When advertisers are free to promote their goods to children, they fuel an obesity epidemic that is in no one's best interest.

This balancing of freedom and well-being will no doubt strike some people as a call to cede political authority to philosopher kings. There is no agreed-on way, after all, of establishing the proper balance. We can't make logical trade-offs between, say, three points of freedom and five points of well-being. There's no established method for choosing between moods and capabilities. Balancing such incommensurable goals is the purview of people like moral and political philosophers.

Paul Dolan, a British economist who has worked closely with Daniel Kahneman, contends that social scientists should get out of the business of moral and political philosophy and stick with scientifically measurable and comparable phenomena. Like Kahneman, he favors basing policies on well-being—on people's moment-to-moment experiences. Health, capabilities, employment . . . these things should only matter to policy makers if they measurably influence people's well-being. Only by keeping to clean, precise measures of well-being, Dolan contends, can we avoid the need for philosopher kings.[22]

The problem with this view, of course, is that it already embodies a particular moral and political philosophy. It asserts that the goal of policies should be to maximize people's moment-to-moment well-being. It thereby concludes that there's nothing wrong with a world populated by happy slaves. What's more, even if we accepted this philosophical view (for it *is* a philosophical view, not a scientific view, and certainly not an economic view), we would still have to figure out what we mean by moment-to-moment well-being. If such well-being is equated with mood (happiness, anger, contentedness, boredom, etc.), then we need to figure out how much weight to give to different emotions—should extreme anger be balanced out by extreme joy?[23]

We have no choice, in modern society, but to make the kinds of choices that even philosophers have not yet figured out how to make. When economists used to believe that freedom maximized well-being, the choice seemed easier. We didn't have to choose between separate goods but could achieve one good—well-being—by maximizing another good, namely, freedom.

Science cannot tell society what to maximize or how to trade off things like freedom and well-being. The best science can do is to help us recognize what it is we're choosing between.

Maximizing What We Measure

Even though economists like Paul Dolan would like to live in a world that doesn't require philosopher kings—in which all policies aim toward one simple goal—most economists have long been comfortable in a much more complicated world, requiring scientists like themselves to measure many incomparable things. Economists have traditionally measured GDP, in part according to the assumption that countries that maximize their wealth will also be improving their citizens' well-being. At the same time, economists have also developed measures of unemployment, recognizing that wealth and jobs do not always go hand in hand and that societies often care about both of these economic outcomes. Economists have also measured things like income distribution, recognizing that people care not only about how wealthy their country is, but also about how that wealth is distributed.

Policy makers have never, then, been content to base economic policies on a single measure, like GDP. Indeed, they haven't even restricted themselves to purely economic measures. They have also measured infant mortality, crime, air quality, and the like. These disparate measures leave policy makers with the impossible job of balancing these very different aspects of quality of life. Increasing wealth may come at the expense of the environment, for example, and policy makers need to figure out how to set this balance.

Behavioral economics, then, hasn't created the need for philosopher kings. Instead, it has made the need more apparent. By showing that freedom can reduce well-being, it has forced policy makers to think more clearly about the goals of their policies, and has even prompted some governments to invest resources to better assess people's emotional well-being.

Behavioral economics has made the complex job of policy making even more complex. But in the process, it has given us a whole new set of reasons to push back against those people—in academia, on cable news shows, in the blogosphere—who propose simple solutions, who think that well-being begins and ends with liberty.

CHAPTER THIRTEEN

Can Government Combat Obesity Without Becoming a "Nanny State"?

THE DECATUR, Georgia, sports bar *Mulligan's* offers its patrons a sandwich that I would have sworn existed only in the imaginary world of Homer Simpson: a hot dog, wrapped in a beef patty, deep fried in oil, slathered in melted cheese, topped with chili, a dash of onions, and, to top it off, a fried egg. Known as "the Hamdog," this particular meal, on its own, probably keeps four Georgia cardiologists gainfully employed.

David Harsanyi lovingly describes the Hamdog in the opening paragraphs of his libertarian manifesto, *Nanny State*. In the book, Harsanyi decries the "officious activists who would like to deny me the self-determination and pleasure of eating a Hamdog." He then goes on to describe the terrible things that happen when nanny states get carried away protecting the people under their charge, creating regulations designed to do "whatever they can to stop us from eating."[1]

In criticizing government regulations, libertarians like Harsanyi frequently draw on the metaphor of the nanny state, knowing that this rhetorical device will conjure images of overbearing, prudish people who, while perhaps well intentioned, can't seem to let children be children. Even worse, this particular nanny, the nanny state, treats adults like children. If a grown man wants to indulge in a Hamdog, why should the government intervene? If he wants to drive a motorcycle without a helmet or an SUV without a seat belt, shouldn't he, as an adult, be free to do as he pleases? When the government enacts laws to criminalize such behavior, Harsanyi contends that it is treating them like children.

Google the phrase *nanny state*, and you'll quickly find hundreds of antigovernment links. Grover Norquist will show up, naturally, as he has made a point of referring to the nanny state while promoting his book *Leave Us Alone*.[2] You'll also find other emotive phrases recurring across these sites. One of my favorites is a book titled *A Nation of Sheep*, in which the government isn't portrayed as treating people like children but, instead, as if they were mindless animals.[3]

You're probably wondering what the nanny state was doing to prevent Harsanyi from swallowing a Hamdog. Did the Georgia legislature outlaw the sandwich? Were Decatur police jailing overweight people? Were the feds denying Social Security and Medicare benefits to people with high cholesterol?

Harsanyi is worried that all these kinds of things might happen. After all, the government ultimately relies on coercion to enforce its laws. And governments do use such powers to protect citizens from each other. Crimes against person and property can lead to imprisonment and loss of some rights.

But this level of coercion is rarely used by governments to control behaviors that affect only the people engaging in the behaviors. If I vandalize your property, the government will punish me, maybe even imprison me. But if I destroy my own property in a fit of rage, the government usually leaves me alone.

What, then, does Harsanyi say that the nanny state is doing to influence our waistlines? The worst he can say is that the government is "scaremongering," even (gulp) threatening to tax food manufacturers. This may sound mild, but Harsanyi is concerned that the Twinkie fascists, as he calls them, are just warming up, "gaining momentum and influence at a startling pace."[4]

Political extremists of all persuasions are often paranoid about the slippery slope, worrying that any tiny concessions they make will lead to complete absolution of their position. Gun rights activists worry that if the government requires businesses to conduct criminal checks on customers before selling them guns, law-abiding citizens will soon not be able to purchase hunting rifles. Pro-choice activists worry that if a state imposes a waiting period for women and girls requesting abortions, all abortions will soon be illegal.

Flaming moderate that I am, I don't live in paranoia of the slippery slope. I know we can sensibly regulate gun sales and abortions without banning either activity. I recognize that there is no middle ground that will satisfy extremists. Good policy making rarely makes everyone happy. But I hope and believe that the government can help us tackle a problem like obesity without causing us to slide toward a cholesterol-free police state.

In this final chapter, then, I'd like to take a brief look at the ways governments can combat obesity, from the win-win alternatives promoted by the soft paternalists, to more intrusive alternatives (although nothing approaching a police state). Along this continuum of government alternatives, I won't pretend to know when we enter a nanny state. Or if you prefer to consider all government interventions to be nannying behavior, then I won't try to state when that nannying shifts from wise leadership to obtrusive bullying. My goal is not to tell you what the government should do, but instead to lay out what it can do, and hope that people who care about the health of the general public will push back against extremists who'd rather have a fat and free citizenry than one that has a hope of living healthier and happier lives.

Soft Paternalism and Rock-Hard Abs

In this book, I've laid out examples of unconscious and irrational forces that influence people's decisions, sometimes in ways that cause us to act against our own best interests. I have presented these examples to show a flaw underlying common justifications for libertarian policies.

Indeed, advocates of soft paternalism have shown that an understanding of people's irrational side can point us toward policies that improve people's well-being without threatening their liberty. If we believe, for example, that most people would be better off if they saved more money for retirement, then we can arrange for part of their income to go directly into a retirement account unless people choose to redirect it elsewhere.[5] Such a policy doesn't constrain people's freedom, even though by making such a deposit the default option, it increases the amount of their income that they put away for a later use. Similarly, soft paternalists have shown us that mandating better information about financial transactions, such as adjustable rate mortgages and rent-to-own deals, could help people make wiser decisions.[6]

But what does soft paternalism tell governments to do about the obesity epidemic? Two of the new paternalists, Dick Thaler and Cass Sunstein, thought a great deal about obesity, even illustrating their method of combining libertarianism and paternalism with an imaginary cafeteria. They ask readers to contemplate a cafeteria owner who must decide in what order to lay out food along the cafeteria line. As it turns out, the psychology of cafeteria behavior results in people filling their trays disproportionately with the food they encounter early in the line. That means that if this cafeteria owner places desserts early in the food line, many people will fill their trays with such desserts before reaching healthier fare. If this cafeteria owner were motivated to serve her customers' best interests, however, Thaler and Sunstein point out that she could rearrange the food, putting the desserts at the end of the line, so that people would be more inclined to place healthy food on their trays. In doing so, the cafeteria owner would be encouraging healthy eating behavior without diminishing her customers' freedom.

As this example points out, it is possible to reduce the consumption of unhealthy desserts without denying people the right to eat those same foods. But unfortunately, this example doesn't point toward easy policy recommendations. The government is unlikely to mandate the location of apple pies or Hamdogs in cafeteria lines.

Indeed, the obesity epidemic is a very difficult test case for soft paternalists. The government can try to influence the obesity epidemic. But it is unlikely that a simple nudge will do the job. That means that when we think about how to reduce obesity, we probably won't face the kind of win-win situation we see with retirement planning. Instead, we need to consider a broader range of policy options and then implement (and evaluate) those policies that appear to set the proper balance between liberty and well-being.

And what are our policy options? Let's next consider a policy alternative that Harsanyi warned us about in the opening paragraphs of his book. Let's talk about taxes.

Taxes and Financial Incentives

To many libertarians, the word *taxes* is even more evocative than *nanny state* in eliciting the horrors of heavy-handed government. Republicans in the United States often speak as if no tax can be good tax, and, indeed, have won a fair number of elections by labeling their opponents as tax-and-spend liberals, with an emphasis on the *tax*ing part. But of course, the government needs to levy *some* taxes. So the only real questions are how much tax revenue the government should collect and from what sources.

Putting aside the first question, of how much money the government needs, we should think about how best to use the tax code to promote important social goals. Republicans, for example, are comfortable using the tax code to influence people's decisions to marry and have children. Why not use the tax code to promote healthy eating behavior?

In fact, the tax code is often a very rational way of influencing people's behaviors without unduly restricting their liberties. For example, the government could offer tax rebates to people with healthy body weights, much the way health insurers offer rebates to people who don't smoke. Along those same lines, it could subsidize healthy foods, or tax unhealthy ones, in order to encourage people to eat more wisely. Or the government could subsidize the cost of fitness centers, and of transportation to and from such centers, for low-income people whose neighborhoods aren't suitable for regular exercise.

Financial incentives like these, when not too extreme, influence people's behavior without restricting their options. If a tax were to make, say, the Hamdog 10 percent more expensive, people would still be free to enjoy such, um, delicacies if they wanted to. They would be less likely to do so, of course. Some people, faced with the higher price, would shift to a cheaper alternative—maybe they'd hold the fried egg. Others would eat the Hamdog but come to Mulligan's a bit less frequently because of its increased cost.

Financial incentives are a promising way of combating obesity because they treat people like rational adults at the same time that they recognize that people aren't always rational. Such incentives acknowledge people's rationality by giving them freedom and by understanding that, as economists have shown us over the years, prices *do* influence people's demands for goods and services. But policies that change the cost of healthy versus unhealthy foods also recognize that people aren't completely rational. Such policies recognize the irrational forces that feed the obesity epidemic—the less-than-optimal decisions that all of us make in our lives and the limits all of us experience in our self-control.

Market extremists, in overemphasizing the rational side of human nature, often don't acknowledge this flip side. In describing his own experience with the Hamdog, for example, Harsanyi writes that he could only stuff half of it into his stomach before filling up: "As a human being, it seems I possess a certain level of self-control. I gather that if I, a dreadfully weak and easily seduced man, can control myself, most Americans can do even better. Most can still find pleasure in eating and reward and self-control. Two concepts that nannies, it seems, can't wrap their minds around."[7]

But as anyone who has followed data on the obesity epidemic should realize, people can have self-control without having *enough* self-control. They can be rational without being perfectly rational. Policies that raise the costs of unhealthy foods are promising because they are compatible with both the rational and the irrational sides of human nature. They play to both our strengths and our weaknesses. Such policies recognize that if people were completely rational, we wouldn't need to be dissuaded from eating fatty food or sugary snacks through taxes. They also recognize that if we were completely irrational, such financial incentives wouldn't have any effect on our behavior.

This financial approach has a strong and relatively successful precedent in cigarette taxes. As any economist will tell you, when cigarette prices rise, cigarette use declines.[8] Careful analyses have shown that such declines aren't equivalent across all groups of people. The "elasticity" of cigarette consumption—the rate at which use changes with a rise in price—varies across people. Those who are strongly addicted to tobacco may not change their use much at all with a modest change in price.[9] Some will inhale their cigarettes more deeply and thereby get more nicotine out of each cigarette. Therefore, cigarette taxes will undoubtedly cost many heavy smokers a lot of money because they won't be able to muster the self-control to reduce their habit. On the other hand, cigarette taxes dissuade many young people from becoming smokers, and reduce casual smokers' use enough that many won't hit the magic threshold at which they become addicted to nicotine.

Cigarette taxes are a form of government paternalism. Like a doting parent, the government is trying to protect people from their own worst instincts. Tens of thousands of young people have avoided tobacco addiction because of such taxes. Most don't realize what a favor their government has performed for them.

Early government efforts are under way, now, to change financial incentives in a way that will improve people's eating habits. New York City, for example, recently announced that it was hoping to pass "green cart legislation" to increase the number of food carts offering fresh fruits and vegetables to residents of low-income neighborhoods.[10]

Keen observers of U.S. politics will recognize the strangeness of this proposal, given that the United States is, in effect, subsidizing unhealthy foods right now through its farm bill, a piece of legislation that lowers the price of sweeteners like sugar and high-fructose corn syrup. Michael Pollan has pushed to refer to such legislation as a "food bill" rather than a farm bill, to emphasize how such subsidies are influencing people's eating habits. Pollan hopes that greater awareness that the food bill is contributing to the obesity epidemic will cut into popular support of the bill, support that arises currently out of a nostalgic desire to help struggling farmers.[11]

I share Pollan's desire to phase out harmful farm subsidies. But the political stars are not yet aligned to fulfill our desires. When George W. Bush wisely vetoed the farm bill in 2008, his veto was overturned by a congress unwilling to fight farm interests.[12]

Can Financial Incentives Cure Obesity?

I have little doubt that a combination of snack taxes, farm bill phaseouts, and other financial incentives could reduce obesity rates in the United States. But I'm also doubtful that these financial interventions, on their own, would have a major impact on people's body weights, because too many powerful psychological forces are stacked up in favor of our increasing abdominal girth. A mere tweaking of vegetable prices, relative to fat and sugar, is not going to turn people into health food aficionados.

Consider an experiment that Leonard Epstein and his colleagues conducted among a group of middle schoolers. In the experiment, Epstein gave the kids some money and laid out a mixture of their favorite junk foods and their favorite healthy snacks. He then let them purchase whichever foods they desired. Across groups of students, however, he varied the amount of money they were allowed to spend, and also varied the relative price of the junk foods and healthy snacks. Sometimes the kids had very little money and faced a choice between expensive carrots and cheap chocolate chip cookies. In these circumstances, the kids gobbled up the cookies. But what happened when Epstein made the junk food items more expensive? Most of the time, the kids simply stuck with the junk foods, settling for a small number of cookies (three instead of, say, five) rather than substituting apple slices or carrot sticks for the increasingly expensive Chips Ahoy.[13]

Epstein's study suggests that the elasticity of demand for foods like carrots is pretty flat when carrots must compete with processed fare. This type of research has significant implications for how best to influence kids' eating habits at schools. A quasi-libertarian approach, for example, would lower the price of carrots and apple slices in vending machines in order to entice kids to buy these foods. If Epstein's study held true, however, this policy wouldn't have much effect. A more burdensome alternative would be to raise the price of snack foods. This would reduce vending machine purchases of such foods. But if the goal is to encourage kids to eat healthy foods, we might need to ban snack foods from school vending machines altogether.

Epstein's kids are not alone in spending their cash on junk food rather than veggies. When the government provides low-income families with food stamps, for example, most families don't use the extra cash to pay for otherwise unaffordable Brussels sprouts.

Instead, they purchase even *more* junk food. The government could, theoretically, change the finances of the food industry enough to halt the obesity epidemic. But these actions would need to be draconian, and they'd undoubtedly lead to the end of many political careers (and to the beginning of many black-marketing opportunities). Financial incentives, alone, won't stop the spread of obesity. But careful use of tax policy, and other financial levies, should be part of our solution to this epidemic.

Restaurant Regulation

By most estimates, a large portion of the obesity epidemic can be attributed to people's increased tendency to buy food that is prepared outside of the home.[14] In the United States, for example, some economists estimate that the majority of calories are now consumed outside the home.[15] By regulating restaurants and food carts, the government could potentially make a serious dent in the size of people's waistlines.

Consider New York City's effort in recent years to ban trans fats from city restaurants.[16] The world of fats is very confusing, with saturated, monounsaturated, and polyunsaturated fats having been prominently displayed on U.S. food labels for years now. Trans fats have been added to this list of polysyllabic varieties only recently, making us consumers even more confused than we used to be. But trans fats deserve their own place on the food label because they are uniquely harmful foods. Most trans fats are not naturally occurring, but are created by food scientists, who place extra hydrogen atoms into vegetable oils so that the oils will remain solid at room temperature. This solidity has made trans fats a popular ingredient in many baked goods. If you've eaten a doughnut in the last couple of years, you've ingested an unhealthy dose of trans fats.

Unfortunately, trans fats exhibit another unusual ability: they are unusually good at clogging people's coronary arteries and leading to heart attacks.[17] They are even worse for people's health than the saturated fats we have been taught to avoid.

Concerned about the health effects of trans fats, the New York City Department of Health approached restaurants and asked proprietors whether they would voluntarily reduce the use of trans fats in their foods. The Health Department even educated restaurants about alternative oils.[18] Unfortunately, the voluntary program was a complete failure.[19] So finally, the city decided to ban trans fats from its restaurants.

The Health Department was confronting what it saw as a market failure. New Yorkers eating out at restaurants had no knowledge of the trans fat content of the meals they were ordering. And it would have been very difficult for restaurants to provide such information, with menus changing so rapidly as they do in many restaurants. Therefore, the Health Department decided that the easiest approach was to simply impose a ban on trans fats in city restaurants. This ban imposes a one-time cost on restaurants. The restaurants will have to rejigger their recipes to take advantage of alternative healthier oils. But having studied the alternatives carefully, the Health Department was convinced that this rejiggering would be relatively simple and that, with the number of calories being consumed each day in New York City restaurants, it could prevent a substantial number of heart attacks, a benefit of its policy that it felt outweighed the costs of the rejiggering.

Mandating Information

Should New York City have considered a less coercive way of reducing trans fat consumption? Should it, instead, have developed regulations that would compel the food industry to provide consumers with consistent and explicit information about the products they buy? Is an informational approach the best way of combating obesity without unduly restricting liberties?

Information regulations put some libertarians in an awkward position. Opposed by nature to government bureaucracy, some libertarians instinctively abhor any regulations that would require the makers of consumer goods to give information to consumers, arguing that governments should not force McDonald's to display how many calories are in a Big Mac, or require manufacturers to tell consumers how many grams of trans fat there are in a frozen dinner. They object to such regulations on the grounds that they restrict market liberty and thrust huge expenses on food manufacturers.

But on the other hand, libertarian philosophy is based in large part on the moral value of letting people make informed choices about their lives. And how can people make such choices if companies aren't willing to give them information about their products? Indeed, one could argue that the FDA food label regulations developed in the late '80s have made the food market more like a true free market, because they have armed consumers with information that they can use to make purchasing choices.[20]

Wouldn't it be nice, when buying refrigerators, automobiles, and other such products, to know the true cost of using them? Wouldn't it be nice to know the true costs of payday loans and credit card fees? If regulations forced companies to give this information to people, consumers might avoid short-term spending sprees that reduce their long-term financial and emotional well-being. If mortgage companies had been under stricter regulations, to inform people about the potential financial consequences of adjustable rate mortgages, perhaps the housing crisis that hit the United States in 2007 would not have been so severe.

Along these lines, New York City has proposed a new policy that would require chain restaurants to prominently display calorie information on their menus and menu boards.[21] This regulation, opposed strongly by chain restaurants, aims to help consumers decide how much food they really want to consume.

Of course, giving people information will only improve the world if the information leads people to make better decisions.

Free markets fail if consumers don't have easy access to important information relevant to their purchasing decisions. But markets also fail if people don't make rational use of the information they're given. And behavioral economics has taught us that we can't count on people to be rational all the time.

Calorie information, for example, could easily backfire. For starters, people have little knowledge of how many calories are "right" for them to eat. And they don't always understand the information on the FDA food label. Consequently, the information may not help them make better decisions.[22]

In addition, restaurants may find ways to alter people's perceptions about how many calories are appropriate in any given meal. I could imagine a burger chain adding a Hamdog to its menus with the primary purpose being to make the rest of its burgers look healthier by comparison. In my own research, I have discovered that I can change the way a given choice feels to people by altering the information I give them about *other* choices.[23] Indeed, people often have difficulty evaluating choices in isolation—does a 300-calorie burger sound healthy to you?[24] It would if I compared it with a 500-calorie burger, but not if I showed you a 200-calorie alternative. When people don't know how to evaluate information, they become more easily manipulated.

Calorie counts also may fail to improve people's eating habits because such dry statistics won't be able to compete with glossy pictures of juicy burgers. In fact, I am sure that for a subset of the population, high calorie counts will look more manly or like a better bargain. No surprise to me, therefore, that early efforts to control appetites by publishing nutritional information have failed.[25]

The Power of Persuasion

Given that information alone may not suffice to encourage better eating habits, policy makers should consider yet another approach to combat obesity—an approach that structures people's choices in ways that will lead them to make better choices, not through incentives or coercion, but through emotional or even unconscious psychological forces. Such an approach would go beyond boring statistical displays of calorie information or tedious data about carbohydrate and fat calories, to labeling food with evocative images that create aversion to foods that aren't healthy. Think about how effective the poison label has been in keeping people from ingesting poisonous materials. The word *poison*, in large type, would never have had as much impact as that skull and crossbones picture. If we want to discourage Burger King customers from ordering Whoppers, and encourage them to eat the healthier items on the menu, we need to appeal not only to their intellect, but also to their emotions.

The government can play the role of persuader rather than rely only on coercion. In doing so, it should take advantage of what scientists have learned about human nature. We know that a dry appeal to the rational risks of smoking won't stop most kids from lighting up. Far better an uninformative ad campaign that plays on kids' emotions, like the Truth campaign, which has worked by appealing to teenagers' suspicions that adults at tobacco companies are trying to manipulate them. If experts are convinced about what's in people's best interests, then they should find persuasive ways to convince people to behave accordingly.

And while the government considers more persuasive ways of encouraging healthy eating habits, it should consider reducing the persuasive powers of those people who are currently trying to sell consumers these same unhealthy products, especially those companies directing their advertisements at our children. Currently, the United States ranks number one among developed countries both in the rate of obesity and in the proportion of its GDP spent on advertising.[26] I don't think this is completely coincidental. The United States has fewer food industry regulations than most developed countries, too, and such regulations have been shown to statistically predict the rate of obesity in any given country.[27] Most European governments, in fact, regulate advertisements more aggressively than the United States. Similarly, the United States was a leader in allowing pharmaceutical companies to advertise directly to consumers. The permissiveness of the U.S. government toward advertisers no doubt reflects its more promarket orientation.

As I discussed in chapter 11, advertisements often benefit consumers by making them aware of new products and benefit entrepreneurs by giving them more hope for finding financial rewards when they bring innovative products to market. But when the products being advertised are harmful, the government should consider appropriate restrictions. The preponderance of scientific evidence now points to direct causal relationships between calorie-dense food and obesity. Cheetos and Coke are not improving the health of the general populace. The government has a right to step in and see whether it can change the situation.

As with the farm bill, I recognize that powerful interests would align themselves to fight any further regulations of food advertising. No doubt, any such regulation would face legal and practical hurdles too. But watch closely, if this debate picks up steam, for the arguments that these interest groups use to oppose such regulations. Keep an eye out for "informed consumer" language and for talk of market efficiency. After reading this book, you should be more able to pick apart these arguments. Indeed, one of my major goals in writing this book is to help the general public take on those people who think the government's role in our lives should be severely diminished. If we know the flaws in the informed consumer view of the world, in the idea that the market will solve all our problems, we will be better able to find common ground among consumers who want to curb this awful epidemic of obesity.

Unavoidable Influence

It is rarely comforting to learn that you've been manipulated. Teenagers who've been persuaded, because of the Truth campaign, to shun cigarettes may not be happy to learn that the public service campaign has brilliantly played on their adolescent psyche. So when I mention the possibility of developing government educational programs that go beyond merely informing people to persuading them, I understand that many readers will be disturbed.

But why are we often more bothered by government programs that try to influence our behavior than we are by other groups that try to influence our behavior?

For-profit food companies, after all, take advantage of both our rational and our irrational impulses to sell us their products. They inundate us, and our children, with advertisements that they have designed with the help of neuroscientists.[28] The marketplace has mastered the ability to deliver familiar, affordable energy-dense food to us, but we consumers haven't mastered the ability to restrain our consumption. And food manufacturers don't have much incentive to help us develop such restraint. They make money selling us food. Their ads and their packaging are designed to get us to buy their products. Why should we be bothered solely by government influence of our lives, when our behaviors are being influenced by so many other people, people we didn't elect and who we can't throw out of office?

We are harming ourselves by eating too much, and most of us can't help ourselves. And we shouldn't expect the market to develop good solutions anytime soon. The obesity epidemic is a result of market failure—the free market has harmed us. So we need to explore ways to modify markets, to reduce the harms they bring on us.

Given the dire consequences of obesity, we should explore ways that our government can combat the epidemic. As I've pointed out, we shouldn't expect simple solutions to this problem. In fact, if we want to combat obesity, we will ultimately be forced to make some difficult decisions about whether to restrict some valuable liberties to achieve important goals. My hope is that armed with a better understanding of the unconscious and irrational forces that have contributed to the epidemic, we as a society will be more willing to consider some of these alternatives, and test them to see whether they work and whether they achieve our goals at an acceptable price.

Preventive Medicine

I've discussed a few of the ways that we, as a society, can combat obesity. Policy makers face many other alternatives. But let me emphasize one more factor we should consider when weighing our policy alternatives: we need to remind ourselves that once people become obese, their evolutionarily inherited biology conspires against their efforts to lose weight. If we truly want to combat obesity, therefore, our best chance is to focus on preventing more people from becoming obese. We need the kind of government programs that emphasize the parental part of paternalism. Our government, elected by its citizens, should work to develop the kind of cultural environment that promotes healthy eating and exercise habits in our children and in young adult citizens.

Our goal as a society should be to create environments where people don't get obese in the first place. We should work to create neighborhoods and park systems that make it easy for people to get outside and walk or play. We should encourage employers to create opportunities for employees to exercise during working hours. And we should exert most of our efforts on our children—to find ways to prevent the next generation from supersizing itself.

In targeting our efforts at children, we need to assess whether changes in school lunch programs and gym classes help our kids develop healthier habits. No simple jiggering of the school lunch menu will take care of childhood obesity.[29] But if I were czar, I'd pour funding into research on how we can use the schools to develop healthy habits among children and their parents. And if we find successful ways to do so, I'd set up strong incentives for local school programs to implement these techniques.

It is cultural change that I'm after. We need to become a culture that doesn't sit back and watch our kids gorge themselves on chips and videogames, allowing a generation of people to race toward diabetes and cardiovascular disease.

Culture plays an important role in the obesity epidemic, a point driven home by Paul Rozin and colleagues when they studied eating habits in France and the United States. Rozin's team started by calculating the calories contained in comparable meals in the two countries and found that, for example, Big Macs in the United States were substantially larger than those in France.[30] People in the United States like larger meals than do typical French consumers. No great surprise there.

But the cultural gap between the United States and France *was* surprising in another way. Because Rozin's team ensconced itself in restaurants across the two countries and observed not only what people ate, but also how long it took them to eat it. They found out that people in France, despite eating smaller meals, took longer to finish those same meals.[31] The current culture of French dining, even when eating Le Big Mac, is healthier than the corresponding dining culture in the United States.

We can't regulate how long it takes for people to eat their meals, of course. But Rozin's study reveals the important role culture plays in people's health behaviors. If we can nurture the right kind of culture, we will eat more healthfully without losing any pleasure from our meals.

One place to influence culture is in our schools. We can help establish good habits in our children in the hope that these habits will seep over into the nonschool part of their lives. The key to promoting healthy culture is to help our children develop good habits of self-control.

Social psychologists who study self-control have described it as "one of the most precious endowments of the human self," pointing out that problems like depression, aggression, teenage pregnancy, obesity, gambling debts and poor school performance are a result of poor self-control.[32] If we really want to help our kids, we'll help them develop their powers of self-control. This goal is potentially achievable, because self-control is an acquirable skill, a habit that can be taught, an emotional muscle that can be strengthened.[33]

Social scientists have learned that self-control can increase with practice. Then shouldn't our schools make greater efforts to help children develop self-control? Our schools should build character. They should help kids develop successful habits. If we focus solely on math and reading scores, we will have overlooked the role our schools could have played in developing people's self-control. If, instead, we focus on helping kids develop self-control, their math and reading scores should fall in line. Self-control is much more valuable to most adults than algebra and is a skill that, if measured and mastered, will increase the chance that our kids will, yes, master algebra.

If we really want to avoid leaving any of our children behind, we should generously fund education research and find ways to create schools and preschools that build children's self-control. We should think about developing early and valid measures of self-control that can be used to judge how much our kids improve their self-control from the beginning to the end of the school year. Given the role that lack of self-control plays in so many social problems today, self-control should be near the top of our educational agenda. We should be talking more, as a society, about how to build character in our kids.

When I think about the social importance of self-control, I'm tempted to counter Kahneman's call of "Back to Bentham" with an admittedly less catchy call of my own: Return to Aristotle. Jeremy

Bentham believed that the goal of social policy should be to maximize people's happiness. Aristotle had earlier espoused that same goal but had held a very different notion of happiness than Bentham. Aristotle identified several types of happiness, with the pain and pleasure that Bentham would champion being but one example of happiness. Instead, Aristotle aimed for a much deeper kind of happiness. He believed humans should strive for virtue and that virtuous actions should become habits. People should practice temperance and honesty; they should build their own character: "The virtues we get by first exercising them, as also happens in the case of the arts as well. For the things we have to learn before we can do them, we learn by doing them, e.g. men become builders by building and lyre players by playing the lyre; so too we become just by doing just acts, temperate by doing temperate acts, brave by doing brave acts."[34] Aristotle viewed one of the major functions of society as being to create an environment that develops virtuous actions in its citizens. We could do worse than to follow his advice.

Final Thoughts

Would it be a terrible blow to our liberty to build and maintain the kind of recreational facilities that my patients could use to keep physically active? Are we so fixated on cutting taxes that we cannot imagine building the kind of public transport system that would make it easier for senior citizens to head out to the mall for long walks during Michigan winters?

The free market, on its own, won't solve the challenges we face. Indeed, the free market *contributes* to many of the problems I've identified in this book. I'm deeply disturbed that political debates about the issues I discuss in this book have too often been hijacked by free market extremists who squeal "Nanny state!" whenever people propose setting any limits on people's freedom.

If we care about people's well-being, we should pay attention to how people behave, and take measures to regulate markets in ways that promote people's health, happiness, and social functioning. If a gentle nudge will suffice to address a given problem, we'll have sacrificed very little liberty en route to a better society.

If the situation requires more than a nudge, then let's test some more aggressive policies and see whether they work. My approach can be summed up as this: experiment frequently, evaluate rigorously, and revise accordingly. Start out locally or on a small scale, and if a particular policy works, expand it appropriately.

When people fail—fail to eat right, exercise, or stay away from cigarettes; fail to save for their futures or invest time to develop good habits—we should at least be able to go to bed at night knowing that we didn't promote free market policies that doomed them to fail.

People deserve a large amount of freedom. But they also deserve to live well. And when freedom and well-being collide, we should be open minded enough to recognize that carefully calibrated restrictions on our freedom are a small price to pay for a healthier, happier populace.

NOTES

CHAPTER ONE

1. National Center for Health Statistics, *Health, United States, 2006 with Chartbook on Trends in the Health of Americans* (Department of Health and Human Services, 2006).

2. Terumo Europe NV, "Company Profile," http://www.terumo-europe.com/terumo_about.html.

3. A. Smith, *An Inquiry into the Nature and Causes of the Wealth of Nations* (Chicago: University of Chicago Press, 1977).

4. J. Rae, *Life of Adam Smith* (New York: Sentry Press, 1895).

5. R. L. Heilbroner, *The Worldly Philosophers: The Lives, Times, and Ideas of the Great Economic Thinkers* (New York: Simon & Schuster, 1965).

6. J. Buchan, *The Authentic Adam Smith: His Life and Ideas* (New York: W. W. Norton, 2006).

7. N. Davies, *Europe: A History* (Oxford: Oxford University Press, 1996).

8. A. Smith, *The Wealth of Nations* (New York: Penguin Books, 1970).

9. J. Niehans, *A History of Economic Theory: Classic Contributions, 1720–1980* (Baltimore: Johns Hopkins University Press, 1990).

10. M. Friedman, *Capitalism and Freedom* (Chicago: University of Chicago Press, 1962); and F. Hayek, *The Road to Serfdom* (Chicago: University of Chicago Press, 1944).

11. C. Wheelan, *Naked Economics: Undressing the Dismal Science* (New York: W. W. Norton, 2003).

12. E. Schlosser, *Fast Food Nation: The Dark Side of the All-American Meal* (New York: Houghton Mifflin, 2001).

13. D. M. Cutler, E. L. Glaeser, and J. M. Shapiro, "Why Have Americans Become More Obese?" (working paper 9446, National Bureau of Economic Research [NBER], Cambridge, MA, 2003).

14. S. J. Olshansky et al., "A Potential Decline in Life Expectancy in the United States in the 21st Century," *New England Journal of Medicine* 352, no. 11 (2005): 1138–1145.

15. H. H. Maes, M. C. Neale, and L. J. Eaves, "Genetic and Environmental Factors in Relative Body Weight and Human Adiposity," *Behavioral Genetics* 27, no. 4 (1997): 325–351.

16. E. Schlosser, *Fast Food Nation: The Dark Side of the All-American Meal* (New York: Harper Perennial, 2002).

17. Smith, *The Wealth of Nations.*

CHAPTER TWO

1. P. Samuelson and W. Nordhaus, *Economics* (New York: McGraw-Hill, 2004).

2. T. G. Smith, "Reconciling Psychology with Economics: Obesity, Behavioral Biology, and Rational Overeating" (working paper 2006-4, Washington State University School of Economic Sciences, Pullman, WA, 2006).

3. R. E. Lucas Jr., *Models of Business Cycles* (New York: Blackwell Publishers, 1987).

4. G. S. Becker and K. M. Murphy, "A Theory of Rational Addiction," *Journal of Political Economy* 96, no. 4 (1988): 675–700.

5. J. Bentham, *Selected Writings on Utilitarianism* (Ware, UK: Wordsworth Editions, 2001).

6. G. J. Stigler, "The Development of Utility Theory I," *Journal of Political Economy* 58 (1950): 307–327.

7. A. Smith, *The Wealth of Nations* (New York: Penguin Books, 1970).

8. R. D. Collison Black, "Utility," in *The New Palgrave: Utility and Probability*, eds. J. Eatwell, M. Milgate, and P. Newman (New York: W. W. Norton, 1990).

9. R. B. Ekelund Jr. and R. F. Hébert, *A History of Economic Theory and Method* (New York: McGraw-Hill, 1975).

10. Ibid.

11. W. S. Jevons, "A General Mathematical Theory of Political Economy," *Journal of the Royal Statistical Society* (1866): 282–287.

12. P. L. Bernstein, *Against the Gods: The Remarkable Story of Risk* (New York: John Wiley & Sons, 1996).

13. Jevons, "A General Mathematical Theory."

14. P. Newman, "Francis Ysidro Edgeworth," in *The New Palgrave: Utility and Probability*, eds. J. Eatwell, M. Milgate, and P. Newman (London: W. W. Norton, 1987).

15. A. Drewnowski and S. E. Specter, "Poverty and Obesity: The Role of Energy Density and Energy Costs," *American Journal of Clinical Nutrition* 79 (2004): 6–16.

16. C. A. Schoenborn, "Body Weight Status of Adults: United States, 1997–98," *Advance Data* 330 (2002): 1–15.

17. T. J. Philipson and R. A. Posner, "The Long-Run Growth in Obesity as a Function of Technological Change," *Perspectives in Biology and Medicine* 46, no. 3 (2003): S87–S107.

18. D. M. Cutler, E. L. Glaeser, and J. M. Shapiro, "Why Have Americans Become More Obese?" (working paper 9446, National Bureau of Economic Research [NBER], Cambridge, MA, 2003).

19. E. A. Finkelstein and L. Zuckerman, *The Fattening of America: How the Economy Makes Us Fat, If It Matters, and What to Do About It* (Hoboken, NJ: John Wiley & Sons, 2008).

20. Philipson and Posner, "The Long-Run Growth in Obesity."

21. F. Kuchler et al., "Obesity Policy and the Law of Unintended Consequences," *Amber Waves*, June 2005.

CHAPTER THREE

1. D. Kahneman, "Daniel Kahneman Autobiography," in *Les Prix Nobel: The Nobel Prizes 2002*, ed. T. Fraengsmyr (Stockholm: Nobel Foundation, 2003).

2. A. Tversky and D. Kahneman, "Judgment Under Uncertainty: Heuristics and Biases," *Science* 185 (1974): 1124–1131.

3. A. Tversky and D. Kahneman, "Availability: A Heuristic for Judging Frequency and Probability," *Cognitive Psychology* 5, no. 2 (September 1973): 207–232.

4. Ibid.

5. T. Gilovich, D. Griffin, and D. Kahneman, eds., *Heuristics and Biases: The Psychology of Intuitive Judgment* (Cambridge: Cambridge University Press, 2002).

6. D. Kahneman, P. Slovic, and A. Tversky, eds., *Judgment Under Uncertainty: Heuristics and Biases* (Cambridge: Cambridge University Press, 1982).

7. T. D. Wilson et al., "A New Look at Anchoring Effects: Basic Anchoring and Its Antecedents," *Journal of Experimental Psychology: General* 125, no. 4 (1996): 387–402.

8. A. Tversky and D. Kahneman, "Belief in the Law of Small Numbers," in *Judgment Under Uncertainty*, 23–31.

9. S. J. Gould, "The Streak of Streaks," *New York Review of Books*, August 18, 1988.

10. P. Slovic and A. Tversky, "Who Accepts Savage's Axiom?" *Behavioral Science* 10, no. 4 (1974): 368–373.

11. M. Allais, "The Foundations of a Positive Theory of Choice Involving Risk and a Criticism of the Postulates and Axioms of the American School," in *Expected Utility Hypotheses and the Allais Paradox: Contemporary Discussions and Rational Decisions Under Uncertainty with Allais' Rejoinder*, eds. M. Allais and O. Hagen (Dordrecht, Holland: Reidel, 1979).

12. L. Savage, *The Foundations of Statistics* (New York: Wiley, 1954).

13. D. A. Redelmeier, P. Rozin, and D. Kahneman, "Understanding Patients' Decisions: Cognitive and Emotional Perspectives," *Journal of the American Medical Association* 270, no. 1 (1993): 72–76.

14. Kahneman, "Daniel Kahneman Autobiography."

15. B. J. McNeil et al., "On the Elicitation of Preferences for Alternative Therapies," *New England Journal of Medicine* 306, no. 21 (1982): 1259–1262; and K. Armstrong et al., "Effect of Framing as Gain Versus Loss on Understanding and Hypothetical Treatment Choices: Survival and Mortality Curves," *Medical Decision Making* 22, no. 1 (2002): 76–83.

16. D. Kahneman and A. Tversky, "Prospect Theory: An Analysis of Decision Under Risk," *Econometrica* 47, no. 2 (1979): 263–291.

17. Gilovich, Griffin, and Kahneman, *Heuristics and Biases*.

18. D. Kahneman and A. Tversky, "On the Reality of Cognitive Illusions," *Psychological Review* 103, no. 3 (1996): 582–591.

19. H. von Helmholtz, *Popular Lectures on Scientific Subjects* (New York: Green, 1903).

CHAPTER FOUR

1. R. Thaler, *Quasi-Rational Economics* (New York: Russell Sage Foundation Publications, 1991).

2. Ibid.

3. D. Kahneman, J. L. Knetsch, and R. Thaler, "Experimental Tests of the Endowment Effect and the Coase Theorem, *Journal of Political Economy* 98, no. 6 (1990): 1325–1348.

4. E. Fitzsimons, "In the Eyes of a Sickly Baby Girl, My First Lessons in Motherhood," *New York Times*, May 13, 2007.

5. R. Thaler, "Mental Accounting and Consumer Choice," *Marketing Science* 4, no. 3 (1985): 199–214.

6. G. Loewenstein, "Anticipation and the Valuation of Delayed Outcomes," *Economic Journal* 97 (1987): 666–684.

7. G. Ku, A. D. Galinsky, and J. K. Murnighan, "Starting Low but Ending High: A Reversal of the Anchoring Effect in Auctions," *Journal of Personality and Social Psychology* 90, no. 6 (2006): 975–986.

8. M. A. Kamins, X. Dreze, and V. S. Folkes, "Effects of Seller-Supplied Prices on Buyers' Product Evaluations: Reference Prices in an Internet Auction Context," *Journal of Consumer Research* 30, no. 4 (2004): 622–628.

9. Ku, Galinsky, and Murnighan, "Starting Low but Ending High."

10. G. B. Northcraft and M. A. Neale, "Experts, Amateurs, and Real Estate: An Anchoring-and-Adjustment Perspective on Property Pricing Decisions," *Organizational Behavior and Human Decision Processes* 39 (1987): 84–97.

11. X. Gabaix and D. Laibson, "Shrouded Attributes, Consumer Myopia, and Information Suppression in Competitive Markets," *Quarterly Journal of Economics* 121, no. 2 (2006): 505–540.

CHAPTER FIVE

1. J. Quinlan, "Can the Chinese Consumer Save the World?" *Globalist*, November 2, 2007; and Eurostat, "Sector Accounts: Fourth Quarter of 2006: Household Saving Rate at 13.7% in the Euro Area and 11.0% in the EU27," Euro-Indicators news release, June 1, 2007.

2. Bureau of Economic Analysis, *Personal Income and Outlays: March 2006* (Washington, DC: U.S. Department of Commerce, 2006).

3. W. Samuelson and R. Zeckhauser, "Status Quo Bias in Decision Making," *Journal of Risk and Uncertainty* 1 (1988): 7–59.

4. S. D. Halpern, P. A. Ubel, and D. A. Asch, "Harnessing the Power of Default Options to Improve Healthcare," *New England Journal of Medicine* 357 (2007): 1340–1344.

5. C. R. Sunstein and R. Thaler, "Libertarian Paternalism Is Not an Oxymoron," *University of Chicago Law Review* 70 (2003): 1159–1202.

6. E. J. Johnson et al., "Framing, Probability Distortions, and Insurance Decisions," *Journal of Risk and Uncertainty* 7 (1993): 35–51.

7. P. A. Ubel et al., "Pennsylvania's Voluntary Benefits Program: Evaluating an Innovative Proposal for Increasing Organ Donation," *Health Affairs* 19, no. 5 (2000): 206–211.

8. E. J. Johnson and D. Goldstein, "Do Defaults Save Lives?" *Science* 302, no. 5649 (2003): 1338.

9. C. Camerer et al., "Regulation for Conservatives: Behavioral Economics and the Case for 'Asymmetric Paternalism,'" *University of Pennsylvania Law Review* 151, no. 3 (2003): 1211.

10. D. H. Novack et al., "Changes in Physicians' Attitudes Toward Telling the Cancer Patient," *Journal of the American Medical Association* 241, no. 9 (1979): 897–900.

11. P. A. Ubel, "'What Should I Do, Doc?' Some Psychologic Benefits of Physician Recommendations," *Archives of Internal Medicine* 162, no. 9 (2002): 977–980.

CHAPTER SIX

1. G. Kolata, *Rethinking Thin: The New Science of Weight Loss—and the Myths and Realities of Dieting* (New York: Farrar, Straus, and Giroux, 2007).

2. R. M. Henry, "Fat Factors," *New York Times Magazine*, August 13, 2006, 28–33, 52, 54–55, 57.

3. T. J. Philipson and R. A. Posner, "The Long-Run Growth in Obesity as a Function of Technological Change," *Perspectives in Biology and Medicine* 46, no. 3 (2003): S87–S107.

4. N. A. Christakis and J. H. Fowler, "The Spread of Obesity in a Large Social Network over 32 Years," *New England Journal of Medicine* 357, no. 4 (2007): 370–379.

5. N. A. Christakis and J. H. Fowler, "The Collective Dynamics of Smoking in a Large Social Network," *New England Journal of Medicine* 358, no. 21 (2008): 2249–2258.

6. J. C. Lumeng and K. H. Hillman, "Eating in Larger Group Increases Food Consumption," *Archives of Disease in Childhood* 92, no. 5 (2007): 1–4.

7. V. I. Clendenen, C. P. Herman, and J. Polivy, "Social Facilitation of Eating Among Friends and Strangers," *Appetite* 23 (1994): 1–13.

8. B. Wansink, *Mindless Eating: Why We Eat More Than We Think* (New York: Bantam, 2006).

9. R. Raghunathan, R. W. Naylor, and W. D. Hoyer, "The Unhealthy = Tasty Intuition and Its Effects on Taste Inferences, Enjoyment, and Choice of Food Products," *Journal of Marketing* 70 (2006): 170–184.

10. J. Cawley, "The Impact of Obesity on Wages," *Journal of Human Resources* 39, no. 2 (2004): 451–474.

11. A. Offer, *The Challenge of Affluence: Self-Control and Well-Being in the United States and Britain Since 1950* (Oxford: Oxford University Press, 2006).

CHAPTER SEVEN

1. A. L. Bretteville-Jensen, "Addiction and Discounting," *Journal of Health Economics* 18 (1999): 393–408.

2. R. E. Vuchinich and C. A. Simpson, "Hyperbolic Temporal Discounting in Social Drinkers and Problem Drinkers," *Experimental and Clinical Psychopharmacology* 6 (1998): 292–305; W. K. Bickel, A. L. Odum, and G. J. Madden, "Impulsivity and Cigarette Smoking: Delay Discounting in Current, Never, and Ex-smokers," *Psychopharmacology* 146

(1999): 447–454; and N. M. Petry and T. Casarella, "Excessive Discounting of Delayed Rewards in Substance Abusers with Gambling Problems," *Drug and Alcohol Dependence* 56 (1999): 25–32.

3. D. Hume, *A Treatise of Human Nature* (London: Penguin Books, 1739).

4. G. S. Becker and K. M. Murphy, "A Theory of Rational Addiction," *Journal of Political Economy* 96, no. 4 (1988): 675–700.

5. D. Laibson, "Golden Eggs and Hyperbolic Discounting," *Quarterly Journal of Economics* 62 (1997): 443–477.

6. T. C. Schelling, *Choice and Consequence: Perspectives of an Errant Economist* (Cambridge, MA: Harvard University Press, 1984).

7. G. D. Whitman, "Against the New Paternalism: Internalities and the Economics of Self-Control," *Policy Analysis* 563 (2006): 1–16.

8. T. O'Donoghue, and M. Rabin, "Incentives and Self-Control," in *Advances in Economics and Econometrics: Theory and Applications*, eds. R. Blundell, W. Newey, and T. Persson (Cambridge: Cambridge University Press, 2007).

9. Y. Shoda, W. Mischel, and P. K. Peake, "Predicting Adolescent Cognitive and Self-Regulatory Competencies from Preschool Delay of Gratification: Identifying Diagnostic Conditions," *Developmental Psychology* 26 (1990): 978–986.

10. R. F. Baumeister et al., "Ego Depletion: Is the Active Self a Limited Resource?" *Journal of Personality and Social Psychology* 74, no. 5 (1998): 1252–1265.

11. R. F. Baumeister, "The Self," in *Handbook of Social Psychology*, eds. S. Gilbert, S. T. Fiske, and G. Lindzey (New York: McGraw-Hill, 1998); and M. Muraven, D. M. Tice, and R. F. Baumeister, "Self-Control as Limited Resource: Regulatory Depletion Patterns," *Journal of Personality and Social Psychology* 74, no. 3 (1998): 774–789.

12. Y. Wang and M. A. Beydoun, "The Obesity Epidemic in the United States—Gender, Age, Socioeconomic, Racial/Ethnic, and Geographic Characteristics: A Systematic Review and Meta-regression Analysis," *Epidemiologic Reviews* 29 (2007): 6–28.

13. R. Balko, "Government Gets Fat Fighting Obesity," *FOXNews.com*, 2004.

14. S. Smith, "Developing Nations Taking On West's Flabby Look," *Boston Globe*, 2002.

15. D. M. Cutler, E. L. Glaeser, and J. M. Shapiro, "Why Have Americans Become More Obese? (working paper 9446, National Bureau of Economic Research [NBER], Cambridge, MA, 2003).

16. G. Kolata, *Rethinking Thin: The New Science of Weight Loss—and the Myths and Realities of Dieting* (New York: Farrar, Straus, and Giroux, 2007).

17. J. Polivy and C. P. Herman, "An Evolutionary Perspective on Dieting," *Appetite* 47, no. 1 (2006): 1–6.

18. T. G. Smith, "Reconciling Psychology with Economics: Obesity, Behavioral Biology, and Rational Overeating" (working paper 2006-4, Washington State University School of Economic Sciences, Pullman, WA, 2006).

19. M. Cabanac, R. Duclaux, and N. H. Spector, "Sensory Feedback in Regulation of Body Weight: Is There a Ponderostat?" *Nature* 229 (1971): 125–127.

20. Polivy and Herman, "An Evolutionary Perspective on Dieting."

21. R. J. Herrnstein et al., "Utility Maximization and Melioration: Internalities in Individual Choice," *Journal of Behavioral Decision Making* 6 (1993): 149–185.

22. D. Ariely, *Predictably Irrational* (New York: HarperCollins, 2008).

23. R. H. Frank, "The Other Milton Friedman: A Conservative with a Social Welfare Program," *New York Times*, November 23, 2006, http://www.nytimes.com/2006/11/23/business/23scene.html.

CHAPTER EIGHT

1. P. A. Samuelson, "Consumption Theory in Terms of Revealed Preference," *Economica* 15, no. 60 (1948): 243–253; and P. A. Samuelson, "Numerical Representation of Ordered Classifications and the Concept of Utility," *Review of Economic Studies* 6, no. 1 (1938): 65–70.

2. D. Kahneman, P. P. Wakker, and R. Sarin, "Back to Bentham? Explorations of Experienced Utility," *Quarterly Journal of Economics* 112, no. 2 (1997): 375–405.

3. J. Bentham, *An Introduction to the Principles of Morals and Legislation* (Oxford: Clarendon Press, 1907).

4. P. Schyns, *Income and Life Satisfaction: A Cross-National and Longitudinal Study* (Delft, Netherlands: Eburon, 2003); and E. Diener, J. Horwitz, and R. A. Emmons, "Happiness of the Very Wealthy," *Social Indicators Research* 16 (1985): 263–274.

5. P. A. Ubel, *You're Stronger Than You Think: Tapping into the Secrets of Emotionally Resilient People* (New York: McGraw-Hill, 2006).

6. N. D. Weinstein, "Community Noise Problems: Evidence Against Adaptation," *Journal of Environmental Psychology* 2 (1982): 87–97.

7. A. Stutzer and B. S. Frey, "Commuting and Life Satisfaction in Germany," *Information zur Raumentwicklung* (2007): 179–189.

8. D. Kahneman et al., "Would You Be Happier If You Were Richer? A Focusing Illusion," *Science* 312 (2006).

9. N. Paumgarten, "There and Back Again," *New Yorker*, April 16, 2007.

10. D. Kahneman et al., "Would You Be Happier?"

11. P. Brickman, D. Coates, and R. Janoff-Bulman, "Lottery Winners and Accident Victims: Is Happiness Relative?" *Journal of Personality and Social Psychology* 36, no. 8 (1978): 917–927; M. Csikszentmihalyi, "If We Are So Rich, Why Aren't We Happy?" *American Psychologist* 54, no. 10 (1999): 821–827; and E. Diener et al., "The Relationship Between Income and Subjective Well-Being: Relative or Absolute?" *Social Indicators Research* 28 (1993): 195–223.

12. C. K. Hsee et al., "Medium Maximization," *Journal of Consumer Research* 30 (2003): 1–14.

13. L. L. Carstensen, D. M. Isaacowitz, and C. T. Charles, "Taking Time Seriously: A Theory of Socioemotional Selectivity," *American Psychologist* 54, no. 3 (1999): 165–181.

14. D. K. Mroczek and C. M. Kolarz, "The Effect of Age on Positive and Negative Affect: A Developmental Perspective on Happiness," *Journal of Personality and Social Psychology* 75, no. 5 (1998): 1333–1349.

15. H. P. Lacey, D. M. Smith, and P. A. Ubel, "Hope I Die Before I Get Old: Mispredicting Happiness Across the Lifespan," *Journal of Happiness Studies* 7, no. 2 (2006): 167–182.

16. M. Ross, "Relation of Implicit Theories to the Construction of Personal Histories," *Psychological Review* 96, no. 2 (1989): 341–357.

17. J. Riis et al., "Ignorance of Hedonic Adaptation to Hemo-Dialysis: A Study Using Ecological Momentary Assessment," *Journal of Experimental Psychology: General* 134, no. 1 (2005): 3–9.

18. D. M. Smith, S. L. Brown, and P. A. Ubel, "Mispredictions and Misrecollections: Challenges for Subjective Outcome Measurement," *Disability and Rehabilitation* 30, no. 6 (2007): 1–7.

CHAPTER NINE

1. H. B. Veatch, *Rational Man: A Modern Interpretation of Aristotelian Ethics* (Bloomington: Indiana University Press, 1962).

2. C. Darwin, *The Expression of the Emotions in Man and Animals* (New York: Dover Publications, 2007).

3. *New York Times*, "Researcher Testifies on Peril in Smoke," April 26, 1997.

4. G. Collins, "Lawyer Is in Round No. 2 Against Tobacco Industry," *New York Times*, April 14, 1997.

5. G. Collins, "Jury in Florida to Decide Landmark Tobacco Case," *New York Times*, May 3, 1997.

6. W. K. Viscusi, *Smoking: Making the Risky Decision* (New York: Oxford University Press, 1992).

7. Ibid.

8. Ibid.

9. G. S. Becker and K. M. Murphy, "A Theory of Rational Addiction," *Journal of Political Economy* 96, no. 4 (1988): 675–700.

10. T. Harford, *The Logic of Life: The Rational Economics of an Irrational World* (New York: Random House, 2008).

11. M. Mahar, "Small Solace: RJR Suers Claim Moral Win," *Barron's* 77, no. 19 (1997): 13.

12. National Cancer Institute, http://www.cancer.gov/.

13. C. Lerman et al., "Mammography Adherence and Psychological Distress Among Women at Risk for Breast Cancer," *Journal of the National Cancer Institute* 85, no. 13 (1993): 1074–1080.

14. B. Fischoff and W. Bruine de Bruin, "Fifty-fifty=50%," *Journal of Behavioral Decision Making* 12, no. 2 (1999): 149–163.

15. L. M. Schwartz et al., "The Role of Numeracy in Understanding the Benefit of Screening Mammography," *Annals of Internal Medicine* 127, no. 11 (1997): 966–972.

16. W. K. Viscusi, "Comment: The Perils of Qualitative Smoking Risk Measures," *Journal of Behavioral Decision Making* 13 (2000): 267–271.

17. B. Fischoff, "Hindsight ≠ Foresight: The Effect of Outcome Knowledge on Judgment Under Uncertainty," *Qual Safe Health Care* 12, no. 4 (2003): 304–311.

18. A. Fagerlin, B. J. Zikmund-Fisher, and P. Ubel, "How Making a Risk Estimate Can Change the Feel of That Risk: Shifting Attitudes Toward Breast Cancer Risk in a General Public Survey," *Patient Education and Counseling* 57, no. 3 (2005): 294–299.

19. P. D. Windschitl, R. Martin, and A. R. Flugstad, "Context and the Interpretation of Likelihood Information: The Role of Intergroup Comparisons on Perceived Vulnerability," *Journal of Personality and Social Psychology* 82, no. 5 (2002): 742–755;

G. F. Loewenstein et al., "Risk as Feelings," *Psychological Bulletin* 127, no. 2 (2002): 267–286; and M. L. Finucane et al., "The Affect of Heuristic Judgments of Risks and Benefits," *Journal of Behavioral Decision Making* 13 (2000): 1–17.

20. J. E. LeDoux, *The Emotional Brain: The Mysterious Underpinnings of Emotional Life* (New York: Simon & Schuster, 1996).

21. R. B. Zajonc, "Preferences Need No Inferences," *American Psychologist* 35 (1980): 151–175.

22. R. E. Nisbett and T. D. Wilson, "Telling More Than We Can Know: Verbal Reports on Mental Processes," *Psychological Review* 84, no. 3 (1997): 231–259.

23. N. Ambady et al., "Surgeon's Tone of Voice: A Clue to Malpractice History," *Surgery* 132 (2002): 5–9.

24. Zajonc, "Preferences Need No Inferences."

25. D. P. Baker, "Florida Jury Finds R.J. Reynolds Not Negligent; Tobacco Firm Had Argued Smoking Is Personal Choice," *Washington Post*, 1997.

26. B. Zikmund-Fisher et al., "Alternate Methods of Framing Information About Medication Side Effects: Incremental Risk Versus Total Risk Occurrence," *Journal of Health Communication* (forthcoming).

27. B. J. Zikmund-Fisher et al., "Does Labeling Prenatal Screening Test Results as Negative or Positive Affect Women's Responses?" *American Journal of Obstetrics and Gynecology* 197, no. 5 (2007): 521–526.

28. J. S. Lerner et al., "Effects of Fear and Anger on Perceived Risks of Terrorism: A National Field Experiment," *Psychological Science* 14, no. 2 (2003): 144–150; and D. A. Small et al., "Emotion Priming and Attributions for Terrorism: Americans' Reactions in a National Field Experiment," *Political Psychology* 27, no. 2 (2006): 289–298.

29. D. Kessler, *A Question of Intent: A Great American Battle with a Deadly Industry* (New York: Public Affairs, 2001).

CHAPTER TEN

1. *Wall Street Journal*, editorial, "Lasik Lessons," March 10, 2006.

2. R. Pear, "A. M. A. to Develop Measure of Quality of Medical Care," *New York Times*, February 21, 2006.

3. A. B. Hubbard, "The Health of a Nation," *New York Times*, April 3, 2007.

4. A. Kastrati et al., "Analysis of 14 Trials Comparing Sirolimus-Eluting Stents with Bare-Metal Stents," *New England Journal of Medicine* 356 (2007): 1030–1039; and R. Moreno et al., "Meta-analysis Comparing the Effect of Drug-Eluting Versus Bare Metal Stents on Risk of Acute Myocardial Infarction During Follow-up," *American Journal of Cardiology* 99 (2007): 621–625.

5. T. Bodenheimer, "High and Rising Health Care Costs; Part 1: Seeking an Explanation," *Annals of Internal Medicine* 142, no. 10 (2005): 847–854.

6. P. A. Ubel, *Pricing Life: Why It's Time for Health Care Rationing* (Cambridge, MA: MIT Press, 2000).

7. S. S. Brehm and M. Weinraub, "Physical Barriers and Psychological Resistance: Two-Year-Olds' Responses to Threats of Freedom," *Journal of Personality and Social Psychology* 35 (1977): 830–836.

8. E. Clark, *The Real Toy Story: Inside the Ruthless Battle for America's Youngest Consumers* (New York: Free Press, 2007).

9. R. B. Cialdini, *Influence: Science and Practice* (Boston: Allyn & Bacon, 2001).

10. S. Worchel, J. Lee, and A. Adewole, "Effects of Supply and Demand on Ratings of Object Value," *Journal of Personality and Social Psychology* 32 (1975): 906–914.

11. R. J. Levine, *The Power of Persuasion: How We're Bought and Sold* (Hoboken, NJ: John Wiley & Sons, 2003).

12. B. Shiv, Z. Carmon, and D. Ariley, "Placebo Effects of Marketing Actions: Consumers May Get What They Pay For," *Journal of Marketing Research* 42, no. 4 (2005): 383–393.

13. J. D. Glater and A. Finder, "In New Twist on Tuition Game, Popularity Rises with the Price," *New York Times*, December 12, 2006.

14. D. Cantor, "The Business of Medicine: The Extraordinary History of Glaxo, a Baby Food Producer, Which Became One of the World's Most Successful Pharmaceutical Companies (Book Review)," *Bulletin of the History of Medicine* 76, no. 3 (2002): 646–648.

15. R. Adaval and K. B. Monroe, "Automatic Construction and Use of Contextual Information for Product and Price Evaluations," *Journal of Consumer Research* 28 (March 2002): 572–588.

16. J. Huber and J. McCann, "The Impact of Inferential Beliefs on Product Evaluations," *Journal of Marketing Research* 19 (August 1982): 324–333; and D. Tull, R. A. Boring, and M. H. Gonsior, "A Note on the Relationship of Price and Imputed Quality," *Journal of Business* 37 (April 1964): 186–191.

17. M. V. Pauly, "The Economics of Moral Hazard," *American Economic Review* 58, no. 3 (1968): 231–237.

18. K. Rove, "Republicans Can Win on Health Care," *Wall Street Journal*, September 18, 2007.

19. A. Hubbard, "A Tax Cure for Healthcare," *Wall Street Journal*, July 24, 2007.

20. J. Cohn, *Sick: The Untold Story of America's Health Care Crisis—and the People Who Pay the Price* (New York: HarperCollins, 2007).

21. Rove, "Republicans Can Win on Health Care."

22. J. Stossel, "Sick Sob Stories," *Wall Street Journal*, September 13, 2007.

23. J. Carreyrou, "Legal Loophole Ensnares Breast-Cancer Patients," *Wall Street Journal*, September 13, 2007.

24. B. McCaughey, "Cancer Killers," *Wall Street Journal*, September 14, 2007.

25. H. G. Welch, *Should I Be Tested for Cancer? Maybe Not and Here's Why* (Berkeley: University of California Press, 2004).

26. J. P. Kassirer, *On the Take: How Medicine's Complicity with Big Business Can Endanger Your Health* (New York: Oxford University Press, 2004).

27. S. M. Asch et al., "Comparison of Quality of Care for Patients in the Veterans Health Administration and Patients in a National Sample," *Annals of Internal Medicine* 141, no. 12 (2004): 938–945.

28. S. Lueck, "Bush's Medicare Plan Likely to Ignite Partisan Fight," *Wall Street Journal*, February 16, 2008.

CHAPTER ELEVEN

1. W. P. McKinney et al., "Attitudes of Internal Medicine Faculty and Residents Toward Professional Interaction with Pharmaceutical Sales Representatives," *Journal of the American Medical Association* 264, no. 13 (1990): 1693–1697.

2. R. J. Levine, *The Power of Persuasion: How We're Bought and Sold* (Hoboken, NJ: John Wiley & Sons, 2003).

3. A. F. Shaughnessy and K. K. Bucci, "Drug Samples and Family Practice Residents," *The Annals of Pharmacotherapy* 31, no. 11 (1997): 1296–1300.

4. M. L. Azcuenaga, *Advertising Regulation and the Free Market*, http://www.ftc.gov/speeches/azcuenaga/lima.shtm.

5. G. S. Becker and K. M. Murphy, "A Simple Theory of Advertising as Good or Bad," *Quarterly Journal of Economics* 108, no. 4 (1993): 941–964.

6. A. W. Gouldner, "The Norm of Reciprocity: A Preliminary Statement," *American Sociological Review* 25 (1960): 161–178.

7. D. T. Regan, "Effects of Favor and Liking on Compliance," *Journal of Experimental Social Psychology* 7 (1971): 627–639.

8. L. R. Goldberg, "The Development of Markers for the Big-Five Factor Structure," *Psychological Assessment* 4, no. 1 (1992): 26–42.

9. W. D. Hoyer and D. J. MacInnis, *Consumer Behavior* (Boston: Houghton Mifflin Company, 2004).

10. E. Peters et al., "Adult Age Differences in Dual Information Processes," *Perspectives in Psychological Sciences* 2 (2007): 1–24.

11. K. Helliker, "This Is Your Brain on a Strong Brand: MRI's Show Even Insurers Can Excite," *Wall Street Journal*, November 28, 2006.

12. N. Schwarz, "Meta-cognitive Experiences in Consumer Judgment and Decision Making," *Journal of Consumer Psychology* 14 (2004): 332–348.

13. L. Lee, S. Frederick, and D. Ariely, "Try It, You'll Like It," *Psychological Science* 17, no. 12 (2006): 1054–1058.

14. E. Schlosser, *Fast Food Nation: The Dark Side of the All-American Meal* (New York: Houghton Mifflin, 2001).

15. T. N. Robinson et al., "Effects of Fast Food Branding on Young Children's Taste Preferences," *Archives of Pediatrics & Adolescent Medicine* 161, no. 8 (2007): 792–797.

16. M. Wakefield et al., "Effect of Televised, Tobacco Company-Funded Smoking Prevention Advertising on Youth Smoking-Related Beliefs, Intentions and Behavior," *American Journal of Public Health* 96, no. 12 (2006): 2154–2160.

17. M. Talbot, "Little Hotties: Barbie's New Rivals," *New Yorker*, December 4, 2006.

18. Hoyer and MacInnis, *Consumer Behavior*.

19. Ibid.

20. E. Clark, *The Real Toy Story: Inside the Ruthless Battle for America's Youngest Consumers* (New York: Free Press, 2007).

21. J. Saranow, "This Is the Car We Want, Mommy. Car Makers Direct More Ads at Kids (and Their Parents)," *Wall Street Journal*, November 9, 2006.

22. S. Dal Cin et al., "Smoking in Movies, Implicit Associations of Smoking with the Self, and Intentions to Smoke," *Psychological Science* 18, no. 7 (2007): 559–563.

CHAPTER TWELVE

1. J. Bentham, *An Introduction to the Principles of Morals and Legislation* (Oxford: Clarendon Press, 1907).

2. P. A. Samuelson, "Consumption Theory in Terms of Revealed Preference," *Economica* 15, no. 60 (1948): 243–253.

3. D. Kahneman, P. P. Wakker, and R. Sarin, "Back to Bentham? Explorations of Experienced Utility," *Quarterly Journal of Economics* 112, no. 2 (1997): 375–405.

4. W. N. Morris, "The Mood System," in *Well-Being: The Foundations of Hedonic Psychology*, eds. D. Kahneman, E. Diener, and N. Schwarz (New York: Russell Sage Foundation, 1999), 169–189; R. M. Sapolsky, "The Physiology and Pathophysiology of Unhappiness," in *Well-Being*, 453–469; J. E. LeDoux and J. Armony, "Can Neurobiology Tell Us Anything About Human Feelings?" in *Well-Being*, 489–499; and P. Eckman and E. L. Rosenberg, eds., *What the Face Reveals* (New York: Oxford University Press, 1997).

5. D. Kahneman et al., "Would You Be Happier If You Were Richer? A Focusing Illusion," *Science* 312, no. 5782 (2006): 1908–1910; and D. Kahneman et al., "A Survey Method for Characterizing Daily Life Experience: The Day Reconstruction Method," *Science* 306, no. 5702 (2004): 1776–1780.

6. E. Diener and M. E. P. Seligman, "Beyond Money: Toward an Economy of Well-Being," *Psychological Science in the Public Interest* 5, no. 1 (2004): 1–31.

7. B. Schwartz, "Choice Cuts," *New Republic Online*, 2004.

8. R. Layard, *Happiness: Lessons from a New Science* (New York: Penguin, 2005).

9. R. H. Frank, "How Not to Buy Happiness," *Daedalus* 133 (2004): 69–79.

10. H. Johns and P. Ormerod, *Happiness, Economics and Public Policy* (London: Institute of Economic Affairs, 2007).

11. M. S. Packe, *The Life of John Stuart Mill* (London: Martin Secker & Warburg, 1954).

12. T. Sowell, *On Classical Economics* (New Haven, CT: Yale University Press, 2006).

13. J. S. Mill, *Autobiography* (London: Longmans, Green, Reader, and Dyer, 1873).

14. Ibid.

15. J. S. Mill, "Utilitarianism," in *The Utilitarians* (Garden City, NY: Anchor Press/Doubleday, 1973).

16. P. A. Ubel, *You're Stronger Than You Think: Tapping Into the Secrets of Emotionally Resilient People* (New York: McGraw-Hill, 2006).

17. A. Sen, *The Standard of Living* (Cambridge: Cambridge University Press, 1987).

18. Ibid.

19. A. Sen, "Capabilities, Lists, and Public Reason: Continuing the Conversation," *Feminist Economics* 10, no. 3 (2004): 77–80.

20. R. F. Kennedy (speech at the University of Kansas, Lawrence, KS, March 18, 1968, http://www.jfklibrary.org/Historical+Resources/Archives/Reference+Desk/Speeches/RFK/RFKSpeech68Mar18UKansas.htm).

21. W. Wilkinson, "In Pursuit of Happiness Research: Is It Reliable? What Does It Imply for Policy?" *Policy Analysis* 590 (2007): 1–41.

22. P. Dolan, "In Defence of Subjective Well-Being," *Health Economics, Policy and Law* 3 (2008): 93–95.

23. A. Kreuger et al., "National Time Accounting: The Currency of Life" (working paper, 2007).

CHAPTER THIRTEEN

1. D. Harsanyi, *Nanny State* (New York: Broadway Books, 2007).

2. G. Norquist, *Leave Us Alone: Getting the Government's Hands off Our Money, Our Guns, and Our Lives* (New York: William Morrow, 2008).

3. A. P. Napolitano, *A Nation of Sheep* (Nashville, TN: Thomas Nelson, 2007).

4. Harsanyi, *Nanny State*.

5. R. Thaler and C. R. Sunstein, *Nudge: Improving Decisions About Health, Wealth and Happiness* (New Haven, CT: Yale University Press, 2008).

6. C. Camerer et al., "Regulation for Conservatives: Behavioral Economics and the Case for 'Asymmetric Paternalism,'" *University of Pennsylvania Law Review* 151 (2003): 1211–1254.

7. Harsanyi, *Nanny State*.

8. G. S. Becker, M. Grossman, and K. M. Murphy, "An Empirical Analysis of Cigarette Addiction," *American Economic Review* 84 (1994): 396–418.

9. R. L. Ohsfledt, R. G. Boyle, and E. I. Capilouto, "Tobacco Taxes, Smoking Restrictions and Tobacco Use," in *The Economic Analysis of Substance Use and Abuse*, eds. F. J. Chaloupa et al. (Chicago: University of Chicago Press, 1999).

10. City of New York, "Mayor Bloomberg and Speaker Quinn Announce Green Cart Legislation to Improve Access to Fresh Fruits and Vegetables in Neighborhoods with Greatest Need," news release, News from the Blue Room, NYC.gov, December 18, 2007.

11. M. Pollan, *In Defense of Food: An Eater's Manifesto* (New York: Penguin Press, 2008).

12. D. Stout, "Farm Bill, in Part and in Full, Wins Passage," *New York Times*, May 23, 2008.

13. L. H. Epstein et al., "Purchases of Food in Youth: Influence of Price and Income," *Psychological Science* 17, no. 1 (2006): 82–89.

14. I. Rashad, "The Economics of Obesity," *Public Interest* 156 (2004): 104–112.

15. A. Offer, *The Challenge of Affluence: Self-Control and Well-Being in the United States and Britain Since 1950* (Oxford: Oxford University Press, 2006).

16. D. B. Caruso, "Next for NYC Trans Fat Ban: Enforcement," *Washington Post*, December 10, 2006.

17. A. Ascherio and W. Willett, "Trans Fatty Acids: Are the Effects Only Marginal?" *American Journal of Public Health* 84 (1994): 722–724; and J. Dupont, E. Feldman, and P. White, "Saturated and Hydrogenated Fats in Food in Relation to Health," *Journal of the American College of Nutrition* 75 (1994): 190–192.

18. G. Hornstra and R. Mensink, "Alternatives to Nutritional Trans Fatty Acids," *World Review of Nutrition and Dietetics* 75 (1994): 190–192.

19. S. Angell, personal communication with author, 2007.

20. D. Kessler, *A Question of Intent: A Great American Battle with a Deadly Industry* (New York: Public Affairs, 2001).

21. New York City Department of Health and Mental Hygiene, "Board of Health Votes to Invite Public Comment on New Calorie Listing Proposal for Chain Restaurants," news release, October 24, 2007.

22. R. A. Krukowski et al., "Consumers May Not Use or Understand Calorie Labeling in Restaurants," *Journal of the American Dietetic Association* 106, no. 6 (2006): 917–920.

23. B. J. Zikmund-Fisher, A. Fagerlin, and P. A. Ubel, "'Is 28% Good or Bad?': Evaluability and Preference Reversals in Health Care Decisions," *Medical Decision Making* 24, no. 2 (2004): 142–148.

24. C. K. Hsee, "The Evaluability Hypothesis: An Explanation for Preference Reversals Between Joint and Separate Evaluations of Alternatives," *Organizational Behavior and Human Decision Processes* 67, no. 3 (1996): 247–257; and C. K. Hsee et al., "Preference Reversals Between Joint and Separate Evaluations of Options: A Review and Theoretical Analysis," *Psychological Bulletin* 125, no. 5 (1999): 576–590.

25. Krukowski et al., "Consumers May Not Use or Understand Calorie Labeling."

26. Offer, *The Challenge of Affluence*.

27. D. M. Cutler, E. L. Glaeser, and J. M. Shapiro, "Why Have Americans Become More Obese?" (working paper 9446, National Bureau of Economic Research [NBER], Cambridge, MA, 2003).

28. S. Elliott, "Is the Ad a Success? The Brain Waves Tell All," *New York Times*, March 31, 2008.

29. L. Belkin, "The School-Lunch Test," *New York Times Magazine*, August 20, 2006, 30–35, 48, 52–55.

30. P. Rozin et al., "The Ecology of Eating: Smaller Portion Sizes in France Than in the United States Help Explain the French Paradox," *Psychological Science* 14, no. 5 (2003): 450–454.

31. Ibid.

32. R. F. Baumeister, "The Self," in *Handbook of Social Psychology*, eds. S. Gilbert, S. T. Fiske, and G. Lindzey (New York: McGraw-Hill, 1998); and M. Muraven, D. M. Tice, and R. F. Baumeister, "Self-Control as Limited Resource: Regulatory Depletion Patterns," *Journal of Personality and Social Psychology* 74, no. 3 (1998): 774–789.

33. M. Muraven, R. F. Baumeister, D. M. Tice, "Longitudinal Improvement of Self-Regulation Through Practice: Building Self-Control Strength Through Repeated Exercise," *Journal of Social Psychology* 139, no. 4 (1999): 446–457.

34. R. McKeon, ed., *The Basic Works of Aristotle* (New York: Random House, 1941).

INDEX

moral behavior, Bentham on, 119, 120
moral philosophy, 16, 201
multiple selves concept, 97-98
Murphy, Kevin, 15, 95, 96-97, 134-135,
    145, 174-175

Nanny State (Harsanyi), 205
nanny state approach to public policy,
    205-206, 224
Neale, Margaret, 59-60
needle manufacturing, and division of
    labor, 4-6
neoclassical economics, 8, 117
newness of product, and judgment
    about quality, 158-161
New York Times, 52, 155
Nordhaus, William, 14
Norquist, Grover, 206
Northcraft, Gregory, 59-60
numeracy, and risk estimation,
    138-139

obesity
    advertising and, 200
    behavioral economics and, 30
    biological explanations for, 80-81
    children and, 210, 213
    economic consequences of, 89
    exercise costs and, 14, 26-27
    financial incentives and, 210-211,
        212-214
    food choices related to, 10, 11,
        213-214, 219
    food technology advances and,
        28, 81
    free markets as cause of, 10-11, 28,
        89, 220
    genetics and, 10, 89
    health problems and, 89
    information about food products and,
        215-217
    irrational choices and, 87-88, 210, 211
    knowledge of causes of weight gain
        and relevance to, 14
    libertarian view on dealing with, 30

longevity changes over generations
    and, 10
medical solutions to, 81
nanny state approach to, 205,
    206-207, 224
paternalism in approach to, 208-209
personal responsibility and, 103
persuasion approach to, 217-219
poverty related to, 26, 28
preventive approach to, 221-222
price changes and, 25-26, 80
psychological factors in, 212-213, 218
public policy response to, 29-30, 205,
    206-207, 220-221
rational choice and, 13-14, 25-26, 80,
    81, 82
restaurant regulation and, 214-215
self-control and, 210, 211, 223-224
social consequences of, 89
social networks and, 83
spending decisions and, 213-214
tax codes and remedies for, 210
time costs and, 27, 28, 80
O'Donaghue, Ted, 99-100
organ donation programs, 71-72

pain, Bentham's focus on, 118-120,
    192-193
Paradox of Choice, The (Schwartz), 193
paternalism, 65-75
    asymmetrical, 73
    cigarette taxes as, 212
    default options and, 70
    libertarian, 70, 208
    medicine and, 74-75
    savings plans and, 70
    seat belt laws and, 70
    soft, 208-209
payday loans, 100, 216
personality types, and marketing, 178
personal preferences, and decision
    making, 11, 93-96
personal responsibility, 103
persuasion, and obesity epidemic,
    217-219

public policy approaches to,
126-127
zoning laws and housing choice in,
126, 127
reciprocity, and advertising, 176-177
regression toward the mean, 34
regulation. *See* public policy
reinforcement, and behavior, 33-34
rent-to-own practices, 72-73
representativeness heuristic, 36-37, 38
reptilian brain, and emotion in decision
making, 130-131, 141-144
restaurant
information distributed by, 216
regulation of food products in,
214-215
retirement savings rates, and
unconscious decisions, 67-70
risk
certainty in choices and, 41-42
estimation of, for breast cancer,
136-318, 139-141
hindsight bias and, 140-141
illogical forces in emotional reaction
to, 145-148, 149
interpreting as high or low, 141
life-threatening situations and,
49, 50-51
public policy and reduction of, 145
rational addiction and, 135
rational decision making and, 134
seat belt and helmet usage related to,
147-148, 206
smoking decision making and,
133-134, 136, 218
Rozin, Paul, 222

sales and selling
anchoring effect and, 58, 59-60
eBay prices and, 57-59
loss in mental accounting
phenomenon and, 55
rent-to-own practices and, 72-73
Samuelson, Paul, 14, 22
Savage, Leonard "Jimmy," 41

savings rates
default options in policy governing,
70, 208
unconscious decisions and, 67-70
scarcity
desire in decision making related to,
156-157
pleasure in fulfilling our desire related
to, 156-157
Schelling, Thomas, 97, 98
Schlosser, Eric, 10
school lunch programs, 221-222
Schultz, Theodore, 44
Schwartz, Barry, 193
scientific theories, and data collection,
79-80
screening tests, 165
seat belts
laws mandating, 70, 206
risk and usage of, 147-148
self-control, 100-104
children and, 101, 222, 223
finite aspect of, 102
food stamp distribution timing and,
110-111
income level and, 103-104, 108
market efficiency and, 153
obesity epidemic and, 210, 211,
223-224
problems as internalities, 107-108
public policy and help with,
108-109
smoking and, 211
studies involving, 100-102
Seligman, Martin, 193
Sen, Amartya, 198-199
Slovic, Paul, 49
Smith, Adam
division of labor theory of, 6-7, 8
economic thinking dominated by
theories of, 8-9
value in water/diamond conundrum
and, 16-18, 19
The Wealth of Nations, 6, 8, 25
Smith, Trenton, 15

timing decisions, in food stamp
distribution, 110-11, 213-214
tobacco companies
lung cancer lawsuits and, 130-131, 136
national campaigns for teenagers
from, 182-183, 218, 220
tradition
capitalist enterprise in eighteenth
century and break from, 7-8
Smith on free markets and, 8
workplace controlled by, 7
trans fat, 214-15
transplantation, misremembering
after, 125
Tversky, Amos
anchoring effect and, 58
certainty theory of, 41-42
early work with Kahneman, 34-35
gambling choice studies of, 39-41, 42
loss aversion theory of, 42-44, 50, 52
"Prospect Theory" published
by, 43-44
reaction of economists to studies of,
49-50, 55-56
studies of judgments defying
rationality by Kahneman and,
34, 35, 38-39, 49, 189
Thaler's studies in behavioral
economics and research of, 49-50,
52, 53, 55
typecasting, and advertising, 177-182

unconscious behaviors, and savings
rates, 67-70
unconscious brain systems, and
judgment, 142-143
unemployment
measures of, 202
rational choice and, 15
utilitarianism
Bentham and, 15-16, 196
James Mill and, 196, 197
utility
advertising and maximization of,
175, 185

development of marginal utility
theory on, 18-22
free trade and increase in, 22-23
gambling choice studies of, 40
maximization of, as a measure of well
being, 116, 117-120, 192-193
quantification of, 22, 23-24
Thaler's observations on behavior
and, 48-49
value related to, 52

value
endowment effect and, 51-53
Smith's analysis of, 16-18, 19
utility related to, 52, 89
value in exchange, 17
marginal utility and, 21
Smith on water/diamond conundrum
and, 17
value in use
marginal utility and, 18
Smith on water/diamond conundrum
and, 17, 19
veterans, 107, 108, 166, 168-169
Viscusi, Kip, 132-33, 134, 138, 139, 145,
146, 147
visual clues, and eating behavior, 85-86
visual illusions, 44-45, 85

Wakefield, Melanie, 183
Wall Street Journal, 154, 164, 165
Walras, Leon, 21
Wansink, Brian, 85, 86, 88
water/diamond conundrum
marginal utility and, 18, 21
Smith's analysis of value and,
16-18, 19
Watt, James, 7
Wealth of Nations, The (Smith), 6, 8, 25
weight loss
calorie in/calorie out theory of,
104-105
choices and, 104-107
diet and exercise and, 98
evolution and success in, 105-106

ABOUT THE AUTHOR

PETER A. UBEL is the George C. Dock Collegiate Professor of Medicine and Professor of Psychology at the University of Michigan, a general internist at the Ann Arbor Veterans Affairs Medical Center, and Director of the Center for Behavioral and Decision Sciences in Medicine at the University of Michigan. His research uses the tools of decision psychology and behavioral economics to explore topics relevant to the decisions people make and how these decisions affect their health and well-being. A founding member of the World Economic Forum's Global Health Council, he is a leader in exploring the relevance of behavioral science for health policy. Dr. Ubel has won many research awards, including a Presidential Early Career Award for Scientists and Engineers from President Clinton in 2000. He has published articles for lay audiences in the *New York Times*, the *Los Angeles Times*, the *New Leader*, and the *Huffington Post*, among others. He is author of *Pricing Life: Why It's Time for Health Care Rationing* (MIT Press, 2000), and *You're Stronger Than You Think: Tapping the Secrets of Emotionally Resilient People* (McGraw-Hill, 2006). A father of two very energetic boys, he still manages to find time for piano, spicy food, backroad bicycling, and tennis. It must be because of his short commute!